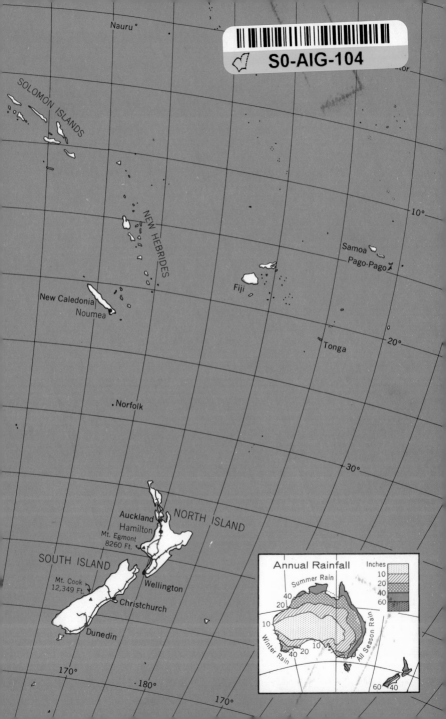

Nauru°

SOLOMON ISLANDS

NEW HEBRIDES

Samoa
Pago-Pago

Fiji

10°

New Caledonia
Noumea

Tonga

20°

Norfolk

30°

Auckland
Hamilton
Mt. Egmont
8260 Ft.

NORTH ISLAND

SOUTH ISLAND

Mt. Cook
12,349 Ft.

Wellington

Christchurch

Dunedin

Annual Rainfall

Summer Rain

Inches
10
20
40
60

40
20

10

10

Winter Rain

40 20

All Season Rain

60 40

170°   180°   170°

The United States and the Southwest Pacific

THE AMERICAN FOREIGN POLICY LIBRARY

CRANE BRINTON AND LINCOLN GORDON, EDITORS

The United States and Britain	Crane Brinton
The United States and the Near East	E. A. Speiser
The United States and the Caribbean	Dexter Perkins
The United States and Russia	Vera Micheles Dean
The United States and South America *The Northern Republics*	Arthur P. Whitaker
The United States and China	John King Fairbank
The United States and Scandinavia	Franklin D. Scott
The United States and Japan	Edwin O. Reischauer
The United States and France	Donald C. McKay
The United States and Turkey and Iran	Lewis V. Thomas and Richard N. Frye
The United States and Mexico	Howard F. Cline
The United States and India and Pakistan	W. Norman Brown
The United States and Italy	H. Stuart Hughes
The United States and Argentina	Arthur P. Whitaker
The Balkans in Our Time	Robert Lee Wolff
The United States and the Southwest Pacific	C. Hartley Grattan

THE
UNITED STATES
AND THE
Southwest Pacific

C. Hartley Grattan

HARVARD UNIVERSITY PRESS

Cambridge, Massachusetts

1961

Distributed in Great Britain by
OXFORD UNIVERSITY PRESS, LONDON

Maps by Robert L. Williams

Library of Congress Catalog Card Number 61–5583
Printed in the United States of America

for

SIR JOHN GRENFELL CRAWFORD

an Australian friend

CONTENTS

Contents

III
World War II and After

Maps

Tables

INTRODUCTION

Our American naval historian of the recent World War, Admiral Morison, cites an arresting example, quoted by Mr. Grattan in this book, of the fact that only yesterday even official American knowledge of the Southwest Pacific was fully a century old: the charts at hand for our use in the 1940's were based in part on the expeditions of the American naval officer Wilkes (born in 1798) and the French explorer Bougainville (born 1729). The instance is no doubt on the overly dramatic side, but it is true that accurate, expert knowledge of this vast area was rare in the United States before Pearl Harbor, and, moreover, this knowledge was scattered in dozens of separate sources. There were available to the general reading public, of course, a great deal of statistical information about Australia, New Zealand, and the islands of Polynesia and Melanesia; a long list of "travel books"; some history, especially of the eighteenth-century Pacific explorations and the nineteenth-century "partage d'Océanie"; and some remarkable, and even more unremarkable escapist literature on the theme of the South Seas. But good critical works of synthesis of human geography, history, cultural anthropology and sociology (or if these terms seem pretentious to you, just good plain reporter's descriptions of the way things are) were sadly lacking, especially when compared with what we could turn to for lands like Great Britain, France or Germany.

Mr. Grattan was, then, obliged to do a good deal of pioneering work in writing this excellent volume. No one had done quite the same task before him, and as he himself points out in his preface, the kind of solid monographic work on relations between the United States and the Southwest Pacific which exists for our relations with other parts of the world (save perhaps for most of Africa south of the Sahara) was scarce indeed. Fortunately, he had a long head start of some thirty years of direct personal experience with these lands and their peoples and possessed the kind of intimate intuitive knowledge for which academic or library scholarship in itself is no substitute. In these decades during which he has traveled and worked in the area, talked with all sorts of people, written much for what we Americans call the quality magazines, and steadily built up a superb scholarly expertness in the field, he has acquired the skills which have made this book possible. It is a fair-minded, realistic, but not a debunking book. It is a book that should do good work in this world of ours, which is indeed One World in so many senses materially, but is still many little worlds of tastes, habits, ideals, ambitions; is still *humanly* a divided world that needs understanding almost as much as it needs preaching. Mr. Grattan's modestly introduced section of "bibliographical notes" is a remarkable *tour de force;* I know of no critical bibliography of the subject approaching it in usefulness. It is also good to have in this volume, where it belongs as much as anywhere, a treatment of the status of the Antarctic continent in our world and in particular of American policies toward the use of that humanly empty land mass that may yet yield to human technologies.

This volume was begun under the editorship of the late Professor Donald C. McKay, who, with Mr. Sumner Welles, was responsible for the first fifteen volumes of the American Foreign Policy Library. My coeditor, Professor Lincoln Gordon, and I wish to take this occasion to pay special tribute to the planning skills and administrative energies of Donald McKay, without which the Library could hardly have come into being. We are both keenly aware of our debt to our predecessors, and shall be content if we can see through to completion an undertaking that must always bear the imprint of their minds.

Crane Brinton

Cambridge, Massachusetts
October 1, 1960

PREFACE

During the thirty-odd years since the author first visited the Southwest Pacific, he has seen the relation of the United States to the area undergo a remarkable transformation, from something close to indifference — though on the American side, at least, friendly indifference — to intimate foreign-political, defensive, and — increasingly — economic relations. World War II transformed the situation; it is a watershed in the history of the United States and the area. As is true of the general transformation, occasioned by World War II, of American relations with the outside world, the transformation of relations with the Southwest Pacific was wholly unplanned and almost utterly unanticipated. Only a very few Americans foresaw the impact on Australian-American relations which the long-anticipated war with Japan would have. The Americans did not expect the war to go outside the North Pacific, the long-term focus of their interest in Pacific Basin affairs.

This book is so constructed as to take that overarching fact into full account, as a glance at the Table of Contents will show. But if World War II is really the hinge upon which the book swings, the author has chosen to try to provide a suitable preface to the climactic episode. He has, therefore, attempted first a sketch of the area and its place in world affairs, since this is not widely understood in America, and second to indicate the history of the relations of the United States with the area up to *circa* 1941, since this is an almost unknown passage in Pacific Basin affairs, interesting in itself and vividly illustrative of the circuitous way in which the Americans have arrived at their present definition of relations with the world.

Unfortunately little monographic work has been done on United States–Southwest Pacific relations, though the field requires so much, and the sketch given here is really more suggestive than exhaustive. What the writer has really done has been to bring into focus thirty years of reading in the relevant materials and take his assists where he has by chance found them. Perhaps this will encourage monographists to fill the obvious gaps and insufficiencies. In telling the story he has of necessity indicated some elements of the domestic history of the area, but that really remains a story quite untold here.

How does one properly acknowledge assistance and comfort in an adventure in understanding that has continued for over thirty years? I think I can only say that I again thank my numerous friends who reside in Australia and New Zealand for their help and their sympathetic reception of what I have written about the Southwest Pacific in books, magazines, and newspapers since I first set eyes upon it, and addressed my attention to it, so long ago.

C. Hartley Grattan

Katonah, New York
July 1, 1960

The United States and the Southwest Pacific

PART I ON THE CHARACTER OF THE AREA

1. The Area in the World Today

There is no standard definition of the Southwest Pacific, but here it will be taken to include the autonomous Commonwealth countries of Australia and New Zealand, the variously owned and controlled Pacific islands south of the equator, and Antarctica. The term "Australasia" was once very commonly applied to much of this large and rather complex area, but it has lost its popularity, partly because the area is not, as the term may be taken to imply, culturally to be associated with Asia, whatever may be the case geographically, because it blankets out New Zealand, and because it never in any case referred to Antarctica. "Oceania" is still occasionally employed to designate most of the area, but as Australia and New Zealand have gained in identity, and are usually referred to separately, "Oceania" has come to refer chiefly to the islands. The use of the word "Oceania" to cover Australia, New Zealand, and the islands now has a slightly old-fashioned flavor; it persists in use as though to illustrate a cultural lag. It is perhaps odd to include Antarctica in the Southwest Pacific, but the rationale for doing so is that from the earliest days Australia and New Zealand have either been jumping-off places, or points of first return, for travelers to the far south. Captain James Cook himself initiated the practice, and whether one travels by sail or steam or air, it still continues. Moreover the Australian sector of Antarctica is the largest single sector claimed by any power, and the New Zealand sector is strategically located and includes in the Ross Sea one of the principal entryways to the great southern continent. There is logic and comprehensiveness in the term "Southwest Pacific."

The area is a segment of the Pacific Basin, and a principal preoccupation of its foreign politics is what is going on in the Basin and in the immediately contiguous areas of south Asia, but it has vital economic and political linkages outside with the North Atlantic world. As a southern hemisphere area it looks *north* at the politics of the Basin and world politics, not east or west, though culturally, politically, and economically it is part of what is loosely called the Western world. It is an outpost of the West, a rather isolated outpost. It looks north with apprehension because its sense of areal security has sharply declined in recent times. The people of the area feel that ultimate menaces (including Communism) to their security in the Pacific come from the north, and they currently believe that vitally significant help in maintaining their position must also come from that direction. Australia particularly, and New Zealand only to a slightly less acute degree, is aware that it is under the overhang of Asia. Indonesia hangs above it like an umbrella. Beyond Indonesia is all that we call South and East Asia, including Communist China, for which the Australians have tried to popularize the term "Near North." The distances involved are greater than is commonly realized, but they nevertheless are relatively short when compared to the distances between the United States and these places or Europe and the same places. Employment of European terminology long gave the residents of the Southwest Pacific a sense of remoteness from Asia. They long had a strong sense of security in spite of an occasional reflection on the facts of geography. The very term "Far East" conveyed no particular sense of closeness to Australia or New Zealand. They were prime beneficiaries of Pax Britannica, profiting from the power in Asia that the British had, but that power was conceived of as separating or protecting them from Asia. Their political, economic and cultural identification with the homeland of British power intensified their sense that they were isolated but insulated in

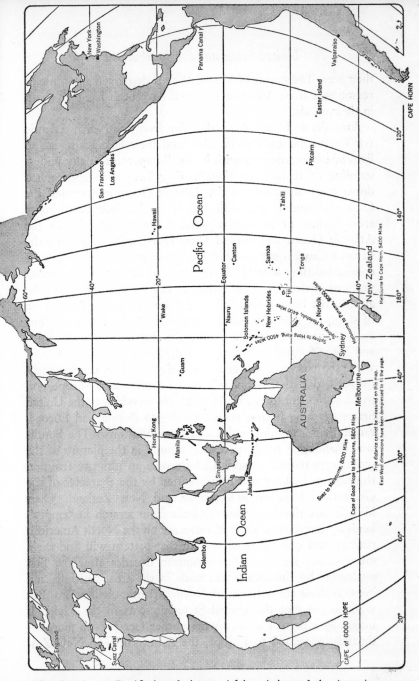

The Southwest Pacific in relation to Africa, Asia, and the Americas

their area. The events of World War II destroyed any sense of remoteness from Asia that may still have been hanging about in their minds.

Australia and New Zealand derive from the North Atlantic (or Euro-American) civilization, and their linkages to it and lines of communication with it are all-important to any understanding of them. Traditionally they have been approached down the eastern side of the Atlantic Ocean and around the Cape of Good Hope, with a shift to the Suez Canal route around 1870, or alternatively down the western side of the Atlantic Ocean and around Cape Horn, with a shift to the Panama Canal route about 1914. These are very long lines of communication, whether in the days of sail, as in the earliest years of settlement, or of steam, as in later years. Even in the air age, the lines, which follow a different pattern from those of ships, are still long. Cables and wireless shortened the time factor without really shortening the distances. For Australia and New Zealand the lines have led, since the establishment of white settlements at the end of the eighteenth century, chiefly to the British Isles, secondarily to the continent of Europe, and to a lesser extent to North America. (In an odd way the United States has long been a transit avenue to Britain and Europe, rather than a terminal point of communications.) The Southwest Pacific has for its part long figured in the picture of the world as a remote extension of Europe, an ultimate frontier, this way of looking at it being ratified by the character of the civilizations built up in Australia and New Zealand. Their histories are those of countries built from scratch in "empty" lands by Europeans. Their histories are on the North American pattern, and nobody familiar with that pattern will find them outrageously strange. Thus seventeen decades after the first settlement by Europeans was made in the area, Australia and New Zealand are outposts of North Atlantic civilizations. But whereas the face the United States presents to the Pacific is integrally a part of a body whose other face is even more intimately presented to Europe, the Australians and New Zealanders are *in the Pacific* and attached to Europe only by their long lines of communication by sea or air.

These peoples are drawn to the United States only partly by the cultural similarities, more by the power the United States wields in the Pacific Basin. Up to World War II Australia and New Zealand gravitated almost exclusively around British power in the East and the Pacific. Their interest was in Singapore, not Pearl Harbor; in British capital, not United States capital; in British cultural exports, not American; in London's politics, not Washington's. World War II transformed the situation, though not as completely as superficial consideration of the situation might lead one to suppose. Australia and New Zealand still closely associate themselves with Britain, as the Suez episode of 1956 illustrated, but they now balance this with close attention to and in some particulars collaboration in what the Americans are doing. As recently as 1940, as this writer well knows, the suggestion that war in the Pacific would bring Australia into the American "orbit" was widely resented in Australia, but that is what happened, and today the need for being in that orbit is axiomatic in Australia's thinking about foreign policy. Only political romantics, oriented to the left, deny it or try to escape from it. Eyes are inevitably pulled to the northeast, to North America. That is one important effect World War II had on the area.

The association of Australia and New Zealand with the United Kingdom is a fundamental fact about them. In the beginning it was a relationship of colonies and mother country, and the evolution of the colonial relationship into the present-day Commonwealth relationship is not only significant in the histories of the Southwest Pacific countries in their slow change toward autonomous maturity, but it is also illustrative of the continuity of a basic orientation toward world politics. From the historical chance that they began their histories as British "possessions" and have uninterruptedly continued within the British system, they have derived a political dogma of *loyalty* to Britain which in foreign affairs has meant accepting the obligation to go to war when Britain went to war. In fact, it is only recently, in historical perspective, that the theoretical right of a Commonwealth associate to contract out of United Kingdom foreign-policy obligations has been admitted, but in Australia and New Zealand that theory has had only limited significance in practical politics. Rather the predominant tendency — there is, of course, a current of minority opinion — has been to continue support of the United Kingdom while developing particularistic regional policies, different from the United Kingdom's if need be, for which primary responsibility has been assumed. This will be developed later. For many decades there was no real choice in the matter, but Australia and New Zealand long heavily discounted what choice existed.

The Suez route, for almost nine decades now the traditional economic, political, and cultural route to and from the point of origin of both Australia and New Zealand, has long been denominated a "lifeline" and still is one. The symbolic and actual importance of that line of communications to the two nations has long been very great. It is, in a sense, the rope that ties them to Europe. In both World Wars these countries figured prominently in the fighting that went on in North Africa and the Middle East. Anzac — the collective noun made of the initials of the Australian and New Zealand Army Corps — is imperishably associated with that brilliantly mismanaged adventure known to history as Gallipoli. Australia and New Zealand are still involved, willy-nilly, in Near Eastern politics, and still in large measure in association with the United Kingdom. How far they will harmonize their views with those of the United States, which has reached the area from the opposite direction, remains to be seen, but probably to the extent that the United Kingdom does.

It is Suez — the Middle East — which gives these nations their peculiar interest in the large and now enigmatic Indian Ocean. Australia, of course, has a long coastline on the Indian Ocean, with a hinterland mostly of low economic utility, unless minerals, including oil, redeem it. In the ocean, she has taken over islands from Britain in recent years. She has pioneered an air route across it to Africa. New Zealand, wholly within the Pacific, has keen interest in the ocean in terms of communications. For the greater part of the Western history of the Southwest Pacific the Indian Ocean has been a British lake — since 1815 at least. Now its definition is changing. In World War II the Japanese almost penetrated it in a decisive way and the United States contributed to its defense, notably with submarines. Today it figures as a Commonwealth lake — no longer, properly speaking, as a British lake. India, Pakistan, Ceylon, Malaya, Australia, New Zealand, and South Africa have primary responsibilities for its condition, while Britain figures only by virtue of her East African colonies, her colonial remnants in Asia, and her general Commonwealth associations. It is not improbable that the defensive job assumed by the Commonwealth will one day come to rest in southwestern Australia. The Indian Ocean is a boundary of the Southwest Pacific, but guaranteed communications across it are vital to its well-being on present-day foundations. What influences its future influences the foreign political views of the Southwest Pacific countries; and this means their involvement in Near Eastern politics and the politics of Africa and Asia.

Emphasis has fallen here on the relations of Australia and New Zealand with the United Kingdom. It must also be taken into account that both are members of the association of nations now called The Commonwealth. This is hardly the place for any elaborate exploration of the subtleties of this relationship, but it is necessary to note that it brings the Southwest Pacific countries into a special relationship with India, Pakistan, Ceylon, Malaya, and the Union of South Africa in their general neighborhood, with Ghana on the west coast of Africa (and prospectively with Nigeria), with Canada as close neighbor of the United States in North America, and, above all, with the United Kingdom. From our present point of view, their relationship with the United States is to some indefinable degree conditioned by the relations of the United States with the

Commonwealth in general and with particular members, notably the senior member, *primus inter pares*, the United Kingdom. Moreover, the sense that Australia and New Zealand have of their maturity and strength as members of the world political community is in some subtle degree intensified by their association with the Commonwealth. It enhances their status both in their own eyes and in the eyes of the other people. It is an intangible of considerable weight in any equation to which they contribute in their own private persons, as in their relations with the United States.

On this showing, then, Australia and New Zealand, the key countries of the Southwest Pacific, are outposts of the North Atlantic civilization in the Pacific Basin, related by geography and communications with South and East Asia, the Middle East and Africa, linked to the Commonwealth and with especial intimacy to the United Kingdom, associated with the United States by virtue of the exigencies of contemporary world politics and, above all, by the logic of power in the Pacific. All of their interests and most of their involvements place them logically against the U.S.S.R. and China in the dominant power-struggle of our time.

2. Australia

The continent of Australia, a geologically ancient land, lies between south latitudes 15° and 40°. In area it is almost as large as the United States: Australia 2,974,581 square miles, the United States 3,022,387 square miles. About 40 per cent of the continent lies within the tropics, but of the states of the Commonwealth (which were from their various founding dates to 1901 separate British colonies), New South Wales, Victoria, South Australia, and Tasmania are wholly within the temperate zone, while Queensland is 54 per cent within the tropics, Western Australia 37 per cent and Northern Territory 81 per cent. The coastline is 12,210 miles long and has but few striking features, the most notable being the Gulf of Carpentaria in the north, where in 1606 the first European discovery of the continent was made, and the Great Australian Bight in the south. The continent is not rich in good natural harbors, though Port Jackson, the harbor of Sydney in New South Wales, is rated one of the best in the world. Off the coast of Queensland is the Great Barrier Reef, one of the most entrancing natural features the world contains.

The words which spring spontaneously to the mind to describe the Australian continent are old, dry, and warm. These words are more important than the gross area in helping us to understand the nature of Australia and, when we fully understand how they apply, we grasp the point that while Australia can undoubtedly carry many more than the ten millions who currently live there, its carrying capacity is nevertheless out of gear with its gross size. Only about one-quarter of the continent, mostly in the southeastern portion, is available for close settlement. If by the end of the twentieth century there are twenty-five million people living in Australia, this will be more because the area of settlement currently outlined is fully and scientifically exploited than because in the intervening years territory now lying idle has been brought into use. Australia's future lies more in the application of the findings of science and technology, as they progressively unfold, less in bringing "virgin soil" into use.

It is the geologists who make one realize that the visual impression of antiquity which one gains in flying over the continent is scientifically accurate. It is, to them, "one of the great 'shields' of the earth," containing some of the world's land longest continuously above the sea. The Australian continent has been stable a very long time. It lacks young mountains, products of geologically recent activity. There are no active volcanoes in Australia today, and no volcanic action is suspected much short of 10,000 years ago. There is a large area in the west of Australia which is believed to have remained "virtually unchanged" for 1,500 million years, and in other parts of the continent are areas dating back 1,000 million and 600 million years. The shield of Australia is extraordinarily rigid. It is probably 200 million years since there were any significant, or violent, earth movements.

The result is that over these long periods of time the continent has been weathered down to a vast peneplain. Erosion has made Australia what it is today. A glance at a map of the physical features reveals that the greater part of the continent has an elevation of between 656 and 1,640 feet only, and a goodly portion is less than 656 feet above sea level. The only significant mountains are strung along the eastern coast and extend into Tasmania. The highest peak among them, Mount Kosciusko, reaches but 7,316 feet, but the average elevation is only 2,000 to 3,000 feet. Other elevated portions of the continent are the Macdonnell and Musgrave Ranges in the center, scenically striking by all reports but not at maximum above 5,000 feet high, and areas of even less height in central and northern Western Australia and South Australia. A broadly conceived description defines six topographical divisions: (1) the narrow eastern coastlands between the Pacific Ocean and the mountains; (2) the eastern mountain system; (3) the central lowlands to the west of the mountains; (4) the great western plateau; (5) the western coastal plain; and (6) the South Australian hoists and rifts.

A fairly clear idea of how dry the continent is can be obtained from the following figures, which establish the contrast between Australia and North America.

Distribution of Total Rainfall by Inches per Year (percentage)

	Over 40	20″ to 40″	Under 20″
Australia	11	22	67
North America	18	30	52

Within the continent there are five main climatic regions. Drawing upon the categories employed by Dr. John Andrews of the University of Sydney, but rephrasing his descriptions to place them in relation to the current political map and to include other relevant points, we have the following.

(1) *Uniform Rain Region* "with a warm to hot summer, which is intermediate between the northern wet summer and the southern wet winter," a region which begins a little north of Brisbane in Queensland and sweeps south across New South Wales and Victoria and includes Tasmania. In the southwest of Queensland and the west of New South Wales it gradually changes into the great Arid Region (Region 3 below). A part of the west of Victoria lies in the Winter Rains Region (Region 2 below). This region includes the larger part of the economic heartland of present-day Australia. Area 456,000 square miles.

(2) *Winter Rains.* This includes the southwestern "island" in the state of Western Australia, roughly that portion south of a line from Geraldton on the Indian Ocean diagonally

across to where the Western Australia-South Australia border touches the Great Australian Bight, plus the coastal areas of South Australia and the portion of the west of Victoria referred to above. The balance of South Australia and all of the rest of Western Australia, except a portion of the latter in the extreme north, falls into the Arid Region (No. 3). Area 290,000 square miles.

(3) *Arid Region.* This vast region covers the geographical heart of Australia, embracing the southwestern portion of Queensland, New South Wales west of the Darling River, most of South Australia, the bulk of Western Australia, and at least half of Northern Territory. It reaches the southern coast, dividing the portions of No. 2 above that fall in Western and South Australia. It dominates the western, or Indian Ocean, coast, for a long distance. It is the second largest area of arid land in the world, exceeded only by the Sahara. Area 1,660,000 square miles.

(4) *Tropical Eastern Coast.* This is a "finger" of country along the Pacific Ocean in Queensland between the mountains and the sea, characterized by "uniform rain or summer maximum." Area 94,000 square miles.

(5) *Northern Tropics.* This region, characterized by winter drought and summer monsoonal rains, begins back of the coastal mountains in Queensland and sweeps across the northern portion of the state, Northern Territory, and the extreme north of Western Australia, reaching the Indian Ocean. Area 470,000 square miles.

These categories, while illuminating to a point, do not reflect all the factors involved. Nothing has been said, or can very satisfactorily be said in a brief compass, about the distribution of the falls of rain over months or in relation to the growing seasons, the erratic nature of the rainfalls, prevailing temperatures, prevailing high rates of evaporation which reduce the effectiveness of the rain that falls, about the susceptibility of all of Australia to droughts, often devastating, nor about the soils and topography as limitations on the economic use of the land. If all these factors were closely examined, it would be easy to accept Dr. Andrews' conclusion that "no continent has so large a proportion of its total area that must be classed as agriculturally worthless" and to find highly illuminating his further observation — surely a classic complaint about the weather — that "Australia is unfortunate in that her tropical areas lie too far south to receive the heavy, well-distributed rains of the wet tropics, while much of southern Australia lies too far north to receive the good, well-distributed rains of mid-temperate regions."

Each Australian state is a congeries of subregions, of which a close student or resident acquires a knowledge, but it would involve us in too much detail to discuss them exhaustively here. The consistent feature in almost every continental state is that if one proceeds inland from any principal coastal city one runs through a series of belts defined fundamentally by rainfall and rather quickly ends up in the low-rainfall Arid Region. The only mainland state or territory that does not include any of the Arid Region within its borders is Victoria. The island state of Tasmania is rather different. It is the only state which appears altogether green from the air, but in includes much very rough country which, though amply watered, is not suitable for close settlement.

An American can get some idea of what Australia is "like" if he thinks it is "like" west of the hundredth meridian in his own country and leaves out the Rocky Mountains.

An illustration of the prevailingly dry character of the continent is the fact that there is but one significant river system, the Murray-Darling-Murrumbidgee system in the southeast. This system supports the major irrigation works of the country. It is almost wholly within low-rainfall country, and its principal river, the Murray, flows at one stage close to the Arid Region, and at another, through the Winter Rains Region, on its way to the sea. What keeps the river going is that it carries waters derived from the melting snows of Kosciusko. The Murrumbidgee is wholly within country of very moderate rainfall and the Darling wholly within truly dry country. The Murray system does not have a high annual flow as the world's great rivers go. The Colorado of the United States, to which it can fairly be compared, has a mean annual discharge in millions of

acre feet of 163, but the Murray, Australia's principal irrigation resource, has but 10. One of the features of the hydro-
electric-irrigation scheme that is based on the eastward flowing
Snowy River in southeastern New South Wales, also fed by
Kosciusko snows, is to feed the Snowy waters through tunnels
under the mountains into the Murrumbidgee and thence to the
Murray, thus increasing the possibilities of irrigation along the
route in New South Wales, Victoria, and South Australia. Although snow falls in other parts than around Kosciusko, a
severe limitation on irrigation in Australia is the absence of
useful westward-flowing, snow-fed rivers. It is not lack of enterprise that makes the actual and potential irrigation areas of
Australia so small in relation to the areas of land needing water;
it is lack of water to use. Water is Australia's outstanding resource deficiency; its conservation and economical utilization
are constant concerns; and her scientists are naturally keen
students of rain physics, the moderation of evaporation from
storage places, and other water-providing and -conserving proposals. The development of a low-cost method of desalting
water will be of major significance to Australia. Much capital
must be invested successfully to utilize the scarce resource of
water to the maximum.

To supplement water from precipitation, there are at least
eighteen known underground water basins in Australia, some
of very limited area, but one of them, the Great Artesian Basin,
is the largest in the world. Exploitation of artesian water began
in the 1880's. The Great Basin covers an area of 550,000 square
miles, mostly west of the coastal mountains, in Queensland
(mainly), New South Wales, South Australia, and Northern
Territory. It supplies over a thousand flowing bores in Queensland alone, and almost all of Queensland sheep and around one-
fifth of its cattle are watered from them. It is also greatly
significant for sheep watering in New South Wales and South
Australia. Speaking generally, that is the importance of all of
the underground supplies: they provide water for animals in
country where surface supplies are at a high premium. They are

of lesser significance as suppliers of water for human consumption and of still less as suppliers for irrigation, in both of the latter cases because of high mineral content.

From the economic point of view the vegetation is valuable insofar as the grasses have been useful for pasture and the trees useful as commercial timber. The pastures of Australia today cover a wider area than the original distribution of vegetation would indicate, for trees and shrubs have been cut off to allow the development of grasses in regions of good rainfall. It was the natural grasses in their aboriginal distribution that were the first major economic resource exploited. Today one important aspect of the intensification of the use of resources is the development of artificial pastures, including irrigated pastures. The trees of Australia are predominantly eucalypts — hardwoods — and the country is not and never has been rich in varieties usable as commercial timbers. Indigenous softwoods are not at all abundant. About nine-tenths of all commercial forest land today carries eucalypts. Commercially speaking, the best timber is found in areas of 40 to 50 inches of rainfall per annum, and such areas are neither numerous nor extensive in relation to the whole. The tropical rain forest of northern Queensland produces both hard- and soft-wood timber, some of the former being highly decorative in color and texture; the subtropical rain forest of southern Queensland and northern New South Wales produces softwoods, and the cool temperate rain forest of Tasmania is also exploited. Probably the most interesting example of well-managed, perpetual-yield, forested areas are the karri and jarrah forests of southwestern Western Australia. As a consequence of its softwood deficiency, Australia is a heavy importer. A triumph of technological ingenuity is the use of eucalypts in papermaking.

No indigenous plants, save pasture grasses, a few shrubs that are drought-time supplements to the grasses, and the timber trees, have contributed significantly to the Australian economy. For all practical purposes the economic plants of Australia have been introduced from overseas and acclimated. (The same generalization can be made about the economic animals.) But it would leave the picture incomplete not to refer to such famous noneconomic plants as the bizarre waratah, the overpoweringly fragrant boronia — in fact to the very rich variety of wild flowers, especially in Western Australia, and to the lovely flowering trees. By the same token it is perhaps necessary to call to mind from among the indigenous animals the kangaroo (or, more accurately, the family of kangaroos), the koala, the platypus, and all their fascinating companions, as well as the rich bird life of the continent, not least among it the emu, which, with a kangaroo, figures on the national seal, and the innumerable and often troublesome "insect wonders." Australia is richly endowed in all that makes naturalists, amateur and professional, very happy. As a final note on this general subject, to which the hand of this writer is but ill adapted, attention may be called to introductions of plants and animals that mis- or backfired, notably among the animals the rabbit, against which a constant war is waged, since it is destructive of pastures, and the many plants which have become noxious weeds, like the prickly pear. The war against the prickly pear, which once heavily infested millions of acres, is a classic epic of economic entomology.

The first really successful economic pattern was the pastoral, primarily the raising of sheep for wool, with cattle a secondary consideration. The wool industry was based upon imported and selectively bred animals fed upon the indigenous grasses. The economic story of the first sixty years of Australian history is an account of how a free economy based on wool production emerged from the constrictions of the penal colony Australia was founded to be and long continued chiefly to be in the eyes of British officialdom. Wool early provided Australia with a valuable commodity, and it has remained throughout its history the nation's most valuable single export. It was the wool growers who first explored the country in detail in their search for grass. It was the pastoralists, too, who pioneered the use of the low-rainfall country and who today, aside from the scattered miners, chiefly account for its use, either for sheep or, in the north especially, cattle. But the vast dry areas have never carried the bulk of the animals depastured. Rather they have always been tributary areas in relation to the better watered parts of the continent, where most of the sheep and cattle are found today as they were yesterday. It is, however, the very large stations in the far outback, on which it is a matter of acres to the sheep or cow (instead of cows or sheep to the acre) that give a touch of romance, in the eyes of foreigners, to the pastoral industry.

Agriculture in the sense of crop growing has a history running back beyond the beginnings of wool growing in the 1820's, but until the 1880's it was a struggling industry, peripheral to pastoral activities. Fierce political battles were fought between the aspiring farmers and the established graziers over ways and means of gaining access to the land believed to be suitable for crop growing. The land adjudged suitable for agriculture was also the best grazing country, and it was in the possession of the pastoralists — "locked up" by them, in the phrase of the day. The problem was to give the farmers legal access to land the graziers held. The political campaigning around this problem, or question, began in the 1860's and, in spite of all difficulties — and they were many — the farmers won out. But mere access to the land proved not enough to establish farming securely. It took time to carry out the requisite experiments with seeds, fertilizers, and cultivation methods, to provide satisfactory transport both at home and to overseas markets (including refrigeration for perishables), to develop or import and adapt the needed machines, and so on. (The primary fertilizer in use in Australia today is "superphosphate," prepared from phosphate rock obtained from islands in the Pacific, notably Nauru.) The chief farm crop became wheat, grown by dry farming methods on large farms with an extensive employment of machines. Wheat became second only to wool as an export commodity. It occupied, in the end, a vast belt of country west of the coastal mountains between the mountains and the Arid Region from southern Queensland across New South Wales and Victoria, down through Tasmania, around to South Australia and, skipping the Arid gap, over into Western Australia. In the process of defining the wheat belt the farmers probed the Arid Region, much as American wheat growers did in the West, but they have now beaten a retreat from it. Around wheat growing a bewildering range of other crops provided the basis for lesser agricultural economies in climatically favorable areas, mostly all in or on the seaward side of the wheat belt, like cane sugar on the Tropical Eastern Coast (Region 4 above) of Queensland, irrigation crops (tropical and semitropical fruits, grapes for table and wine, rice, et cetera) along the Murray River, or temperate fruit orchards in Tasmania. Dairying found its place in well-watered coastal valleys in all states, with a concentration in Victoria. Australia became, and still remains, one of the major food exporting countries of the world.

It is noticeable that the progress of the land industries in Australia has been and still continues to be chiefly a matter of more intensively using an area which was first explored and occupied by the pastoralists. (A conspicuous exception to this generalization is the sugar country of tropical Queensland.) Economic Australia, in terms of the land industries, may be defined as consisting of a finger of country north from Brisbane along the coast of Queensland, the huge triangle of country roughly marked off by a line drawn from Brisbane across to the head of Spencer Gulf in South Australia, plus the pendant island of Tasmania, and the inland "island" of southwestern Western Australia. All else is tributary to this economic heart of Australia.

Manufacturing has also found its location within the heart of the country, notably in New South Wales, Victoria, and South Australia. The needed resources are either there, or can be assembled there at reasonable cost, and so are the markets. Manufacturing began in Australia with only the protection of distance, but after the gold rushes the colony of Victoria took the lead in exploring the uses of protective tariffs. However, it was not until after the federal government was established in 1901 that protective tariffs were employed on a nationwide basis to encourage industrialization. The systematic development of modern industry really dates from the establishment of steel production in Newcastle, New South Wales, in 1915 on the basis of New South Wales coal and South Australian iron ore. Since then there have been periods of slow progress, notably during the Great Depression of the interwar period, but no real turning back, and the industrial pattern has become progressively more complex. The impressive development program which has engaged Australian energies since World War II has fundamentally been a program of industrialization. Heavy industry today is chiefly centered on the New South Wales coal fields north and south of Sydney. A Victorian industrial complex, centered on Melbourne, is based upon electricity generated from brown coal. A third impressive complex is developing in South Australia. Today Australia has around 55,000 factories, representing more than 200 different industries. In proportion to the size of its population, Australia is now one of the most intensively industrialized of countries. More people work in factories than in the land industries, a fact which contradicts the general impression overseas that it is a land of sheep stations and crop farms. Australia is also marked by the elaborate development of the tertiary, or service, industries and occupations.

The mining of the base metals which modern industry uses began over a hundred years ago when copper was produced in South Australia, but base-metal mining really got on its feet in Australia in the seventies and eighties of the last century, when the country became an important producer of lead and zinc. In the world market, Australia was an important producer of industrial metals long before it had the domestic industry to use any significant quantities. Today the range produced is wide but not all-inclusive in relation to industrial needs. New deposits of important minerals are, however, constantly being discovered, especially as modern prospecting techniques come into play over more and more of the likely country. Although a map indicating the known mineral deposits shows a striking concentration of them within the economic heart of the continent, it has long been the case that deposits of the first — sometimes of the greatest known — magnitude have been found and developed in the dry tributary areas. As remarked before, mining is, next to pastoral activities, a principal industry of these areas, and the discovery of new mineral deposits and their development is a principal hope of making more profitable use of them. Celebrated and long-established base-metal mining centers in the Arid Region are, in the east, Broken Hill in southwestern New South Wales and Mt. Isa in northwest Queensland. The gold-mining city of Kalgoorlie in Western Australia is similarly located. It is indicative of prospects that the most important deposits of uranium have been found in the outback of South Australia and in Northern Territory and that recently a very large discovery of bauxite, to be elaborately and quickly brought into production, was found on the remote western side of Cape York peninsula in northern Queensland. The well-known iron ore deposit at Yampi Sound on the northwestern coast of Western Australia is an older illustration of the same point.

However, as Australia today is not self-sufficient in all the minerals used in modern industry, so it cannot be assumed that it will one day become so as discoveries are made. The situation will shift and change, perhaps consistently for the better for some years, but like the United States, Australia will always be dependent on outside supplies to some degree and in some particulars. In some respects the situation can be improved by tapping the resources of its island neighbors, notably the Melanesian neighbors like New Caledonia and New Guinea. The outstanding deficiency is petroleum. While experts do not yet despair of finding oil on the Australian continent, the hard fact is that to 1960 no significant pool had been discovered. Oil imports are naturally very large in the total absence of domestic supplies. They are drawn from the Persian Gulf, Indonesia, and Borneo. A feature of the trade in recent years has been the building of large refineries at strategic points around the coast. Australia has become an exporter of refinery products. It is building a petrochemical industry.

As to power, Australia's coal reserves are the largest in the Southern Hemisphere. The black coal fields of New South Wales are the largest and best in the Commonwealth. Queensland has a number of important fields, but the total reserves are short of the New South Wales quantities. Tasmania has one good field of moderate quality. South Australia's coal is of poor quality and limited in quantity, but Western Australia has quite large reserves of moderate to poor quality coal. Victoria, with but limited quantities of black coal, has very large quantities of brown coal; the famous Yallourn-Morwell field, which is intensively exploited, has reserves of no less than 10,200,000,000 tons.

The water-power resources of the continent are naturally limited. Nevertheless, the Snowy River power-and-irrigation scheme in southeastern New South Wales is a truly gigantic project, which among other things will link the New South Wales and Victorian electricity distribution systems, thus joining together the two largest industrial complexes of the continent, enormously increasing the available electric power, and confirming the point that here is the heart of Australia. However, impressive as Snowy River is, a reliable estimate has it that hydroelectric stations will never supply more than 15 per cent of Australia's needs for electricity, though this figure may be increased if the potential hydroelectric power of New Guinea can be tapped for continental use. Tasmania is, of all the states, best endowed with water-power resources. Thus far its electricity has chiefly been applied industrially to the treatment of minerals, notably bauxite. As one of the world's most important producers of uranium, Australia looks forward with

confidence to profiting to a major extent from atomic power.*
Meanwhile power generation in Australia rests upon coal, with
supplements from oil and water power, in that order of significance.

To devise and operate a transport system which will efficiently and cheaply serve their economy is a problem which
has thus far baffled the Australians. The complaint today is that
transport charges make a larger contribution to the cost structure of industry than in any other country in the world. In
part this is probably inevitable, given the nature of the continent, the dispersed pattern of exploitation dictated by that
nature, and the distribution of population which has resulted
from it, but, taking all explanations into account, the burden is
nevertheless reckoned excessive. All the standard means of
transportation are employed: roads and motorized passenger
and freight carriers, railways, airplanes, coastal ships, ocean-
going freight and passenger carriers, and intercontinental airplanes. Of these, air transport is the most efficiently utilized.
Australia has one of the best domestic air service networks
in the world, and overseas services of equal value. But the older
elements of the transport service are not of comparable merit.
The rail systems were first developed on a state basis and were
designed to funnel traffic to a single port which was also the
capital city. Only Queensland escaped this pattern, for, being
long and relatively narrow, it built lines inland from strategic
points and then connected them by a coastal line. All efforts
thus far to link the several state systems into a national system

* In the *Seventh Annual Report*, 1958–59, of the Australian Atomic
Energy Commission, it is stated (p. 31), "It is likely that nuclear power
stations will be economic for installation first in South Australia and
Northern Queensland, the first units being commissioned about 1970.
Between 1970 and 1980 nuclear power should also become economic in
Southern Queensland, Tasmania and Northern Territory. . . . With the
development of more advanced forms of reactors . . . nuclear power
should be competitive in the remaining States — New South Wales,
Victoria and Western Australia — by about 1980. . . . It must be
emphasized, however, that technical developments could entirely change
the outlook in a comparatively short time."

have failed, not wholly because of the great cost of imposing a uniform gauge upon a multiplicity of gauges — each state has its own. A Brisbane-Sydney-Melbourne-Adelaide line of uniform gauge will be a reality within the next few years, and it will be a great improvement, but it will not solve the problem of continental rail transport in Australia. The fundamental problem of railway management is how to handle the lines on which traffic densities are low. These came into existence in all states when railways were being built for developmental purposes, but the development has never been of a character that adequately supports railway service. Moreover, this over-extended group of systems is deeply influenced by changing modes of transportation. Road and air transport of passengers and freight is cutting into railway traffic and revenues. The railways are today taking traffic away from but one competitor, the coastal vessels. In short, transport in Australia, as in other countries, is in the process of redefinition of the most economic means, and the established carriers are suffering from it. How the problem will be worked out will depend upon public under-standing of the general situation, especially as a problem in economics. It is important that Australia have as efficient and cheap transportation as can be provided, but today it is not clear what the means should be, or how the alternative means should best be balanced.

The population of Australia today has passed 10,000,000 and is rising. A reasonable expectation is that it will reach 20,000,000 by the end of the twentieth century, at the present rate of increase. The people are concentrated in Regions 1, 2, and 4, in that order of importance, and Region 1 strikingly predomi-nates. The characteristic pattern of distribution within each state is for a high proportion of the people to live in a single city which is often a seaport and always the state capital, a far smaller proportion to live in small provincial centers, and the remainder in rural areas. Australia is urbanized to an astonishing degree.

This pattern has consistently been supported by the nature

of rural activity involving a small labor force of high productivity, this justifying the concentration of population at the export-import centers, where the services, long important in the Australian economy, also naturally had their seats. The pattern has been confirmed by the location of factory industry and it seems improbable that any deliberate policy of decentralization can materially change it, though the inland provincial urban areas — including some specially established around industrial enterprises — may in the future experience a rather faster rate of growth than hitherto. Today 7 out of

Table 1. Concentration of population in urban or rural areas, by percentage.

State or territory	Principal city	Climatic region	Population distribution (per cent)		
			Metropolitan urban	Provincial urban	Rural
New South Wales	Sydney	1	50	22	28
Victoria	Melbourne	1	60	11	29
Queensland	Brisbane	1	36	23	41
Tasmania	Hobart	1	30	29	41
South Australia	Adelaide	2	59	10	31
West Australia	Perth	2	54	10	36
Northern Territory	Darwin	5	0	23	77
Australian Capital Territory	Canberra	1	0	90	10
Commonwealth	—	—	51	18	31

every 10 Australians live in urban areas and 5 out of every 10 in metropolitan areas, while only 3 out of 10 live in rural areas. This may comport oddly with the common vision of Australia as a country of sheep stations, wheat farms, sugar farms, irrigation plots, mines in isolated desert locations, and so on, but while the elements out of which this false vision is constructed unquestionably exist, they must be combined with other factors,

most of which have been mentioned above, to explain the reality reflected in the figures — the true Australian reality. The average Australian of today works, not on a sheep station, but in a factory, an office, or in one of the service industries.

The Commonwealth is one of the great trading nations of the world; its trade per head is normally three times that of the United States. Traditionally it has been closely integrated into the British imperial trading system, and while the proportion of exports going to and imports coming from the United Kingdom has declined in recent years, indicating a desirable dispersion of trade, the heaviest concentration is still upon the United Kingdom as the principal trading partner. Just short of half of all imports come from the United Kingdom and around one-quarter of the exports go to the United Kingdom. The trade with other Commonwealth countries is of far less volume, though enough to bring the proportion of exports to such countries to about half of the total, and imports to two-thirds of the total. Trade with non-British countries is widely dispersed over the world. Japan is the most important non-British trading partner, with the United States normally in second place. Trade with Asia may be decisive in Australia's future, and in any case expansion of exports, including manufactures, is necessary to sustain Australia's pace of growth.

Australia is a conspicuous member of the so-called "Sterling Area," predominantly but not exclusively an association of Commonwealth countries whose monetary systems are linked to "sterling," or the monetary standard of the United Kingdom, and who are associated as traders with the United Kingdom and other members of the group. Normally Australia is a member of the Sterling Area which runs a deficit in dollars; in a characteristic year it does not earn all the dollars it requires to settle its obligations in the United States. One of the persisting conundrums for the Australians is how to achieve a fundamental correction of this situation, but no solution has thus far been found, largely because of the real and artificial limitations on the demand for Australian exports in the United States.

In addition to the heavy concentration of current commodity trade on the United Kingdom, a large quantity of private capital from the United Kingdom is invested in Australian land industries, manufacturing, banking, and so on. Of that part of Australia's public debt held abroad, by far the greater proportion is held in the United Kingdom. The sharp rise in American private investment in Australia since World War II has not disturbed the position of the United Kingdom private investors as the principal suppliers of capital. It has simply made American capital far more conspicuous. It should not be thought, however; that United Kingdom capital dominates the Australian economy; it does not. Australian-owned capital is clearly predominant, taking the economy as a whole. The overwhelming proportion of Australia's public debt is also held domestically. But a fear of the effects of heavy investment of foreign capital, analogous to the fear that plagues the Canadians, is intensifying. Criticism is directed largely at the Americans simply because they are the principal non-British investors. The involvement of Australia in the trading-monetary Sterling Area makes her financial position in London a primary concern at all times; and this cash-nexus is the material foundation of the political and cultural orientation toward the United Kingdom.

Since World War II Australia has been rapidly expanding its economy and taking in large numbers of immigrants. The national income has been rising steadily, and capital investment, both from domestic sources, and from the United Kingdom, the United States, and international lending institutions, has been very great. It is one of the capital-hungry countries of the world. Most of the private capital has gone into manufacturing, while government investment has gone to provide the necessary services to industry, like electricity supply, and other "public works" needed to serve a larger population and a more complex economy. About 65 per cent of all investment has been private, 35 per cent public. Like most of the rapidly expanding countries, Australia has not avoided a considerable inflation, caused largely by sharp competition for scarce domestic resources, and partly at times by high prices for exports, notably wool. One consequence of this has been a marked tendency to overimport, leading to the periodic imposition of import controls. Nevertheless, there is agreement that Australia's expansion is in general sound, though not without soft spots stemming from tariff protection and subsidies. The problem of high costs in manufacturing urgently requires solution. The high costs are thought to derive from such factors as low volume of production in relation to overhead costs, occasioned by the relatively small domestic market, weakness in managerial skills, trade-union attitudes and practices with regard to productivity, and transport costs, but not the costs of welfare-state benefits, which are, in any case, small vis-à-vis the wages bill. The growth of industry in Australia has not lessened her dependence on foreign trade; it has not made her more self-sufficient, but rather has redefined the nature of her dependence as expressed in the imports required. As an exporter, she is still basically dependent upon primary products, but one of her important aspirations is strongly to enter the international market for manufacturers.

The Commonwealth of Australia is one of the several monarchical members of the Commonwealth of Nations. Queen Elizabeth II is Queen of Australia, as she is also Queen of the United Kingdom, Canada, and the other monarchical associated countries. The government of the Commonwealth of Australia is a federally organized system, composed of the six colonies — now states — that had been founded between 1788, when the first settlement was made in Australia, and 1859, when Queensland was separated from New South Wales and set up as a colony. Tasmania was settled in 1804 as an offshoot of New South Wales and became a separate colony in 1825; Victoria was settled from Tasmania in 1835 while it was still a district of New South Wales and was given separate status in 1851; Western Australia was settled directly from England in 1829; and South Australia was settled directly from England in 1836.

Northern Territory, in the charge of South Australia from 1862, became the federal government's responsibility in 1911. After protracted discussion, the representatives of the six colonies agreed upon a federal constitution, which was proclaimed in 1901. The Queen's representative in Australia is the Governor-General, who is usually, but not always, a distinguished citizen of the United Kingdom, appointed with the advice and consent of the Australian government. Governors-General not from the United Kingdom have been Australians, one a distinguished judge, the other an able political (Labour Party) leader.

The federal constitution represents a conscious effort to write a document adapted to Australia and acceptable to the Australian public while profiting from experience with a federal system elsewhere. In the course of over half a century of operation, there has been a marked tendency for the power of the federal government to increase at the expense of the states, especially by exertion by the federal government of the power of the purse. At present the states, while still carrying heavy responsibilities, are dependent financially on the federal government. On the other hand, efforts to increase federal power in fields other than finance have normally been resisted by the voters at constitutional referenda. The politics of constitutional amendment is a very confused and confusing subject.* There is considerable sentiment in Australia in favor of a unitary government, but it is not widespread enough to support systematic constitutional revision to that end. On the other hand, there is but little really able argumentation in defence of states' rights, though the voters usually ratify that position. The result is an uneasy and unsatisfactory compromise, a compromise, moreover, that is less a consequence of reasoned plan than of past piecemeal decisions on particular questions. The

---

* The literature on constitutional alteration is enormous. The section of the constitution involved is #128. A recent contribution to the discussion is *Report from the Joint Committee on Constitutional Review, 1959* (Canberra: Commonwealth Government Printer, 1959). The Australian constitution can only be amended by referendum.

need for fundamental constitutional revision is recognized, but it is hard to imagine it being undertaken in the present condition of the public mind. Some additional patchwork changes may, however, be made.

There is a House of Representatives and a Senate. In the House representation is on a population basis, but each state uniformly has ten members in the Senate. At present there are 121 members of the House, plus two nonvoting members from territories, distributed among the states as follows: New South Wales 47; Victoria 33; Queensland 18; South Australia 10; Western Australia 8; and Tasmania 5. The majority party (or coalition of parties) in the House takes charge of the government, the party leader (or leader of the senior party of a coalition) becoming Prime Minister. All members of a Cabinet must be members either of the House or the Senate. Both by constitutional provision and by virtue of earned prestige, the House is the most powerful and important legislative body. The Senate, while not without power, has never quite gained the prestige it was intended by the constitutional fathers to have. What brings the Senate conspicuously into the public eye is its power of obstruction when its majority complexion is different from that of the House. Aside from the existence of such a situation, the actions of the House are decisive.

The government of the Commonwealth is organized departmentally, but it is a rather more fluid arrangement than in some countries, for in Australia departments are customarily established and abolished rather freely as the character and volume of public business shifts and changes with the changing times. Rather than from a naming of the departments in existence at any particular time, a better idea of the structure of the government can be obtained from a functional analysis, the classification based on "service rendered." Such a classification, recently made, gives eleven headings, as follows: (1) financial and economic policy; (2) defense; (3) external affairs; (4) production, transport, and communications; (5) development; (6) regulation of industry and commerce; (7) legal, protective, and judicial services; (8) health, education, and social welfare; (9) research and information services; (10) territorial administration; (11) internal administrative services. Analysis of these categories would reveal that an Australian government carries out the functions traditional for all English-speaking countries and also a wide variety of activities which reflect the accumulated peculiarities of the Australian governmental scene. The Australians have long taken an instrumental view of government; it is a useful device for doing what appears to need doing. Therefore concealed under the categories are such enterprises as Qantas Empire Airways, a globe-girdling airline, the government-owned and -operated Commonwealth railways, commissions concerned with the production of phosphate and aluminum, a Commonwealth-owned trading bank, the National Library, the National University, and so on through a bewildering variety of production and service undertakings. Australians traditionally have expected and accepted a good deal of government. They still do. The vast and complicated Commonwealth structure has been superimposed in the last fifty years on the six state governments. Only local government has never been elaborated to any great extent in Australia.

For the last thirty-odd years there have been three parties active in federal politics, two on the "conservative" side, and Labour. It is necessary to put conservative in quotes because the predominant "conservative" party is not entirely conservative by overseas conceptions. The Labour Party has been represented in the federal parliament from the beginning; it has a continuous history. It is, however, definitely prone to devastating internal quarrels of an ideological character, and on occasion these have led to disastrous splits and the appearance of *two* Labour parties in the federal sphere. One of the two "conservative" — or better, anti-Labour — parties, the Country Party, has a continuous history since its first appearance on the federal scene in 1920, but the other "conservative" party has a remarkably discontinuous history. It has several times been dissolved, reformed, and renamed. At present it is known as the

Liberal Party. The Labour Party will not enter coalitions. Either it rules alone or it does not rule. It is the two "conservative" parties that form coalition governments and have consistently done so since 1923. Oddly, it is the unstable "conservative" party that has always been the senior member of the coalitions and has consistently provided the Prime Minister. Country Party men have been Prime Minister only under such unique circumstances and for such short periods as to make the occasions mere oddities of Australian politics. It is fairly clear what the Labour Party represents; it represents, fundamentally, the unionized workers (though it is not to be explained as wholly the creature of the trade unions), and the leftward-oriented voters of any social status. It is ostensibly a socialist (though not a Marxist) party, but really it favors a mixed economy, though the exact composition of the mixture is but vaguely and impermanently defined, plus as elaborate a welfare system as can be placed on the law books. The Liberal Party is oriented toward free enterprise, but it has accepted a good deal of state enterprise inherited from the past and such installments of the all-out Welfare State as have been legislated. The core of its political strength is apparently the urban business groups and their sympathizers. It is protectionist, but so, in its way, is Labour. The Country Party is really more of a pressure group than a party, or is a pressure group organized as a political party. It is spokesman for the well-to-do rural interests. Both Labour and the "conservative" parties command a hard core of thick-and-thin supporters and elections are therefore determined by "the floating vote." To win elections the parties must induce this vote to "float" in the proper direction, and this necessity keeps them all in reasonable relationship in their election appeals with the prevailing outlook of the Australian people. Labour cannot afford to get too socialistic, the anti-Labour parties too conservative. If this be true, then the Australian federal electorate is normally vaguely liberal, with occasional deviations a little to the left. At least this appears to follow from the relative success of the opposing groups in federal politics. The "conservatives" have held office since 1901 for more years than Labour. However, this way of assessing the situation definitely understates the influence Labour has had in federal affairs, for during its periods in office it has initiated many important policies, and established institutions, that have survived all the chances and changes of politics. Moreover it must not be overlooked that Labour, when out of office, is always the Official Opposition and, when internally cohesive, is a check upon the conservatives and a latent or active threat to their continuance in power. Labour is the only alternative to "conservative" rule the Australian federal electorate has. In some of the states, notably Queensland and New South Wales, Labour has had far greater success, and in no state except South Australia is its record of office-holding poor. Voting in elections is compulsory.

It is manifestly impossible to capture all facets of a country as complex as Australia in a short series of factual statements, even when they are pieced out by the free use of generalization. There still remains the problem of conveying to the reader what Australia is "like."

As to physical likeness, the acceptable analogy to suggest to Americans is with the southwest of the United States. As to the people, they are overwhelmingly of British derivation, but there have long been minority groups of different national origin — Germans and Italians, notably — and since World War II, with heavy immigration, representatives of still other European nationalities have become numerous too. The Australians are still less diverse in their national origins than are the Canadians, but if immigration keeps up they will approach more and more to the Canadian condition. A missing ingredient, from the American point of view, is a permanently resident colored population. Australia's immigration policy has long been designed to keep out black, brown, and yellow peoples as permanent residents, and the cumulated exceptions (like the Chinese) are relatively inconspicuous. (The Australian aborigines are, of course, colored, but they are few — 50,000 full-bloods, 25,000 half-castes — and not commonly seen in the cities, being largely an outback people.)

But if the Australians are predominantly of British origin, that does not tell us everything about their character today. Insofar as they are Australian they deviate from British norms. There is beyond question a distinctively Australian character, and Americans normally find it readily acceptable, but how to render it succinctly in words is a bit of a puzzle. If the writer may repeat himself, the Australians seem to be organized emotionally much like the Americans, but their intellectual furniture is different, more British. They are democratic in their manners, often unnecessarily aggressive in their egalitarianism. As George Orwell might have put it, they do not believe that anybody can possibly be more equal than anybody else and if he tries, he must be cut down to size right away. Normally they are open-spirited, hospitable, not ordinarily given to introspection, sardonic in outlook (rather than optimistic or pessimistic), and willing to give anything reasonable by way of a scheme or idea a "go." They are inveterate improvisers and not usually disposed to labor hard and long for an ultimate perfection of finish. They can work hard under harsh conditions, but they tend to define group norms for what is reasonable application and to look coldly upon a lone individual who violates the norms. They seem to regard work as the "curse of Adam," not as a proper end of man, and they therefore have traditionally placed a high value on leisure. They seem less inclined than Americans to glory in accumulating "things," but a passion for gadgets, encouraged by "hire-purchase," is rising visibly. The national ideal of a home is a single-story cottage house (a "box-for-living") in a garden. They are beer drinkers, but the *avant-garde* is actively exploring the virtues of the excellent domestic wines. Their leisure they devote to fun-and-games. They are inveterate gamblers, devotees of the horses. Intellectuals are rare among them, and their prestige is minimal but improving currently.

Australia is a "laboristic" country. It is rather less of a workingman's paradise than has been alleged by Australians trying to sell Australia to Australians, but to a very great extent social policy is calculated to benefit the worker. The trade unions are powerful, and in politics there is the Labour Party. Generally speaking the articulated ideals which have found expression in the lively literature of the country are working class rather than middle class. It would take a clever analyst indeed to show why Australia, a child of the nineteenth century, failed wholeheartedly to accept middle-class ideals as the prevailing ideals of the nation (as America did), but rather chose to glorify the workingman. Yet this was done within a capitalist scheme of society and has continued within a society still basically capitalist in spite of all the efforts to water it down with something called "socialism." Moreover, the Australians, a highly urbanized people, believe, or profess to believe, that the "true Australia" is to be found in the outback, as so many Americans believe in the primacy of rural virtues (and as the urbanized Romans likewise did so very long ago). Whatever the way in which the situation is defined, it is a fairly obvious fact that the urban and the rural middle classes of Australia have had to battle to sustain their ideals; they have never been in a position easily to impose them. The political parties that command middle-class support were once described by a brilliant Australian historian as "the parties of resistance" — resistance to laboristic policies and pressures. Retreat before them has often been their strategy of holding office. Why the Australian middle classes were forced to take up a stance of resistance is a complicated story, and why their parties have nevertheless ruled the Commonwealth for more years than Labour, since its founding, is another.

The Australian mind is flexible and given to improvisation. It tends to proceed from case to case, settling each issue as it arises in terms relevant at the moment the decision must be made, taking full account of the necessity for compromise. It is only uncommonly doctrinaire, and even when it appears to be, or is accused of being, it is usually a matter of the emotions rather than the mind. Australians ordinarily have a bias or prejudice in favor of a particular orientation toward life rather than an intellectualized philosophy which supplies criteria of judgment. There is, for example, no discernible Labour ideology in the sense of an elaborate structure of carefully articulated ideas, but rather it is a matter of a cluster of policies about specific current issues, some determined by reference to Labour's traditional stands, some improvised at the moment, all reflecting an emotional orientation in favor of the "working bloke" — "the battler" preferably, though the "no-hoper" if need be. Labour's doctrinaires, always a minority, ordinarily based in the trade unions, are a minority pressure group within the Party, always needling, rarely triumphant. They habitually harass. Australian utopianism is vaguely socialistic in character.

To take a different field, in religion the Australians are more apt to be nominal than fervent believers; they appear to lack any passion for theology, any active disposition to try the varieties of religious experience. The major churches are the Church of England and the Roman Catholic. There seems to be a strong feeling among Australians that religious beliefs should be kept apart from one's thinking about secular and mundane affairs; and when an effort is made to mix the two, feelings are outraged. Secularism should rule, except when one is at one's devotions. Public education, for example, is free, compulsory, and secular. None of the universities is church-sponsored or church-maintained; all ten of them draw upon public funds for support and are secular. Australian literature, painting, music, theater, ballet are secular in atmosphere. Moreover, Australian secularism is normally a very placid affair. Australians customarily strive for no dizzy heights and plumb no vasty deeps. There is a strain of provincialism in the Australian mind. Australians regularly get out of step with their more cosmopolitan overseas friends by occupying too long a once-fashionable position that the restless vanguard has left behind. Their minds are apt to be occupied by images of the way things were the day before yesterday; it took World War II, for example, to force many Australians to accept that changed position of Britain in the world which the British themselves had acknowledged at the Washington Conference of 1920, if not earlier. There are, of course, many very cosmopolitan Australians, but it is only lately that they have begun to live at home. The tradition is for them to live abroad. This is called the export of talent. Australia has supplied the world with a vast deal of talent over the decades; Britain would be noticeably poorer without her gifted Australians. It is a measure of Australia's increasing maturity that this particular export is declining and that there is evidence that some of the ability that went overseas to flourish is going to be attracted back to Australia. Australia has been fertile of talent for a long time, but its society was not complex enough to provide careers for the talented, especially those seeking to make careers in science, the arts, and the academic specialties, the high utility of which is not obvious to earth-bound minds. Today all that is changing, and rapidly. Australia is on the move.

As actors on the international stage the Australians are very much in character when they are seeking to promote what best serves their own interests while taking account, by way of compromise, of the other fellow's point of view. In many respects they are easy collaborators, sophisticated in the arts of agreeable association. They are, ordinarily, an easy people with whom to get along, but they insist upon a decent respect for their own conception of their worth and opinions, occasionally with fierceness.

3. New Zealand

New Zealand and Australia are so often linked together by overseas writers and treated as though they were somehow identical in character and outlook that their separateness and distinctiveness is obscured, even implicitly denied. Of course a great many people know very well that they are both autonomous nations, but there is a disposition to think that, generally speaking, it is difficult and hardly worthwhile to discriminate the differences, or to make much of them in terms of international politics. There is enough in this notion of generalized identity to make it very provoking to New Zealanders and those foreigners who are appreciative of the differences and feel they are worth careful attention. In this book, for more than merely tactical reasons, the differences will be treated as very real and will receive something like adequate emphasis.

To begin with, Australia occupies a continent, is developing on a continental scale, and is more and more thinking continentally, while New Zealand consists fundamentally of but two sizable islands. The islands of New Zealand are "off" the coast of Australia to the southeast, but they are 1,200 miles off. New Zealand is really one group in the great "system" of islands in the Southwest Pacific; before the coming of the white man it was a distinctive part of the Polynesian world, and it had become culturally different from its geographical associates specifically because it happened to be wholly temperate in climate.

The incoming whites used the indigenous resources as the foundation for a variant of the Western economy, and this reduced its Polynesian character to the vanishing point. There is more of a Polynesian flavor in Americanized tropical Hawaii than in Anglicized temperate New Zealand. New Zealand today is a Western nation, predominantly British in character, in this respect like Australia, but not identical with it. It has remained "colonial" in its attitudes longer than Australia — there appears to be a lag of three or four decades. For example, there is a marked tendency to date the emergence of a distinctly New Zealand literature only from the nineteen-thirties, whereas the Australians customarily refer back to the eighteen-nineties. It is an outpost of the West in the Pacific world, linked to the North Atlantic world from whence its civilization was derived, but very remote from it. Unlike Australia, which has an Indian Ocean face, it is wholly in the Pacific. If about the same forces of geography and world politics operate on it as on Australia, and the responses are always comparable and frequently identical in kind, there is nevertheless enough free play in the situation for New Zealand to be a bit different. If these forces have led to formal collaboration in external affairs between New Zealand and Australia, that does not mean that New Zealand has been, or is being, absorbed by Australia. Neither is its separateness discounted by the fact that Australia has long been something of a "metropolitan" country to New Zealanders. They have long made careers in Australia in considerable numbers and are especially conspicuous in high places today. New Zealand elected separateness when she rejected the proposal of the Australian colonies to join them in the federal system they were discussing in the late eighteen-nineties. The comparability and the identity are in part attributable to the influence Australia, as the larger and longer settled of the two, has had on New Zealand, but the roughly similar geographical positions of the two land masses and their identical political and cultural traditions and loyalties are even more important.

The core of the complex of islands which is New Zealand is the two large islands known simply as North and South, stretching from 34° to 47° south latitude. Taken together, they provide a territory just a little larger than Great Britain and Northern Ireland. The main islands are about a thousand miles long, running southwest-northeast. The maximum width is 280 miles, the average 120. South Island, the larger of the two, is 58,093 square miles in extent, while North Island contains 44,281 square miles. In population and economic development the North Island is by far the more important. About two-thirds of the total population of 2,175,000 resides there, and all but about 5 per cent of the Maori population of 137,000. The shape of the country gives it an extended coastline, but it is not well endowed with natural harbors.

The islands have a long geological history, but unlike Australia they do not have a history of prolonged stability. New Zealand is a hilly and mountainous country, the South Island decidedly more mountainous than the North. In the South Island truly Alpine conditions are found. Mount Cook, the highest peak of all, rises to 12,349 feet, almost five thousand feet higher than any point in Australia. There are more than 50 peaks of over 9,000 feet in the country, of which only one (Ruapehu) is in North Island. The most famous and scenically grand North Island peak, Egmont, in Taranaki, rises in splendid isolation to 8,260 feet. Glaciers of magnitude are found among the South Island mountains. Both islands have numerous lakes, 6 in North Island, 18 in South, and swift-flowing rivers, 25 in North Island, 48 in South, none of which is more than 200 miles long and most of which are less than 100. New Zealand lies in the earthquake and volcano belts that circle the Pacific Basin (but miss the Australian continent). It has a number of active volcanoes and hot springs, especially in the North Island, and, while its seismicity is high, comparatively few major destructive quakes have been experienced in historic times. The most recent of magnitude occurred in 1931. People who have heard that New Zealand is a land of scenic grandeur ordinarily hold in the mind's eye a vision of great mountains, glaciers, hot springs, grandly situated lakes, and fast-flowing rivers.

A graphic presentation of New Zealand's land forms shows, as the foregoing would suggest, but a limited area of plains country, and that widely scattered, a good deal of steep hill country, some so-called downland, a bit of plateau, and a good deal of mountainous country.

Climatically most of New Zealand can be described as "maritime" or "ocean." Because of the considerable length of the country there are marked variations from the warm far north to the cool far south, and because of the high mountains, other variations caused by elevation, but the islands are entirely within the temperate zone and as a whole the climate is cool-temperate-moist, without marked seasonal variations. Mean air temperatures range from 58° in the north to 40° in the south. The topography influences the distribution of rainfall, especially in South Island, but the range is from 25 to 50 inches in the settled areas, quite evenly distributed over the year, and very reliable. The high country and the mountains, especially in South Island, receive considerable falls of snow, some of which feed glaciers.

In its aboriginal condition New Zealand was predominantly a forested country. Perhaps seven-tenths of the country carried forest. In the process of settlement, the forested land has been reduced to 25 per cent, and, what is equally significant, the remaining indigenous forests, consisting of slow-growing trees, are a rapidly declining commercial resource. Great reliance will in the future be placed upon exotic forests, and it is fortunate that under New Zealand conditions several exotic softwoods thrive remarkably. On the basis of these, the production of woodpulp, newsprint, and so on, has recently been started on a grand scale. The most considerable nonforested natural grasslands were found in South Island. In North Island the forests were eliminated to allow the establishment of pastures of exotic grasses. In considerable measure pastures, natural and man-made, account for the economic history of New Zealand.

New Zealand is primarily a pastoral country. The basic farm organizations are dairy, livestock, and crop. Over 38,000,000 acres are devoted to dairy cattle, beef cattle, and sheep, producing butter, cheese, meat, and wool, but only slightly more than 2,000,000 acres are used for field crops. About 84 per cent of the dairy cows (mostly Jerseys), 55 per cent of the sheep, and most of the beef cattle are found in North Island. The Canterbury District of South Island is a principal crop-growing area, producing a large proportion of the wheat, oats, barley, pea, grass seed, and potato crops. The high efficiency of New Zealand's animal industries is well known; they provide the underpinning for a high standard of living.

In spite of the rather difficult topography of the islands, a road network of reasonable adequacy has nevertheless been developed. The trend is decidedly in favor of passenger traffic by road as against railway, in private motor vehicles, of which New Zealand has a proportionately more ample supply than Australia, and public-transport vehicles. It is likely that the same trend would be shown in freight transport if the traffic were not controlled to the advantage of the railways. The railways of New Zealand have in general a traffic density comparable to those of Australia, but the density is twice as great in North Island as South. The system, government-owned, is usually able to show a profit on operations but not to pay interest on capital. It consists of two separate units, one on each island. The problem of uneconomic branch feeder lines is acute. Coastwise shipping is relatively unimportant, but as one of the world's great international traders, New Zealand is fully served by overseas shipping. New Zealand has the highest per capita foreign trade in the world. The major ports are Auckland — by far the busiest of all — Wellington, Lyttleton (port of Christchurch), and Dunedin. These account for four-fifths of the goods moved in and out of the country, Auckland for half of this proportion. As in Australia air transport is of increasing importance both for domestic and overseas traffic. About 40 per cent of all passenger departures overseas are now by air. New Zealand has elaborately developed its domestic air services, although the longest possible flight is 926 miles and the average flight is but half the world's average, or 240 miles. A highly significant development is an air freight service linking the railways across Cook Strait.

The islands are not rich in minerals and they are not likely to become the seat of any large heavy industries, though an iron and steel industry is possible. They lack adequate resources of both coal and iron, though neither is absent. Such manufacturing as has developed is of the kind called "light" and is still closely related to the processing of primary produce, though diversification beyond this has been going on for many years. Today about one employed person in five works in a factory, and about 70 per cent of the factory workers are in North Island. Most of the factory units are small. Auckland is the principal manufacturing city by numbers employed, but Lower Hutt, near Wellington, has the most intense concentration of relatively large units. The other principal manufacturing centers are Christchurch and Dunedin. The power basis of this development is hydroelectricity; New Zealand's factories rely heavily on electric motors. The country's hydroelectric resources are, proportionately, very great. They were reserved to the Crown as long ago as 1903, so the current very impressive developments are government enterprises. It is now believed that only by the further development of factory industry can New Zealand hope to sustain its present standard of living while continuing to increase its population.

Auckland, Wellington (including Hutt), Christchurch, and Dunedin — in that order — are the most populous urban areas. Although about two-thirds of all New Zealanders are urban residents, the urbanization is not really as intense as Australia's because moderate-sized towns are more numerous. It is one of these — Hamilton — that is currently the fastest growing urban area in the country. There is a drift to the towns at work in

New Zealand as rising productivity on the farms releases labor. The Maoris are affected by it; the largest single urbanized Maori group is in Auckland. The total population is rapidly increasing both by natural increase and by immigration. It is forecasted that by the year 2000 there may be 4,800,000 people in New Zealand.

Although the constitution of 1852, which is still in force, but much amended, provided for a pseudo-federal system under which several provinces with fairly extensive powers were associated with a central government, New Zealand has had a unitary government since 1876, when the then-existing provinces were summarily abolished. Up to 1950 the legislature consisted of two houses, but in that year the upper house was abolished, leaving the legislature unicameral. The British parliamentary forms are followed. The leader of the majority party in the legislature becomes the Prime Minister. He is assisted by a Cabinet drawn from the single house of the legislature. It is a well-established tradition in New Zealand that state power shall be used instrumentally to effectuate a wide variety of social and economic purposes. The resultant structure of executive government is therefore now quite complex. There are over forty central departments. Usually these are distributed among no more than sixteen ministers.

Two parties, the Labour Party and the National Party, dominate the political scene. Neither can be thoroughly understood apart from the social and intellectual context in which it functions, but in a general way it may be hazarded that Labour is more disposed to invoke the state power in the direction of economic affairs and the redistribution of the national income, while the National Party leans away from this, though it cannot hope to escape established practices. Both are parties of national appeal, but Labour leans heavily upon the urban, unionized workers, while the National Party has a traditional association with the farmers. Leaving aside the effect on the voting of transient small parties and the independent candidates, the electorate is normally quite evenly divided between the two major parties. Victory at the polls can be by a very narrow margin. Essentially the two existing parties represent deviations from the "lib-lab" outlook of the eighteen-nineties, when New Zealand attracted the world's attention for "advanced" legislation, the one party inheriting the conservative components of that effective but rather amorphous synthesis, the other developing the laboristic components. A farmer-based split-off from Liberalism won office as far back as 1912, but the laboristic wing first came to power in 1935.

Much energy has been expended by commentators, domestic and foreign, on trying to define the social tone of New Zealand. With reasonable justice it can be said that New Zealand has an administered capitalism designed to achieve a maximum of equality by the systematic socialization of income through elaborate social services and other devices. Equality is the operative ideal, rather than freedom. New Zealand writers point out emphatically that the emphasis is upon equality of *material* welfare. But as it has thus far proved impossible to devise a system of equal rewards for differential services to society, inequalities of income and property holdings exist in New Zealand as elsewhere. Probably, however, they are more muffled in New Zealand than elsewhere. It is the struggle for basic equality in the material fundamentals of welfare, rather than for excellence of the mind and spirit, that led a distinguished New Zealand historian to remark, "New Zealand is on the same track as the rest of Western Civilization, and maybe a little further toward the triumph or disaster which lies at the end of the road." There are signs that the established national ideal may, because of its manifest deficiencies, be ever more pungently criticised by the intellectuals in the next few years.

4. The Islands

There are almost, but not quite, as many ways of looking at the islands as there are islands, and to be absolutely inclusive would be exhausting, for it would require that an attempt be made to relate various categories of facts — geological, climatological, anthropological, demographical, political, and economic — to a wide variety of very specific situations. Nor can the problem be handled by concentrating attention upon "important" islands or groups of islands, for the "importance" of the islands has always been a highly fluid conception and still is today. Here the complexity of the islands will be at least partially obscured by the generalizations needed to assist a quick understanding of them.

A useful division of them is into the Polynesian and the Melanesian islands. These terms refer to the indigenes living on them. The Polynesian islands fall within that great triangle that is formed by a line running from Hawaii to New Zealand, eastward to Easter Island, and then back to Hawaii. Historically the Polynesian islands were the first to attract and hold the attention of Europeans, and, as a matter of fact, facts and fancies about them figure in the most vivid image of the islands commonly held in the Western world. The other great division, the Melanesian islands, meaning literally the "black" islands, a reference to the pigmentation of the people, is less well known. (The Polynesians are a brown people.) The Melanesian islands stand west of Polynesia over toward and to the north of Australia. These islands came later than the Polynesian into Western political and economic history, but today they are thought of as the islands of greatest economic potential. Unfortunately they often have difficult climates and they are in the malaria belt. Mostly north of the equator and therefore not relevant in detail to our present concerns, are the Micronesian islands, a world of tiny islands, formerly mostly in the Japanese Mandate, today in the United States Trust Territory. Only one of the Micronesian islands, Nauru, will figure prominently here, though others which happen also to be south of the equator are associated governmentally with either Melanesian or Polynesian groups.

The islands are also divisible into the broad categories of arcuate or "continental" islands on the one hand and the "strewn" islands on the other. "Continental" islands include New Guinea (the largest of all the islands), the Solomons, New Caledonia, the larger islands of the Fiji group, and New Zealand (although it is here treated apart from "the islands" for reasons specified). Most of the "continental" islands fall in Melanesia, though not New Zealand, and the Fijis straddle the cultural border between Melanesia and Polynesia. Most of the "strewn" islands are in Polynesia; or, differently put, Polynesia consists prodominantly of strewn islands, "high" or "low." A more elaborate classification is into five categories, as follows: treeless, dry-forest, or raised coral islands, weathered volcanic islands, and "continental" islands.

The significance of the foregoing distributions for us is that they give a tentative, preliminary, sense of the probable importance of the islands, historically or potentially. On the face of it small strewn coral islands, or atolls, must originally have little importance, but they may acquire importance because of unique resources, geographical position, or marine resources on their foreshores. Thus Canton Island, a treeless coral atoll, after years of unimportance, suddenly became of great importance as a landing place for airplanes when the route from North

America to the Southwest Pacific was pioneered in the nine-teen-thirties, while the Tuamotus, dry-forest strewn atolls, were long quite important because of their resources of pearls and shell. Nauru, a small raised coral island, is vitally important as a major source of phosphate, the basis of the fertilizer chiefly used in Australia and New Zealand in crop-growing and pasture improvement. A case could be made for regarding this small island as the most important single island for Australia and New Zealand today, but it is a wasting resource that is involved. If small islands not of obvious utility in the eyes of their dis-coverers can on closer study or because of changed technology become of great importance, it is nevertheless logical to sup-pose that it is the larger islands that have had and mostly still possess importance. Especially is this true if one's eye is on re-sources for agriculture and mining. While the importance of the larger islands has changed over time, and is still changing, it is to the larger islands like those in the Fiji group, to New Caledonia, and to New Guinea that attention is chiefly directed today. They now overshadow such anciently important large islands (weathered volcanic islands) as Tahiti and Samoa. Fiji is in terms of developed resources probably the most important of the large islands today, with New Caledonia in an ambiguous middle position, and New Guinea regarded as having the high-est potential for the future. The Melanesian islands, if as rich in minerals as alleged, will assume greater and greater impor-tance as time passes.

For historical reasons there is no order, logical or other, about the political status of the islands. The pattern is a curious result of a wide variety of circumstances. At present possession or control of the islands with which we are concerned is shared by the United Kingdom, France, New Zealand, Australia, the Netherlands, the United States, and Chile. In terms of area and population the islands in Australian possession or under Aus-tralian control are the most extensive. In Polynesia the French hold Tahiti and have associated with it the rest of the Society group and a number of minor groups, including the historically famous Marquesas and Tuamotu groups. The United Kingdom possesses Pitcairn Island (the home of the *Bounty* mutineers) and a protectorate over Tonga, the only survivor of all the island monarchies that figure so interestingly in island history. New Zealand possesses the Cook Islands, with which is associated Niue, and the Tokelaus, and is trustee for the larger part of the Samoan group. That part of Samoa not in the charge of New Zealand is a possession of the United States. (Few Americans indeed ever reflect that the United States and New Zealand have a common frontier!) Chile holds Easter Island.

In Melanesia the United Kingdom possesses Fiji, part of the the Solomons group is a British protectorate, and Britain shares control of the New Hebrides with France under a condominium. Australia holds that portion of New Guinea which is called Papua and controls under a United Nations Trusteeship another portion of New Guinea with which are associated outlying islands, including some which belong geographically to the Solomons. The Dutch hold the balance of New Guinea under the name of Irian, but the Indonesians lay claim to it. In Melanesia the French hold New Caledonia and certain associated islands, and share in the control of the New Hebrides, as just remarked. The Micronesian island of Nauru is a U.N. Trust Territory shared by Australia, New Zealand, and the United Kingdom and administered by Australia. In all cases the structures of government are on the pattern of colonial governments with a tempering of local representation in government counsels. Politically the islands today are of the so-called "colonial world," but there are signs of impending change in certain groups.

The holdings of the French and British refer back to the nineteenth-century imperialistic activity of those powers. The Dutch acquired their portion of New Guinea at a late stage of their empire building in the East Indies. The Americans are in Samoa because, decades ago, before the Panama Canal was built, they coveted a convenient coaling station on the route via Cape Horn to the North Pacific. The Chileans inherited

Easter Island from the Spanish. The Australians and New Zealanders hold and control what they do because their geograpically intimate relation to the islands early inspired an imperialistic attitude toward them which, when they themselves were colonies, went unrequited but later was assuaged by transfer of territory to them by the United Kingdom and by the taking of territory from the Germans who were active in the islands until World War I. In fact there is some warrant for saying that the United Kingdom is represented in the islands more because of colonial than metropolitan enterprise. If the colonial imperialists had been closely attended to, all the islands south of the equator might have been British. If some Australian theorists had been listened to at later stages, there might have been a total redistribution of United Kingdom possessions in favor of Australia and New Zealand. But as it has fallen out, the pattern is that just outlined.

Aside from the romantic notions, chiefly propagated by literary people, about the quality of life in the islands, there is probably no subject about which misconceptions are more rife than natural resources. The idea that the tropics are especially and fabulously rich is a fairly ancient one and it has been applied to the islands for many generations. There are, of course, riches in the islands, whether one is talking about resources useful to the indigenous people, or resources prized especially by intruders because of their value in their own civilizations. Judged either way, the case may nevertheless be overstated, especially with regard to particular islands. Overstatements have been exceedingly common down the years and have, indeed, motivated many irrevocable actions which have ultimately benefited neither the islanders nor the intruders. One might with a certain show of reason say that more has been done in the islands on the basis of misconceptions than facts. Much of the grief in the islands today arises from the persistence of misconceptions.

The islanders, who were resident in the islands for many hundreds of years before the Europeans appeared, exploited the resources of the islands and their foreshores in the forms of an economy that was designed to provide subsistence plus a small surplus for the support of cultural activities and a little trade. This is still a fairly accurate description of the economies in which the great majority of the indigenes are still involved today.

The earliest intruders into the islands who had economic purposes were mostly either gatherers — as of indigenous products of the sea like trepang, pearl shell, or whales, or of the shore, like sandalwood — or traders bartering European goods like nails, hatchets, firearms, and cloths for native produce, including foodstuffs highly useful to mariners long at sea. The missionaries stimulated trade and production for trade. At later stages in certain islands, especially those of Melanesia, there was exploitation of the human resources by carrying off the males for work on plantations, notably in Queensland and Fiji, but also to Peru. On islands where the natives could be induced to work European-fashion, the plantations drew upon local peoples for labor. Later still, mining was initiated in the islands, notably in New Caledonia, Fiji, New Guinea, and Nauru. Both mining and plantation agriculture led to the introduction of Asiatic labor in the islands, and in some cases the introduced Asiatics settled down with fateful consequences. The major instance is the settling down of the Indians in Fiji, where they now outnumber the indigenous Fijians.

However in no case have the indigenes wholly accepted, or been wholly absorbed into, the economy of the intruders. The degree to which the intruding money (or market or free-enterprise) economy has affected the native economy is different from island to island, but there has nowhere in this area been any such comprehensive destruction of the old economy as in Polynesian Hawaii. It is generally true that two economies exist, connected by the participation of indigenes in the European economy as laborers and increasingly as small producers of such crops as copra, cocoa, coffee and bananas for the market. Today, except in the most remote and isolated areas of the larger islands, it is practically obligatory for the indigenes to participate somewhat in the European economy in order to underwrite their needs for European goods to which they were given their first introduction decades ago by the pioneer traders. In fact, it is a high policy question how to deal with the use of the exploitable resources with a proper balance between the demands of the intruding Europeans and the needs of the indigenes, whose numbers are increasing and whose economic expectations are rising.

Care for the future of the indigenes on the part of governments can easily cause the intruding free enterprisers to allege that their interests are slighted and the creative role of free enterprise in island advancement underrated. Few issues are more acrimoniously debated today. The trusteeship idea encourages a heavy official emphasis on the present and future welfare of the indigenes, and the future becomes more difficult to calculate when the indigenes begin obviously to increase in numbers. This makes the limitations of island resources rather painfully plain. When, as in Fiji, a non-European intruding people becomes very numerous and also presses competitively on resources, the problem is complex indeed.

It took the indigenes a long time to achieve the effective balance which would allow them to increase their numbers. For over a dozen decades after Europeans first came among the islands in numbers in the late eighteenth century, demographic discussion was largely in terms of depopulation. Not only was there a steady, sometimes precipitate, decline in numbers from the totals first estimated by explorers and other early comers, but such light as could be gained on the past seemed to indicate that at various periods before the white men came the numbers had been greater still. Most of the demographic literature on the islands, and the best of it, deals with depopulation. But since the nineteen-tens evidence has been accumulating that the indigenes are in most places definitely increasing their numbers, and in some places problems caused by actual or incipient overpopulation have appeared. It is roughly estimated that at present there are at least 350,000 Polynesians in the islands south of the equator, and 1,500,000 Melanesians. The most important nonindigenous peoples are the Indians of Fiji, a very rapidly increasing people, now numbering about 160,000. Europeans number upwards of 40,000 or a little more. Chinese total perhaps 15,000. And there are fairly numerous half-castes, but any comprehensive figure for them would be but a rough guess.

The towns are the foci of nonindigenous influences. In them the Europeans are mostly resident as are most of the Chinese, a considerable contingent of Indians in Fiji (although the bulk of the Indian population is rural), and many of the half-castes. Either integrally a part of the town population, or closely associated with it in a satellite, is a native population which is normally the most completely deracinated of all native groups. While in the larger island groups there is a principal town which is the seat of government and the trading, banking, manufacturing,* overseas shipping, and general service center, there are in the more highly developed island groups other towns of lesser but growing significance. From the towns the European influence has spread and is spreading through the island or group as government agents bring the indigenes under control and European economic activities are dispersed. The most important island towns today are Suva in Fiji (population 30,000), Papeete in Tahiti (population 16,000), Apia in New Zealand's Samoa (16,000), Noumea in New Caledonia (20,000), and Port Moresby in Australia's New Guinea (14,000) and Rabaul on the island of New Britain in Australia's Trust Territory of New Guinea. Other but much smaller towns, important in relation to their groups, are Vila in the New Hebrides, Honiara in the Solomons, Nukualofa in Tonga, and Pago Pago in American Samoa.

The exports of the islands cover a wide range, but in quan-

* Manufacturing in the islands consists of industries processing indigenous raw materials for overseas markets, producing consumer goods for local consumption in competition with overseas suppliers, and producing consumer goods without the expectation of overseas competition. Fiji and New Caledonia show the greatest variety of industrial activity.

tity and value the total is often small. The largest single item of export, taking all the islands together, is copra, as it has been for many years. But the islands also export phosphates, nickel, chrome, gold, sugar, fruits, cocoa, coffee, rubber, lumber, meat, hides, native crafts, and marine products. In none of these (aside from native crafts) are the islands a principal world source of supply and in most cases the contribution is a decidedly small percentage of the world total. Imports conform nearly exactly to the pattern one would expect to be necessary to support European-style life and industry under tropical conditions — for example, considerable temperate-climate food — with the trade goods in demand amongst the indigenes in addition. The list includes: foodstuffs (that is, groceries including canned goods), textiles, paper and stationery, tobacco, and so on, and machinery, including vehicles.

While exports and imports are traditionally dispersed among a variety of countries including the United Kingdom, France, Canada, the United States, Japan, Australia, and New Zealand, there is a trend in both trades that favors the constant strengthening of Australia's position as an island trader. However, Australia is a sugar-producer itself, so it absorbs no Fiji sugar, though New Zealand does. It also produces its own bananas, so buys none from Fiji or Samoa. (They go to New Zealand.) But it obtains 99 per cent of its copra from the islands, 94 per cent of its vanilla beans, 20 per cent of its cocoa, 16 per cent of its crude rubber, and 6 per cent of its coffee. It can be expected, as its industrial economy continues to grow, to be more and more interested in island minerals. If oil should be found in New Guinea, the situation would be transformed overnight. Similarly Australia is well placed as a supplier of island needs and its position is improving as its economy becomes more complex. The Australians (and to a lesser extent the New Zealanders) have long been active in island economic affairs as individuals and on a company basis. Several of the largest and best-known island shipping, trading, and plantation companies are Australian, notably Burns, Philp & Company and W. R. Carpenter & Company. Island air services are also mostly in the hands of Australian or New Zealand concerns. The Bank of New South Wales and The Commonwealth Bank have branches and agencies dispersed through the islands. The Bank of New Zealand is in Fiji. Mining outside New Caledonia (which is a French interest, of course) is usually carried on by Australian companies. The Fiji sugar industry is controlled by the Australian company, the Colonial Sugar Refining Company. In spite of the fact that Australia is importing great quantities of capital for home development, some money is available for investment in the islands. If the role of private capital in island development can be more precisely defined than at present, and in a fashion favorable to the private entrepreneur, more Australian capital will find its way to the islands. Insofar as private capital plays a role in the future development of the islands, there is reason to suppose that Australian capital may predominate. However there is also reason to be very uncertain how private capital of Australian origin will be dispersed in the islands, and New Zealand capital also, for there is today a strong tendency to focus interest on those islands for which the country has political responsibility. Thus much Australian private capital may go to New Guinea, if the "climate" is right, rather than to island groups not under Australian political control, like Fiji and New Caledonia. Truth to tell, the future of overseas private enterprise in the islands is a matter of great uncertainty.

From the earliest days of their concern with the islands, the Australians and New Zealanders have thought of them as a defensive screen against foreign enemies. Hence their often expressed concern for keeping them wholly in the hands of the United Kingdom. Opinion has varied a good deal about which islands had the highest defensive importance for whom, but in the only major test — that of World War II — fighting was fiercest in New Guinea and the Solomons, while Japanese objectives for the purpose of isolating Australia and New Zealand from North America were New Caledonia, Fiji, and Samoa.

5. Antarctica

Antarctica is by far the most enigmatic component of the Southwest Pacific as here conceived. It is not only that it has not yet been fully explored, that its economic resources and significances, particularly with regard to continental resources as distinguished from those of the surrounding seas, are obscure, that its strategic significance in relation to world communications and as a base (as for missile warfare) is appropriately shrouded in mist, and that there is currently an effort to keep its politics in abeyance, but also that it is early in the day to say how the continent will ultimately be integrated with the rest of the world. It is treated here as part of the Southwest Pacific on a strong surmise that a very large portion of it — more than half its total area — will in the long run be closely integrated with Australia and New Zealand. The surmise is fortified by references to past history, current activities, and faintly discernible lines of development. Such an integration seems likely to take place even if Antarctica is to some degree internationalized. These points will be developed more fully later.

What we have in Antarctica is a largely ice-bound continent approximately 5,000,000 square miles in extent, the last continent to be discovered by man. Palmer Peninsula (or Graham Land), the vast finger pointing north toward South America, was probably first seen in 1820 by Bransfield; the main continent was first glimpsed by John Biscoe in 1831. The early discoveries were largely by-products of a commercial enterprise — sealing — but the proving of the reality of the discoveries soon passed to adventurers and scientists, in whose hands the definition of its character, and the inventorying of its resources still remains. Mostly a civilian enterprise, there is significant collaboration by the national armed forces, particularly in the case of the United States.

Exploitation of Antarctic resources has thus far remained in those parts of the region more correctly designated sub-Antarctic or in the circumjacent seas, involving sealing and whaling. Known land resources include coal, iron, and a variety of other minerals, but it must be kept in mind that only a tiny fraction of the continental land is free of ice and little is known, except in the broadest geological terms, of what is under the ice. Speculation rules. Use of the known mineral resources waits upon final proof as to quantity and quality and, to a greater extent, upon very high scarcity prices for them in existing or new markets. While the technology of their recovery is at least partly known from exploitation of comparable resources under Arctic conditions, cost of recovery and of transportation to points of use are x-factors in the equation. Other suggested economic uses of Antarctica are for air bases for global routes — for example, Australia and New Zealand to South America — storage depots for surplus foods, sanatoria, and so on. Some informed students of Antarctica dismiss proposed economic uses as delusions of fevered imaginations.

Strategically there is the question of the control of Drake Passage, which is 600 miles wide, between Cape Horn and the South Shetland Islands. If the Panama Canal were ever blocked, or otherwise rendered useless, the route around the Horn to the Pacific would once again become as important as it was for many decades before 1914. In both World Wars use of sub-Antarctica by Germany as enemy of Australia and New Zealand was both suspected and proved. New Zealand maintained coast-watchers in her sub-Antarctic islands from 1941 to 1945.

The continent has also been viewed as a possible location for sites for missile bases. Indeed Antarctica may be viewed as a gigantic backstop of the denfenses of the Southwest Pacific, control of which is vital to Australia and New Zealand. The United States as a collaborator in the maintenance of the security of those nations is necessarily also concerned.

Politically it may be noted that seven nations have lodged claims to territory in continental Antarctica. The claims are organized on the sector principle by which the continent is divided like a huge pie, all claims beginning with a stretch of coastline and converging on the South Pole. The claims are:

Australia — Antarctica Territory, 1933

New Zealand — Ross Dependency, 1923

France — Adélie Land, 1924

United Kingdom — Falkland Islands Dependency, 1908 (also claimed in part by Argentina from 1925 and Chile from 1940)

Norway — Queen Maude Land, 1939

The United States makes no formal claim to any part of Antarctica and refuses recognition to all the claims made. The U.S.S.R. also has made no claim to any specific portion, but maintains a "floating claim" which amounts to the assertion that she must be consulted if and when the division of the continent is finally decided or fundamental changes are made in the current situation. As matters stand, the claimants have only the support that comes from mutual recognition of their claims by one another. There is conflict as to territory claimed only between the United Kingdom, Argentina, and Chile. The territory in dispute is the Falkland Islands Dependency. Only two countries, Germany and Japan, have ever renounced a claim to a portion of Antarctica. At the instance of Australia, Japan renounced her claim in the Treaty of Peace after World War II. It is the policy of the United States to try to keep the territorial claims in abeyance, meanwhile reserving Antarctica as a field of cooperative scientific endeavor. India has formally proposed in the United Nations that Antarctica be internationalized and, while in logic there is a forceful case for this, it seems improbable that internationalization is likely to go beyond the point suggested by the United States.* The alternative is a "scramble for Antarctica" comparable to the scramble for Africa in the nineteenth century, or the less feverish "partage d'Océanie" in the same century.

Activity in Antarctica in recent years, especially during the International Geophysical Year, has had a scientific emphasis, although some of it may on occasion have quite another import in the eye of a suspicious interpreter. It seems likely that this emphasis will continue. The influence of the United States is strongly exerted in this direction. The countries involved in the scientific work are more numerous than the claimants, and much of the work has, indeed, been done in claimed areas by nationals of other powers. Some of the countries have worked in both sub-Antarctica and Antarctica, but only South Africa has wholly confined itself to sub-Antarctica. The participating countries have been Argentina, Australia, Chile, France, Japan, New Zealand, Norway, South Africa, United Kingdom, the United States, and the U.S.S.R.

* See below, page 247, for a description of the treaty of December 1959.

PART II HISTORICAL BACKGROUND

6. The Area Explored

The Southwest Pacific came into the history of the West as a consequence of the so-called "expansion of Europe." Even when the actual exploration was clearly motivated by scientific or religious considerations, the economic motivations of imperialism were never far behind or wholly absent. Exploitable resources were always sought and forestalling rivals by gaining first access to them took many men on tremendous journeys into the unknown. The Spaniards in the sixteenth century sought both souls to save and gold; the Dutch in the seventeenth century sought trading opportunities; the British and French in the eighteenth and nineteenth centuries in rivalry sought to forestall one another in whatever advantages might be found; and the Americans, after the Revolution, entered the region as traders and exploiters of the indigenous resources of the sea and its foreshores.

The Spaniards pioneered Pacific discovery with Balboa's discovery of the very ocean itself at Panama in 1513 and the Portuguese Magellan's first crossing of it in 1519–20. Their probings of the Pacific after these great efforts were relatively feeble. Basing their Pacific power on Mexico and Peru, they established a link across the North Pacific with the Philippines and then did little more. Their efforts to find out what the Southwest Pacific might contain came late in their active imperial history, resulted in the discovery of the Solomon Islands, the Marquesas, and the New Hebrides, but they were unable to make anything of them either as sites for settlements, or for trade, and they missed their real objective: the long-rumored continental landmass, *Terra Australis Incognita*. By 1605 when Torres sailed through the strait separating New Guinea and Australia — a feat the Spaniards carefully forbore to publicize — they were through, save for an abortive effort to gain control of Tahiti after its discovery by the English in 1767 and an equally futile effort to use Easter Island, discovered by the Dutch in 1722, as a base for opposing the incursions of their rivals. Slowly their significant discoveries in the Southwest Pacific, inaccurately located on maps, if not concealed from public knowledge, faded toward the status of geographical myths. The Solomons, for example, discovered in 1595, were not identified again until the Frenchman D'Entrecasteaux finally established their reality in 1792. The Spaniards were able neither to explore the Southwest Pacific themselves nor to keep others out of it.

The Dutch, who reached the Indies in 1595, found the resources there just about sufficient for their energies, and those energies were directed by a private trading company which, generally speaking, begrudged the cost of exploring expeditions. What systematic exploration the company did was by way of forestalling rivals and seeking a new road for raids on their Spanish enemies. Knowing nothing of Torres' feat, they probed for a passage into the Southwest Pacific along the south coast of New Guinea but failed to find it. While so engaged, and quite incidentally, they chanced upon the north Australian coast in the vast Gulf of Carpentaria in 1606, and by abandoning in 1611 the old Portuguese route to the Indies up the east coast of Africa to Madagascar and thence to the Indies across the Indian Ocean, in favor of sailing east from the Cape of Good Hope and then turning north for Java, they eventually made a series of landfalls on the Indian Ocean coast of the same continent. Within a few years the Dutch knew something of the Australian coast from Cape York westward around the Indian Ocean side and along the southern coast to the islands of St. Peter and St. Paul. None of these landfalls revealed country at all attractive to them. In 1642 Governor-General Anthony van Diemen dispatched an expedition which was to travel to the south of Australia on an eastward course to search for new lands with trading resources and a new route to Spanish South America. This expedition, led by Abel Tasman, a strikingly accomplished sailor, discovered Tasmania (Van Diemen's Land to 1852), but touched it at a relatively unattractive point, and then found New Zealand, but from a combination of bad weather and Maori hostility was unable to land. Turning north Tasman discovered some principal islands of the Tongan group, saw some of the outliers of the Fiji group, and then swung north around New Guinea to his starting point at Batavia (Jakarta). Nothing seen proved of much interest to the practical Dutch. The Dutch thus knew of the great continent of the Southwest Pacific and the islands near it. Their misfortune was never to find the continent's exploitable "heartland" bordering the Pacific Ocean coast.

The English, beginning with Sir Francis Drake, entered the Pacific via Cape Horn to prey upon the Spanish at sea and along the coasts. The early voyages were up the west coast of South America and across the North Pacific. William Dampier, a philosophical buccaneer, was on the northwest coast of Australia in 1688 and again in 1699. He found it as unattractive as ever the Dutch had. Gradually the English edged west from Cape Horn before turning north and eventually came among the islands. The most important discovery they made before Captain James Cook came into the area in 1769 was Wallis' discovery of Tahiti in 1767.

The French, for their part, went into the Southwest Pacific in rivalry to the English, as a by-blow, one might say, of the struggles of the two nations in North America, India, and the Indian Ocean. The most important French voyage into the area, between those of Tasman and Cook, was that of Bougainville in 1768. The French continued in rivalry to the English well into the nineteenth century, playing a curiously negative role in the histories of both Australia and New Zealand, as well as the island groups. It was in the islands that they found such imperial satisfaction as was vouchsafed them, as we shall see later. In fact, the French followed the British in what they called the "partage d'Océanie," or the dividing up of the islands among the European powers. New Zealand, an integral part of Polynesia, fell to the British in 1840. By that time the French had been jockeyed into the position of reluctantly tolerated "intruders" into what was vaguely regarded as a British preserve. What was later called the policy of "Oceania for the Anglo-Saxons" was by then a thought of some force among the British colonials.

Captain Cook, the greatest of English oceanic explorers and a major figure of the British eighteenth century, in three voyages between 1769 and 1780 not only reduced the Southwest Pacific to geographical order, leaving only incidental and subsidiary discoveries subsequently to be made, but also went a long way toward performing the same feat for the Pacific as a whole. In 1769 he rediscovered New Zealand, showed it was a pair of major islands, and then sailed west in 1770 and came upon the elusive east coast of Australia, which he traced from a point just above Tasmania — he did not ascertain it to be an island — north to the tip of Cape York. On a second voyage he added some island groups, discoveries and rediscoveries, that brought Spanish findings, notably the New Hebrides, back to the realm of actual knowledge, but the second voyage is even more memorable for the fact that during it Cook brought Antarctica into the geographical picture. He reached a farthest South that stood for many years, but located no land beyond the circle. New Zealand was his base in the locality. The third voyage was only incidentally concerned with the Southwest Pacific; it was rather chiefly concerned with the northwest coast of North America and the Arctic. It was on this voyage that Cook discovered Hawaii, which was, of course, to become in the long run a principal focus of United States power in the Pacific Basin. Cook's voyages confirmed British interest in the Southwest Pacific and led to the most decisive kind of follow-up of discovery: occupation. The British moved into the two places best adapted for settlement colonies, Australia (in 1788) and New Zealand (in 1840). The Australian and New Zealand colonies became relay points for the power of British imperialism; the colonists encouraged — occasionally demanded — British assumption of sovereignty over island groups and resistance to the pretentions of "intruders."

The American adventurers in the Pacific generally, and the Southwest Pacific specifically, appeared just as the great age of discovery was closing and the age of settlement and development on the European pattern was beginning. American activity took place simultaneously with all the significant history of Europeans in the area, save the remotest preliminaries. A New-York-born Tory named James Maria Matra, who was with Cook on the first voyage, figured curiously in the discussions of the establishment of a settlement of Australia; Connecticut-born John Ledyard, who was with Cook on the third voyage, elected to be a citizen of the United States, and was the most ardent early propagandist in the United States for the Pacific as an arena of trade. In 1783 Ledyard published at Hartford, Connecticut, an account of his experiences with Cook which was a mixture of plagiarism of a shipmate's narrative published earlier in London and his own recollections. The book contained a map, also borrowed, which outlined what was known of the Pacific just before Americans entered upon the great ocean. The officially edited version of Cook's journal of the first voyage was pirated in New York in 1774 and in 1783 a book — the same from which Ledyard had plagiarized — was pirated in Philadelphia as an "authentic narrative" of the third voyage. In this rather odd fashion Captain Cook became a patron of America's incursion into the Pacific. The early voyagers all knew what in Cook best served their purposes, even if from pirated or plagiarized texts, or at second hand.

Long after the Americans had become familiar actors on the Pacific stage, the Germans, as a phase of the imperialistic adventures from Bismarck's time through Kaiser Wilhelm II's, played a role in the Southwest Pacific which brought them into collision with the British and the Americans, especially in the Samoan Islands, as will be developed later. The actors in the dramas of Southwest Pacific history have been, therefore, the British and their colonists in Australia and New Zealand, the French, the Americans, the Germans, and the Dutch, but the principal actors for most of the time have been the Australians and the New Zealanders.

7. The Americans and the Pacific

Citizens of the United States have played an active role in Pacific Basin affairs from the earliest years of the Republic. Save omnipresent Europe, no area of the outside world has so persistently held their interest, not even South America, nor has any external area, again save Europe, played a larger role in the thinking of Americans about the national future. The idea of "manifest destiny," the most potent slogan justifying their continental expansion, was in large part a rationalization of their determination to reach the Pacific overland. One reason they wanted to accomplish this was the more easily and efficiently to reach out across the ocean to the Orient, chiefly imagining themselves doing so as traders, but their pursuit of trade in the end caused them to accept territorial responsibilities beyond the Pacific littoral. Oregon and California in the 1840's, Alaska in 1867, the Philippines, Guam, Hawaii, and Samoa at the end of the century, are tokens of their persistent interest in the Pacific Basin. The acceptance of Alaska and Hawaii into the union as states extended the metropolitan territory of the United States into the Pacific Arctic and Polynesia. Prophets and agents of the manifest Pacific destiny of the United States have been, in addition to innumerable adventurers, merchant and otherwise, from John Ledyard on, harvesters of the wealth of the sea and the seashore — fur-traders, whalers, sandalwood and trepang gatherers; explorers, from Lewis and Clark to

Charles Wilkes and Richard Byrd; naval figures like Thomas ap Catesby Jones, Matthew Calbraith Perry, George Dewey, and Alfred Thayer Mahan; religious leaders like Hiram Bingham and his missionary fellows; writers, scribblers, literary men, journalists, and specialists in academic disciplines like Herman Melville, Jack London, Henry Adams, Charles W. Stoddard, James Michener, and Margaret Meade; and political figures like Thomas Jefferson, James K. Polk, William Henry Seward, Theodore Roosevelt, John Hay, Charles Evans Hughes, and, by force of circumstances, or circumstances forced, Franklin Delano Roosevelt, one of whose Delano ancestors, Amasa by name, was a pioneer sealer who complained to the Australian authorities about the ill-usage he experienced in Bass Strait and Tasmania.

The story of Western man in the Pacific Basin, of which the American chapter is but a part, has never been comprehensively told, and the American chapter particularly is still a thing of shreds and patches. It is obviously impossible to supply a seamless garment here, and not simply because our focus of interest is the Southwest Pacific. The Southwest section of the American chapter is, of course, the least studied part of the story, and only toward the end does it rise to the high political level where most of the writers on Pacific affairs prefer to discourse. Americans have neglected it, except insofar as it has come into accounts of their activities which have embraced the whole ocean, because from the earliest days their concern has been — and still largely is — mostly with the *North* Pacific Ocean. The first centers of American interest in the Pacific were Canton in China and the Northwest Coast of North America. Americans went to Canton soon after the Revolution to obtain directly for themselves goods, including tea, hitherto supplied to them via Britain by the East India monopoly. They were active on the Northwest Coast — the Oregon country in its extended definition — as traders with the Indians for furs, particularly of the sea otter, to trade in turn to the Chinese for their coveted products. Between these two was Hawaii, by 1820 the greatest of the Pacific refreshment centers (and something of a trading point in its own right) for the men of furs and the whalers.

This concentration upon the North Pacific brought the Americans very early into contact with the other major Western intruders into the Pacific Basin: the British, the Spanish, and their successors, like the Mexicans, the Chileans, and the Peruvians, the Russians and the French, all of whom played a major or minor role in the North Pacific or on the then regular road to it. With these the Americans carried rivalry to the point of war only with the Mexicans, the Spaniards (though not particularly for a cause related to Pacific affairs), and the British. The war with the Mexicans was part of the American campaign for control of their self-defined continental domain in its Pacific Coast aspect, that with Spain was the portentous Pacific Basin phase of a clash of interests in the Atlantic which owed its Pacific extension largely to the personal initiative of Theodore Roosevelt, and the armed conflict with the British was a phase of the War of 1812. It was in the North Pacific, too, that the Americans eventually found a most formidable Pacific Basin enemy, the Japanese, whom, ironically enough, they had induced out of a carefully modulated isolation to join the so-called comity of nations about nine decades earlier. This war, also, was fundamentally a North Pacific war, the only one of the series fought by the Americans that originated out of issues rooted in Pacific Basin affairs. It was, however, extended southward along the western margin of the Ocean into the Southwest Pacific, and thus brought that area vividly before the American people and led to a collaboration with the nations there that has proved enduring. It is up to an examination of this continuing collaboration that this book leads. It is, however, a collaboration given focus and meaning by the situation in the North Pacific — north of the equator.

Of the two passages from the Atlantic Ocean into the Pacific, that around Cape Horn and that by way of the Cape of Good Hope and the Indian Ocean, the early American voyagers made most use of the Cape Horn route, but they nevertheless often both entered and left the Pacific by way of Good Hope, notably the ships trading out of Salem whose objectives were ports in India, the pepper and spice ports of South Asia, and Canton. There was also early developed a route from the Cape of Good Hope to China around Australia and up the western side of the Pacific, and after the British established themselves in Australia, American ships traveling by way of Cape Horn sometimes called at Sydney on their way to the Northwest Coast or China. These, of course, were sailing ships using what knowledge there was of winds and ocean currents, and what they discovered was grist for the mill of Matthew Fontaine Maury, the great American student of these matters. Even the Boston ships that went to the Northwest Coast for furs before going on to Canton, and which, as implied above, traveled widely in the Pacific en route from home to the Northwest Coast, often returned home via the Cape of Good Hope. The American whalers usually but not invariably, got into the Pacific via the Horn and went home the same way. The sealers mostly used the Horn route outward bound but took their furs to Canton and returned home by way of the Cape of Good Hope.

The only importance this has for our present purposes is that the ships mostly, in early days, or up to 1815, kept to the eastern side of the Pacific, fairly close to the South American coast, when making their way north. Their visits to Spanish ports on that coast on these journeys are more obviously a part of the history of American intercourse with South America than of the Southwest Pacific, and it is significant of the way in which American concerns were balanced that when United States naval vessels were finally stationed in the Pacific they first made their headquarters at the Chilean port of Valparaiso and the Peruvian port of Callao. Historically the only serious attempt to penetrate the Southwest Pacific west from South America — that of the Spanish, working from Peru in the late sixteenth century — was a failure. The only successful Spanish trans-Pacific operations were between Acapulco, Mexico, and

Manila in the Philippines — in the North Pacific. Relations west and east across the South Pacific are tenuous to the present day, although lately an airline from Australia via Tahiti and Easter Island to Chile was plotted. If it is possible to draw any reasonable boundaries around the Southwest Pacific, the eastern boundary is surely to be drawn with reference to the location of the easternmost South Sea islands, and a glance at a map will show that that is a good distance *west* of South America. However, it was early learned how to get to the west among the islands after rounding the Horn, or to get to the east among them by way of the Cape of Good Hope. It was via the Horn that Wallis got into the islands to discover Tahiti in 1767, and Cook made his approach to Tahiti in 1769 by the same route and then proceeded westward to New Zealand and Australia. All this and more was known to the early American visitors to the Pacific via Cape Horn. The mere fact that Americans were in the South Pacific did not mean that they were, willy-nilly, in the Southwest Pacific. It was, in a way, a separate province of the great ocean, not an unavoidable entryway to the North Pacific, where almost all the American ships were bound. If they were to get into the Southwest Pacific it was because they wanted to go there — had some errand there. It is rather remarkable how early the Americans found errands to do in the Southwest Pacific.

8. The United States and the Southwest Pacific to 1816

On the eighth of March 1816 Governor Lachlan Macquarie of New South Wales (in office from 1810 to 1821) addressed a dispatch to his superior in England, Earl Bathurst, detailing at some length a quarrel between himself on the one side and the Reverend Benjamin Vale and Lawyer W. H. Moore on the other. The difficulty had arisen over an American ship. *The Traveller*, Captain William French, which had arrived in Sydney from Canton with tea and other Chinese merchandise consigned to Sydney merchants. She was bound home to the United States. The only remarkable thing about her was that she was the first American ship to visit Sydney after the conclusion of the War of 1812. The Governor granted her liberty of entry as he had other American ships in prewar years, but the Reverend Mr. Vale, supported and advised by Lawyer Moore, seized her as a lawful prize under the British Navigation Act. Macquarie was away from Sydney when this happened and, discovering it on his return, he was incensed. He released the ship to complete its business and proceeded to deal with Vale and Moore in a rather reckless fashion, since it ultimately turned out that, under the law, they were right and he was wrong, and he therefore earned himself a severe rebuke for his handling of the whole complicated situation.

This famous episode calls attention to two points of some interest. First, American ships visiting Australian ports, mostly Sydney in the earliest days, did so with very doubtful legality. They ran either the risk of falling afoul of the regulations of the East India Company's trading monopoly of the Pacific Basin, in force to 1813, since the privileges granted to Americans under Jay's Treaty of 1794 clearly did not apply in Australia, or, at a later stage, the risk of becoming entangled in the Navigation Act. That no American visitor before *The Traveller* was particularly embarrassed for these reasons is attributable, it appears, to the compelling fact that the colony usually desperately needed any merchandise — though not all kinds, as we shall see — the American visitors had for sale. The trading went on under the rule of necessity which the Governors felt free to invoke to justify winking at the violation of law. The other point is not so weighty. It is that although the American visitors to Sydney were always on their way to some other destination, Sydney was never a terminal point of their voyages — still, in the earliest days they called in sufficient numbers to lead the British traders, who were kept away from Sydney by the East India Company's rules, to protest in 1800 that the Americans were monopolizing the Sydney market. Eventually the increasing irrelevance of the rule of necessity and the application of the Navigation Act reduced American trade to negligible proportions.

To his dispatch about the Vale case Governor Macquarie attached a list of the forty-one American ships his assistants said had visited Sydney prior to *The Traveller*. The list gives the names of the vessels, "where from," "year of arrival," and "sailed for." Using these data and taking into account the research that shows that the list was not exhaustive, and taking account also of the general position in the Pacific, it is possible to draw a picture of the activity.

In no year between 1792, when the first American vessel visited Sydney, and 1812, when traffic ceased on the outbreak of war, did more than five American ships call at Sydney in any one year. In three of these years none at all called. The whole business was extremely casual. It was, as a matter of fact, a by-blow of trading voyages to or from China, or to the Northwest Coast, or among the islands, or of sealing activities in the Australian neighborhood, or of whaling voyages.

The very first visitor was the ship *Philadelphia* of Philadelphia, Captain Patrickson. It arrived on November 1, 1792, via the Cape of Good Hope. The call was made as a result of rather ambiguous talks at the Cape the previous year between Captain Patrickson and Philip Gidley King, later governor of New South Wales, when he found the Americans something of a trial. Patrickson on that occasion had offered to carry to Australia for £1,500 part of the cargo of the storeship *Guardian*, which had been badly damaged in a collision with an iceberg while en route to Sydney and which had limped back to the Cape. This offer was refused, though if it had been taken up, the settlement would have had its hardships materially lessened. Patrickson then quizzed King about trading prospects at Sydney, but got no direct encouragement to undertake a speculation, though King nevertheless concluded that he would visit Sydney at some time. When Patrickson actually arrived in Sydney, with a cargo made up in Philadelphia, the authorities, necessitous as always in those years, purchased of him cured beef and pitch and tar, while the military officers bought a miscellany of goods. The *Philadelphia* also made a chartered voyage to Norfolk Island for the government. The second American visitor arrived a month later. This time the sealer *Hope* of Rhode Island (Providence, Newport, or Warren), Captain Benjamin Page, called in, ostensibly for wood and water. It was China-bound with the skins it had collected. It had some goods for sale and sold them. They included rum, fatefully, as will appear. That it had goods to sell apparently means that it had been provided with abnormally abundant stores, including rum, as a speculative hedge against failure of the sealing. There is no reason to suppose that an American whaler visited any inhabited point in Australia until 1805 when the *Ann* of New Bedford crossed over from New Zealand to Sydney.

It is clear enough why Captain Patrickson ventured into Sydney. In those days American traders were peddlers of the seas and Sydney appeared to be a likely stop to make. The *Hope* must have known that there was a settlement at Sydney, for the news of its founding seems very quickly to have reached America. The American consul at Canton, Major (of the Revolutionary Army) Samuel Shaw, knew that the British intended to make a settlement in New Holland (as Australia was then called) a year before it was actually made. He picked up the gossip from visiting East Indiamen who knew that ships under contract would carry out convicts and then proceed to Canton to load tea. But however the very first visitors learned about what to expect, there is no mystery about how the subsequent visitors learned of the place and its trading potential. The third American ship to arrive was the *Fairy* of Boston in 1793, bound for the Northwest Coast. It is a reasonable guess that she got her information from Boston ships returned from Canton. And when the notation "Rhode Island" is found under "where from" it is clear enough that the people of the *Hope* had passed the word along. Three Rhode Island ships visited Sydney in 1794, the only American visitors of that year, one each in 1796, 1798, 1799, and so on. The grapevine of the world of ships was in action. Like the two originals of 1792 they were on their way to some other place, usually China, directly or indirectly. Some of them called simply for wood and water, to repair ship, or to refresh the crew, but a goodly proportion had trade in view. The number of Rhode Island ships — at least ten out of twenty-one in the years 1792–1801 — indicates that the rum trade was a powerful inducement. Rhode Island was a center of the rum trade from before the American Revolution and that there was an outlet for "the stuff" in Australia was undoubtedly a sufficient attraction.

Reverting now to the legality of the trading activities of the

Americans at Sydney, it is clear that all the governors from Phillip, the founding governor, on were supposed to prevent violations of the East India Company's trading monopoly covering the whole Pacific Ocean. In Phillip's Instructions was this passage, repeated in the same form in those issued to every governor of this period, including Macquarie:

> And whereas it is our royal intention that every sort of intercourse between the intended settlement at Botany Bay, or other place which may be hereafter established on the coast of New South Wales, and its dependencies, and the settlements of our East India Company, as well as the coast of China, and the islands situated in that part of the world, to which any intercourse has been established by any European nation, should be prevented by every possible means: It is our royal will and pleasure that you do not on any account allow craft of any sort to be built for the use of private individuals which might enable them to effect such intercourse, and that you do prevent any vessels which may at any time hereafter arrive at the said settlement from any of the ports before mentioned from having communication with any of the inhabitants residing within your Government, without first receiving especial permission from you for that purpose.

Under Jay's Treaty Americans were granted a specific right to trade directly to and from India, but they were otherwise forbidden to trade by sea with British colonies. The American trade with China at Canton was not within the power of the Company or the British Government to challenge; they could only act to prevent unauthorized British ships from engaging in it, as in the case of Australian ships, and the Americans recognized no power of the East India Company or the British Government to interfere with the fur trade on the Northwest Coast of America (or the Hudson's Bay Company to interfere either) or with the seal and whale fisheries in the Pacific Ocean, all of which were either conducted within the ambit of the East India Company's monopoly or involved travel through the area to which it applied. The trade with the Australian penal colony was, however, a horse of another color; it was trade with a British colony and that colony was within the East India

Company's monopolized territory (to the Company's annoyance), so that the American trade with it appears to have been doubly illegal in the absence of any exception in Jay's Treaty like that covering the India trade. To be sure, the penal colony did not seem important enough to be specified in 1794, but the logic of its position is straight enough. The trade was allowed to exist for some years only by virture of a consistent use of the rule of necessity. Necessity was often dire in the early years of the Australian settlement.

Governor Philip Gidley King (in office 1800–1806) was the first governor to find relations with the Americans difficult and confusing and to try to do something positive about them. In large part this was because the trade as it had developed was directly connected with domestic irregularities he was attempting to correct. However, he was unsuccessful in correcting the situation, and his successor, William Bligh, was more than merely unsuccessful also: he provoked an armed rebellion which toppled him from office. The roots of all this trouble, which began about the time of Governor Phillip's departure from the colony in 1792 and continued into Macquarie's administration, were put down when the military were in charge of the colony between the departure of Phillip and the arrival of John Hunter. During that brief period the military set in train practices which concentrated great economic power in the hands of certain officers and their friends, an essential part of which was an effective monopoly of the import trade, including the importation of liquor. They set local prices for imported goods at very high levels, and the liquor trade was especially lucrative under these conditions because local per capita consumption of "rum" was very high, higher than in Britain by far. In the absence of a viable local currency, commodities were substituted, including "rum." "Rum" was the term applied to all high-proof, low-quality liquor. By using it corruptively, especially in barter, the monopolists got many ex-convict farmers into their clutches, often depriving them of title to their land. An important avenue of attack upon the monopoly was through the rum trade, at once an integral element of the monopoly and a kind of symbol of the whole. When Bligh was driven from office, the episode became known to history as the Rum Rebellion.

King was concerned with relations with the Americans during his whole term of office. His first effort was to cut down imports of intoxicants and to use imports of other goods to reduce monopoly prices while also cutting the imports down in quantity, and he further sought a way to limit or eliminate American competition in the exploitation of the resources of the sea and seashore, especially the taking of seals for skins.

On March 10, 1801, he addressed a long dispatch to his superior in England, the Duke of Portland, in which he included a lengthy paragraph on the rum trade. He noted that with the Duke's cooperation the flow of "spirits" from India was under control — it later turned out that he was mistaken about this — but that too much liquor was coming out from England. Even the ships bringing convicts were averaging 8,000 gallons per ship. He continued:

> . . . and such has been the certainty in America of any quantity of spirits being purchased here, that a ship cleared out from Rhode Island for this port with a very large investment of spirits and other articles, the former of which I positively forbade being landed, in consequence of which she left this port, after having compleated her water and refreshments, with upwards of 13,000 gallons of spirits brought here for sale, in which they were disappointed. The master's plea was the assurances of those who had been here before that he could not fail to get an unheard-of profit. At his request I have written the enclosed to the American Minister, in case your Grace should approve it, as the readiest means of preventing the American merchants from sending any more spirits here . . .

The "enclosed to the American Minister," who was Rufus King, read as follows:

Sydney, New South Wales, February, 1801.

Sir,

Mr. Parry, Commander of the American Ship Follensby, having cleared out from Rhode Island for this Settlement and China, and having on board a very large Investment of Spirits, intended for this Market, which His Majesty's Instructions Absolutely prohibits being landed, except in such Quantities as may be necessary for the Domestic use of the Officers and Soldiers, Captain Parry has, therefore, been obliged to depart without selling any part of his Investment, except the Tobacco. As he has requested me to signify that the Landing of Spirits is restricted as above, and that every other Species of Trade is allowed of such as Tar, Salted Provisions, Tobacco &c., I shall be glad if this Communication may prevent the Merchants from risqueing their Property by sending Spirits, &c., hither, the Penalty of landing which, without my Permit in Writing, is Forfeiture of Ship and Cargo.

I have, &c.,

PHILIP GIDLEY KING

About a year later King addressed a letter of similar import to the British Consuls in North America. The ship *Follensbe*, 269 tons, 6 guns, 23 men, Captain James Perry (or Parry) was from Newport, Rhode Island, owned by Vernon & Company and was, as King noted, bound for China. Captain Perry was much annoyed by the frustration he suffered, threatened King with trouble his owners would make, and it was in an effort to avoid difficulties of this kind in the future that King wrote his formal letters to the American Minister and the British Consuls.

Neither the letters nor King's regulations brought the liquor trade wholly under control. King had to send liquor back to India and even to England. On the records available it appears that America and India ran neck for neck as sources of unwanted liquor, with the former having a slight edge. In 1801 King was still encouraging what he comprehensively called "dry goods," or general merchandise. "Whilst I have forbidden a great quantity of spirits being landed," he wrote the Duke of Portland on July 8, 1801, "I have given every encouragement to the dry goods being left, under regulations of price and distribution." But Australian–American trading relations remained in this shape but a short while. On June 14, 1802, King announced that "Goods of all kinds brought for sale by individuals from any Port to the Eastward of the Cape of Good Hope are to pay a Duty of 5 percent *ad valorem* on the price they are laid in at . . ."; and it was especially noted that the duty applied to goods "not of British manufacture." This was another shot at the American traders, as King explained in commenting on the regulation in a dispatch to Lord Hobart dated March 1, 1804. "My reasons for that measure . . . were the encouragement of English manufactures . . . And to prevent as much as possible the intercourse with the Americans . . ." King apparently thought that the Americans had served their turn.

From early in the piece relations with the Americans became mixed up with the vexed question of how to control sealing on the Australian coast. With amazing speed, the Americans engaged in this harsh but lucrative trade pursued their quarry to the remotest coasts and islands in the South Atlantic, South Pacific, and South Indian Oceans after they entered it in 1783 with a venture to the Falkland Islands. Within a decade they were operating near enough to Sydney to make that remote port a reasonable place at which to call to refit, refresh, and trade. The Americans became exceedingly active in sealing on all the coasts and islands around Australia and New Zealand, including sub-Antarctic islands, on which seals showed themselves. The Australians were severely handicapped in the trade by the restrictive regulations of the East India Company, and Governor King did all he could to get the regulations relaxed. He was keenly interested in advancing Australian participation in the business. He sought ways and means to control or get rid of the deadly American competition and to prevent local residents from making deals with American sealers designed to get around the East India Company's regulations.

But the difficulty was that King did not quite know what to do. After the discovery in 1798 of the strait separating Tasmania from the mainland and the observation of seals on the islands of the strait, the Americans who visited these rookeries were obviously within Australian territorial waters, though remote from the principal settlement. Nevertheless the Americans acted as if they were working in an unclaimed place. On May 26, 1804, King issued a Proclamation in which he gave a version of the situation as he saw it and tried to deal with one phase of it:

> Whereas it has been represented to me that the Commanders of some American vessels have, without any Permission or Authority whatever, not only greatly inconvenienced His Majesty's Subjects in resorting to and continuing among the different islands in and about Bass's Straits, for Skins and Oil, to the Hindrance of the Coasting Trade of this Territory and its Dependencies, but have also, in violation of the Laws of Nations, and in contempt of the local Regulations of this Territory, proceeded to build vessels on the Islands in the said Straits, and in other places within the defined Limits of this His Majesty's Territory of New South Wales and its Dependencies to the prejudice and infringement of His Majesty's Rights and Properties therein . . .

To deal with the offense of building ships, King announced that if any so built, with keels over fourteen feet long, should turn up in Australian ports, they could be seized on his authority for His Majesty's use. But he considerably weakened his position by writing into the Proclamation the following:

> And whereas I have some time past requested Instructions how far the Subjects of any European Power in amity with His Majesty may be allowed to procure Skins and Oil on the Islands, Coasts and Bays of this Territory and its Dependencies as aforesaid; until I receive those Instructions I do in the mean time . . .

A Proclamation couched in such terms could hardly settle the questions at issue; and King was still requesting instructions when his term ran out.

It was the custom of the sealers to fight, or be prepared to fight, for possession of a particularly promising sealing ground. The relations between the Australians and the Americans at the Bass Strait grounds deteriorated to the point where violence took place between Americans led by Amasa Delano (President Franklin Delano Roosevelt's ancestor) and Australians led by Joseph Murrell. This collision took place in October 1804 and the event is copiously documented, for both Delano and Murrell wrote accounts of it, but they are so contradictory that any impartial assignment of blame for taking the initiative is now impossible.

But if Governor King could neither keep the Americans out of sealing grounds to which the Australians had far superior claim, nor satisfactorily control their actions on them, he could try to prevent the American sealers from using Sydney itself as a base of operations. He appears to have succeeded fairly well at this.

The War of 1812 cut off the Australian-American trade, but it is reasonably certain that, war or no war, it would have declined at about that time. In 1813 the East India Company lost its Pacific Basin monopoly and the English merchants could freely enter the Australian trade. There seems little doubt that they would have reduced the American trade to very little strictly by competition. However the British government was in no mood to take chances. Macquarie, as we have seen, rather welcomed the prospect of a resumption of the trade after the war, but even as he fell afoul of the Reverend Mr. Vale over *The Traveller*, the following letter was on its way to him from his superior, Earl Bathurst, dated Downing Street, December 11, 1815:

> It is probable that in consequence of the re-establishment of Peace, both in Europe and America, the Ports of the Colony under your Government may be again revisited by Foreign Vessels for the purposes of Trade, particularly by such as are going to China. It therefore becomes necessary to remind you that the Trade of Foreign Vessels with a British Colony is directly at variance with the navigation Laws of this Country; and although this infraction of them might have been tolerated at earlier periods upon the plea of necessity, it cannot now be defended upon such grounds; more particularly since the Colony will henceforth have the benefit of a more regular and free Intercourse with the Mother Country, in consequence of the Act of Parliament, which has given, to all Classes of His Majesty's Subjects, a less restricted Intercourse with the Settlements in the Eastern Seas.
>
> It appears that the chief Article, brought out by these Foreign Vessels, consisted of Spirits of an inferior quality, in payment

for which the Specie of the Colony was exported; and, as there cannot be a doubt that you will receive a sufficient Importation of Spirits either from this Country, or British India, I am to desire that no Foreign Vessel may be permitted henceforth to trade within the Ports of your Government; and, if any such Vessel should arrive for the purpose of refitting, you will take due care that no trade is carried on.

The Americans were the foreigners chiefly in question. In a general dispatch to Macquarie dated April 18, 1816, Bathurst reiterated his instruction. American trade fell away toward none at all, to revive 1833–43, relapse again and revive again in the fifties as a reflex of the Australian gold rushes.

Aside from putting an end to trade with the Americans, the War of 1812 had very incidental impact on Australia. At the outbreak of the war the United States had no naval vessel in the Pacific — it assigned its first to the Pacific in 1817 and established a squadron in 1821 — and apparently had no plans for sending any there. The American merchantmen and whalers in the Pacific were left to the untender mercies of the British. But Captain David Porter of the frigate *Essex*, assigned to a South Atlantic squadron, missed his rendezvous and decided on his own to go around the Horn to attack British whalers in the Pacific. The whaling grounds he chose were those close to the South American coast and Porter had his greatest success around the Galapagos Islands. All told he captured and sent home or destroyed British shipping to the value of two-and-a-half million dollars. He was, of course, operating without a base, and to provide himself with one he resorted to one of the Marquesas Islands, today known as Nukuhiva. At the port of Nukuhiva Porter established a base, built a fort, and on November 19, 1813, formally proclaimed United States sovereignty. The British caught up with Porter when he left Nukuhiva to visit Valparaiso. The *Essex* was destroyed outside that port on March 28, 1814.

Sydney got into this extraordinary business, a wonderful example of reckless Yankee enterprise, when one of the captured British whaleships taken into Nukuhiva was recaptured by a

scratch crew of British sailors and sailed via Tahiti and Rarotonga to Australia. At Sydney the ship was provided with tem-
porary papers and a captain capable of navigating her and
sent to England to be dealt with by the Lords of Admiralty.
Governor Macquarie praised the adventurous sailors in fulsome
terms, but rumors circulated in Sydney that some of them at an
earlier stage had served the Americans rather too faithfully. The
point cannot be clarified.

American privateers, operating in the Atlantic, fell in with
two or three convict carriers out of England or Ireland for
Australia. One, the *Emu*, from Ireland with women convicts,
was captured and sent into New York as a prize, chiefly it
appears because she was carrying an unusually large quantity
of ammunition. The women convicts and the ship's commander
were landed in the Cape Verde Islands. Otherwise it was the
American practice to relieve a convict ship of its ammunition,
accept on board any deserters from its crew, destroy its papers,
and let it go. This procedure involved the convict carriers in
obvious difficulties in completing their voyages to Sydney, but
they appear invariably to have done so. Oddly the convicts seem
to have behaved far better than the crews during the en-
counters, and it is of record that the conduct of one lot was
so exemplary that Governor Macquarie recommended it en
masse for conditional pardon.

9. Sealing . . . Whaling . . . Guano . . . Gold . . . Trade . . .

Up to this point our attention has largely been concentrated on Australia, chiefly Sydney, with incidental references to the islands. The American sealers who worked in the islands apart from those immediately off the Australian coast were chiefly active around South Island in New Zealand and the sub-Antarctic islands to the south of it. The first visit of an American sealer to New Zealand occurred in 1797, when the ship *Mercury* was there. By 1804 American competition was severe at all the known New Zealand rookeries. It was an American sealer named Smith who in 1804 discovered Foveaux Strait, which separates South Island from Stewart Island. The sealers did not, of course, ply their trade north of New Zealand in these waters, though in the eastern Pacific the seals were followed north until the Alaskan rookeries, pioneered by the Russians, were reached. However, the sealers got to know something of the South Sea islands as they made their way to China. This led to discoveries but they were only incidental to filling up the map of the Pacific. The whalers, when they got among the islands, also made discoveries, but only rarely were they islands of much immediate or subsequent significance. The real importance of the activities of the whalers was quite otherwise. When the United States Exploring Expedition of 1838–1842, under the command of Charles Wilkes of the United States Navy (nephew of that thorn in the side of King George III, "that devil Wilkes") was in the Pacific one of the many chores Wilkes did was to plot the whaling grounds of the Ocean. He found that there were fifteen principal grounds in the Pacific "visited by our whalers," of which the following were in the Southwest Pacific:

(a) the offshore ground — over toward the islands from the onshore grounds along the west coast of South America,
(b) in the neighborhood of the Society Islands (Tahiti),
(c) in the neighborhood of the Samoan Islands,
(d) in the neighborhood of the Fiji Islands,
(e) along and to the south of the equator from the coast of South America to the vicinity of the Gilbert Islands,
(f) across the South Pacific between parallels 21° and 27° South,
(g) in the neighborhood of the east coast of New Zealand,
(h) the middle ground between New Zealand and Australia.

The whales were, of course, migratory animals. They moved about the ocean to take advantage of the seasonal abundance of food in certain places or, in the case of some species, to find satisfactory bays in which to give birth to young. They were thus at particular grounds at particular times of the year and the whalers came to have knowledge both of the location of the grounds and the migratory habits. They planned their voyages to take advantage of the movements of the whales.

American whalers, sailing from an American port, first entered the Pacific in 1792. (They were preceded by two years by American whalers of the Rotch fleet based on Dunkirk, France, and both were preceded by British-flag whalers in 1789.) These ships cruised the onshore grounds along the west coast of South America, and these grounds were the principal center of Pacific whaling until the offshore grounds a thousand miles over toward the islands ("a" above) were located in 1818 by a Nantucket captain. It was after the War of 1812 that the American whaling industry really got on its feet and started that expansion which made it dominant in the world until the Civil War.

Before whaling voyages could follow any particular pattern, the pattern had to be uncovered, and it was in finding this pattern that the whalers chanced upon hitherto unknown islands. They discovered no major group, but they added to the map isolated islands and islands within groups — the groups often are scattered over a great many square miles of ocean — which had hitherto escaped detection. As this implies, the charts they used in their work were incomplete, and long after the whalers had traversed great stretches of island-studded ocean, the charts of individual groups were rough and poor. The Fiji Islands were first adequately charted by Wilkes as late as 1840. Many of the wrecks, with which the story of Pacific whaling is punctuated, were caused as much by bad charts as by poor navigation or storms that made ships unmanageable. The richest Pacific grounds were in the North Pacific, particularly for sperm whales, only to be captured on the high seas. They gave the best oil, and the Americans were the pioneers in their capture. This species remained the primary interest of the Americans though they did not disdain right-whales, usually taken in bays to which the whales came to give birth. To the Americans Pacific whaling was primarily a deep-sea enterprise. Their incursions into bay-whaling, ordinarily conducted from stations on shore, were incidental and usually from ships temporarily anchored in a whale-rich bay, as in New Zealand.

This basing of whaling on a ship miles and miles from its home port gave great importance to ports of call at which supplies, especially fresh foods, could be obtained, the crew "refreshed" (a euphemism covering liquor and sex), and the ship refitted. It was this aspect of the business that chiefly brought the American whalers into contact with the local peoples. When the Pacific whaling was confined to the onshore grounds near the coast of South America, the principal port of call was Valparaiso in Chile. When the center of gravity of Pacific whaling began to shift to the North Pacific, Hawaii (especially Honolulu) quickly assumed primary importance. This development came about 1820. Honolulu became so overwhelmingly important that both the Americans and the British appointed official representatives there before they appointed them at any other Pacific island. (The Americans had an officer there before they appointed one in California.) In the Southwest Pacific the principal ports of call were at Tahiti and New Zealand, but there was hardly a significant South Sea island at which American whalers did not call at one time or another and often in numbers during a season. To take care of the business created by frequent calls, American consuls were appointed at Tahiti in 1836 and at New Zealand (Bay of Islands) in 1838. Wilkes added one pro tempore at Apia, Samoa, in 1839. (A consul was first appointed to Sydney, Australia, in May 1836 but he did not enter upon his duties until February 1839; whaling was an incidental consideration. A consul took up duty at Hobart in June 1844; he had far more to do with whalers than the Sydney man, for reasons given below. When a consul was sent to Melbourne in 1852, whaling was not a consideration at all.) The consuls appointed in the islands were at this period accredited to native rulers, for the fiction of native sovereignty was being maintained by the powers. This was the time when native kings and queens played a role in Pacific politics. They did not last long. All but one island monarchical system disappeared before the century was out; the survivor was the Tonga monarchy, which has continued to the present day. The United States had no consul at Tonga in the whaling era.

The whalers in the South Sea islands contributed to a rather complicated situation which can either be interpreted anthropologically as part of a story of cultural contact and change, initiated earlier and still continuing, in which the natives are depicted as adapting themselves to the incoming culture of the west, or politically as part of the process which eventually worked itself out in the "partage d'Océanie." The two phases of the story are obviously closely related one to the other.

The anthropological phase of the story has not yet been studied in a comprehensive way. It is fairly plain, however, that the visiting whalers must be thought of as one of several influences operating in sequence or simultaneously: visiting explorers, who sometimes spent considerable time on particular islands, as Cook and Bligh spent time at Tahiti; deserters from visiting ships, including whalers who sometimes demonstrated the truth that it was easier for a "civilized" man to become a savage than for a savage to become civilized; escaped convicts from the Australian penal colonies; resident traders, missionaries, and settlers experimenting with plantation systems. Insofar as the whalers traded with the natives, they played a role in the encouragement of production for market by the natives, and in this they were collaborators with the missionaries, for the latter tried to direct native energies into production for sale as a kind of moral equivalent of war. This was chiefly the production of foodstuffs, as for example potatoes in New Zealand, in the growing of which the Maori early became expert, pork in New Zealand, Tahiti, and other islands, and other vegetables and fruit. The trade was chiefly barter — local edibles for cloth, made-up clothes, iron and iron utensils, and so on, with which the whalers were regularly stocked for a voyage — but sometimes money changed hands: this the natives usually gave toward the support of the missions. Ordinarily, however, the whalers were not regarded as collaborators with the missionaries, however welcome their trade may have been. There were some pious whaling captains — Quakers from Nantucket and New Bedford, for example — but not many. The crews seem ordinarily to have been anything but pious. Mostly, whatever their views of missionaries and their schemes, the captains were honest. They did not purposefully cheat the natives, but they caused anxiety and anger among the missionaries by exhibiting to the natives modes of conduct that contradicted those the missionaries were attempting to inculcate. The missionaries, for example, tried hard to prohibit the importation of "rum" into the islands for sale to the natives. Many of the captains were prepared to sell "rum," even captains running so-called "temperance ships" — which seems to have meant only that no rum was served to the crew while the ship was at sea. The natives appear to have found "rum" a superefficient substitute for the native intoxicants they had favored earlier, while the missionaries regarded the imported stuff as far more destructive, physically and morally, than the old intoxicants. It probably was. But the natives coveted it and the captains did not scruple about supplying it. The South Sea island trade became as soaked in rum as ever the trade with the North American Indians was with whisky, east or west of the hundredth meridian.

The crewmen who jumped ship at the islands — or were left behind by homeward bound, fully loaded ships to avoid payment of wages — were, more often than not, pretty poor human stuff, not discernibly superior to the escaped convicts from Australia. These men, along with other Europeans engaged in trade and production, introduced the natives to a variety of Western culture which was decidedly not "missionary." Missionary culture in that era was, in the islands south of the equator, a British product. (American missionaries confined their operations to the islands north of the equator, notably Hawaii, by a kind of unwritten compact with the British. The Mormons appear to have been the American denomination first to break the compact and work south of the line.) British missionary culture was an extraordinary mixture of Bible Christianity, fussily Puritan morality, and lower-middle-class economic ideas and aspirations. It comported very oddly with the native culture. On economics the missionaries and the other intruding whites were ordinarily not too far apart, and it was not unknown for missionaries to get altogether too interested in trade and the acquisition of land. With land-grabbing the whalers appear to have had very little to do, though ambitious waifs of the whalers, like David Whinny of Nantucket and Fiji, might indulge in it. On balance, however, it is as impossible to say that the non- or antimissionary influence was all bad as it is to say that the missionary influence was all good. Both were saturated with a comprehensive ignorance of how the welfare of the natives could best be served when so radically contrasted cultures came into contact.

Along with the whalers came the gatherers of such sea products as bêche-de-mer or trepang and such products of the foreshore as sandalwood. No comprehensive study of American participation in these activities has ever been made, though it is well established that they played a conspicuous role during the first six decades of the nineteenth century. Some of the richest documentation of the trades is American in origin. There was a great concentration of such activity in Fiji; and in Fiji of ships and men from Salem, Massachusetts. Economically, however, these activities never achieved the significance of whaling.

Traders established themselves at ports frequented by the whalers and where the gatherers were active. The great Pacific frontier for American traders was, of course, Hawaii, but they were also active at Papeete in Tahiti and at Kororareka (Bay of Islands) in New Zealand.

A good indication of where the concentrations of American activities were is provided by the appointment of consuls by the United States government. The consuls themselves were not in the beginning always Americans, but in the case of the representative at Papeete, a Belgian who later abandoned the American service and joined the French, at Kororareka an Englishman who clearly took the post for the pay involved and for little other reason, and in Samoa also an Englishman, son of the famous missionary, John Williams. At Sydney, however, the early consuls were Americans, and the same was true at Hobart. In common with the other powers active in the area, the Americans backed up their consuls and nationals in the islands by visits of warships operating, in the American case, from the South American stations, while en route to Honolulu. Early cruises among the islands to "show the flag," compose disputes, and sometimes to suggest trade treaties between the United States and the native sovereigns, were headed by such famous figures as Percival, ap Catesby Jones (first to visit Tahiti), Finch, and Downes. Most of these voyages were described in important published narratives which are significant substantive contributions to the literature of the islands. In the early years the visits were chiefly made to islands in Eastern Polynesia, but later on to Western Polynesia and Fiji. A by-product of Finch's visit to Tahiti was the following letter from Pomare Vahine I (*vahine:* woman, hence "Queen Pomare") to President Andrew Jackson, dated September 26, 1829, probably the first official communication from a ruler of a Southwest Pacific island to the government of the United States:

In consequence of your kindness I write a letter to you. You sent a man-of-war formerly to our land, commanded by Captain Jones; he treated us with great kindness. You have now sent another man-of-war commanded by Captain Finch; his kindness to us has also been great. We are highly pleased with his visit. I now write to you to express my gratitude; also to inform you of our present state.

I am a female — the first queen of Tahiti — Queen Pomare I is my name. I am daughter of Pomare II. When he died the government devolved on my little brother; he died, the government then became mine. I am young and inexperienced.

We have cast away the worship of idols, and have embraced the worship of our common Lord. In the year 1814 we embraced Christianity.

We have missionaries on the island, who are dilligent in teaching us that which will promote our welfare. Some have been with us upwards of thirty years.

We have laws by which we are governed. I cannot send you a copy, I being on a visit to my grandfather at Raiatea.

Tahiti and Eimeo are the largest islands in my government. We have not many people; perhaps ten thousand.

There is not much property in my island: arrowroot and cocoa-nut oil are the principal. We have abundance of food, and excellent harbors for ships. Many American vessels call at Tahiti; tell them to continue to call, and we will treat them well.

All kinds of cotton cloth are in demand here for barter: white, printed, blue — shawls, ribbons, axes are all good property to bring to procure refreshments.

We have a new flag given us by Captain Lawes, of the Satellite,

British man-of-war; will you kindly acknowledge it in traversing the seas, and in visiting you, as yours is by us, should that be the case at a distant period.

Captain Finch has made myself, and mother, and aunt, with others, some handsome presents in your name, for which receive my gratitude. We are always glad to see American vessels at Tahiti. Continue to sail your vessels without suspicion. Our harbors are good and our refreshments abundant.

Prosperity attend you, President of the United States of America. May your good government be of long duration.

A proper commentary on this really charming letter would involve telling the history of Tahiti from Wallis' time to 1829, and especial attention would have to be given to that master-piece of understatement, "We have missionaries on the island, who are dilligent in teaching us that which will promote our welfare."

The official American attitude toward the islands differed from that of France or Britain. Back of whatever the French or British might do by way of sending warships into the islands was the possibility that formal possession might be taken of likely islands, though Britain was more reluctant to take this course than France, in spite of constant colonial pressure. At that time, however, it was assumed almost without question that all governments had territorial acquisition as an ultimate purpose, not only in the islands but throughout the world. So universal was the assumption that the very fact that the Americans were active in the Southwest Pacific was taken as evidence that they too were after territory. British suspicion of American intentions in Western Australia in the middle eighteen-twenties, and in such island groups as Fiji at a later time, are part of the record, a kind of counterpoint to American suspicions of British purposes in Texas, Oregon, California, and Hawaii. Whatever ideas the Americans on the various spots may have had, the United States government seems not to have countenanced territorial ambitions in any way in the Southwest Pacific before the 1870's. It rather sought to keep open access by Americans to indigenous resources and the channels of trade. While Wilkes was in the area with his exploring expedition the British finally took sovereignty in New Zealand. Americans of Wilkes' party were present at Captain Hobson's ceremonies at Waitangi. Wilkes took a critical view of the British action, but less because he thought the United States had any territorial ambitions in New Zealand than because he was afraid that a British administration would impede the activities of the American whalers and traders. Wilkes was, as a matter of fact, quite right, for American activities in New Zealand declined from 1840 and the whalers shifted over to Hobart in Tasmania as their principal port of call in the area. The authorities at Hobart took a more sympathetic attitude toward the whalers than had the New Zealanders. It was in recognition of this that an American consul was sent to Hobart in 1844. (There were probably more Americans in New Zealand in the 1830's than for many decades after.) Whether or not because the State Department more or less shared Wilkes' dubiety about British assumption of sovereignty in New Zealand, it is a fact that the American government was slow formally to acknowledge British sovereignty. It took two years to make up its mind. The question became involved (in a fashion that is not clear, since the matter has never been closely studied) with the question of whether or not United States citizens were included among those persons "transported" from Canada to Australia for participation in the Canadian rebellion of 1837. As American Ambassador to the Court of St. James, Edward Everett dealt with the tangle of questions involved. It would be interesting to puzzle out the story in detail. For different reasons, the French were also slow about formally acknowledging British sovereignty in New Zealand. The British citizen who had been the American consul at Kororareka from 1838 played a conspicuous part in persuading the Maori chiefs to sign the Treaty of Waitangi, conveying sovereignty to Britain. He resigned in April 1841 and joined the British administration. Not until January 1843 was American representation put on a secure footing by the proper appointment of a consul who was an American citizen. He was appointed to Kororareka, Bay of Islands, then already fading away, not to the rising town and seat of government, Auckland. The State Department got around to stationing a consul in Auckland only in 1874. It continued to consider Bay of Islands a post until 1917.

But really the Americans seem not to have cared too much about what happened with regard to sovereignty in the islands of the Southwest Pacific. They were, however, deeply concerned about what went on at Hawaii in the *North* Pacific. A rather well-known confirmation of the point is Herman Melville's Appendix to *Typee*. Although he opened his statement with a reference to the French assumption of a protectorate over Tahiti, and in that connection employed such words as "iniquitous" and "piratical," Melville immediately went on to deal at length with Lord George Paulet's actions at Honolulu because, he says, the Tahitian affair "created not half so great a sensation, at least in America, as was caused by the proceedings of the English at the Sandwich Islands." At a later time when American interest in Samoa was very great and the first steps leading up to the acquisition of Pago Pago as a coaling station were being taken, the State Department formally disclaimed interest in what might occur in the Melanesian islands to the west, on the ground that they were properly a British and Australian concern. The Samoan affair was, as we shall see, a sharp deviation from established American policy which such an astute student of American foreign policy as John Bassett Moore regarded as historically fateful.

The exploring expedition led by Charles Wilkes (1838–42) was concerned with far more than the Southwest Pacific, even in the extended definition employed here. Wilkes himself showed an especial interest in fortifying the American claims in Oregon. Historians have taken their keenest interest in his forays into Antarctica. But as a result of their work in the islands the Wilkes expedition made one of the most considerable contributions to knowledge of them in the first half of the nineteenth century. The work was of a quality comparable to that of Captain Cook. This is not generally appreciated. In dealing with Antarctica, Wilkes began with some rather foot-less activities around the Palmer Peninsula, south of South America, where American sealers had operated from the eighteen-twenties, but the activities in which historians take a continuing interest were based on Sydney in Australia. Start-ing from and returning to Sydney, Wilkes sought land to the south and claimed he had seen it. He was in the Antarctic simul-taneously with the Frenchman Dumont d'Urville and immedi-ately preceeding the Englishman James Clark Ross. Part of the land Wilkes saw, d'Urville also saw, and part Ross alleged he not only could not find but actually sailed over. However, it is today generally accepted that Wilkes did locate a good deal of coastal Antarctica and in fact made a basic contribution toward establishing the reality of the continental land mass. In the islands Wilkes and his companions examined the places visited in the light of a greater variety of scientific disciplines than anybody up to that time. What they did far overshadowed any scientific work the English did in the area in the first half of the century and was richer and more varied in results than anything the French did, though the reports were not as charming liter-arily as those of the French. But to this day Wilkes has never been given the credit he deserves for the accomplishments of the expedition. The whole affair was born in controversy, was con-ducted to the accompaniment of controversy, and concluded in a burst of controversy. Although an exhaustive bibliography of the expedition has been compiled, no authoritative critical study of it in all its phases has ever been made and no acceptable life of Wilkes has ever been published. It is a pity.

In his account of his visit to Sydney in 1839, Wilkes observed, "New South Wales is known in the United States almost by its name alone." He therefore wrote about it on the assumption that no small detail was anything less than news to his readers. This is interesting indeed, for it shows that the activities in Aus-tralia — for New South Wales meant Australia to Wilkes — of American traders, sealers, and whalers up to 1839 had neither led to the dissemination of much information about the country at home, nor to the development of much curiosity about it. True Wilkes did not make a survey of American knowledge and opinion to support his generalization and minor evidence to the contrary, bibliographical in character, can be cited. But it seems to have been the case that Americans up to *circa* 1840 took more interest in and knew more about the islands (including New Zealand) than Australia. Herman Melville, who seems to have been the first important American writer for the general public about this part of the world, wrote of life in the islands, chiefly the Marquesas and Tahiti.

The discovery of gold in California in 1848 gave a new twist to the American interest in the Southwest Pacific. While travel to California by sea, whether via Panama or Cape Horn, was confined to the eastern Pacific, traders scoured the islands for foodstuff which could be carried to San Francisco and arrive in saleable condition. Tahitian oranges thus went to market. The merchants of Australia, especially those of Sydney, took an active part in supplying the San Francisco market with flour and coal. And gold-seekers from both Australia and New Zealand flocked to California. Among the Australians were a goodly number of ex-convicts who gave the vigilantes work to do; they went by the name of "Sydney Ducks" or "Coves." Although gold had been discovered in Australia long before this time, the discoveries had always been hushed up on the ground that a rush would destroy convict discipline. But certain Australians in California thought the formations in which gold was to be found remarkably like formations they had seen in Australia. Two such men went back to Australia obsessed with this idea and one made the first discovery in New South Wales, the other in Victoria. This set off the great Australian gold rushes of the eighteen-fifties.

More Americans were attracted to the Southwest Pacific by the Australian gold rushes than by anything else up to that time. More Americans were in Australia during the "golden decade" than at any other period up to World War II. How many went to Australia when the rushes were active and how many stayed as permanent settlers cannot be exactly stated, but anyone familiar with the literature of the rushes and of the decades immediately following, is aware that Americans were a conspicuous element in the population, especially in Victoria. However, one cannot be sure that all the individuals called "Americans" were actually United States citizens, least of all Americans by birth. Many of them were undoubtedly nationals of other countries who had acquired a veneer of Americanism in California or elsewhere in the United States, as indeed was true of the "Americans" in the islands from earliest times. (While the islands were no-man's-lands, the claim to being American was often raised by criminals seeking to escape from the hands of British law officers.)

Many of the gold seekers traveled to Australia from England in American-built clipper ships flying the British flag, and American clippers under the United States flag developed a service from Boston and New York to Melbourne via Cape Horn. The Australian rushes really made a powerful impact on the American mind, and for the first time an "image" of Australia began to take form in it, rather feebly assisted by such a popular writer as W. H. Thomes, who produced for the resultant market *The Gold Hunters in Australia* and *The Belle of Australia.*

Most of the Americans who "rushed" to Australia were "diggers" or miners, but American merchants, conspicuous among them the famous George Francis Train, were active in Melbourne. There was an exodus of American merchants in the late fifties as the gold boom subsided, but a few Americans continued active in the business community for many years. Characteristically, the American merchants in Melbourne took a keen part in the Chamber of Commerce. Americans are known to have played a role in the famous digger rebellion, an armed protest against maladministration of the goldfields, at Ballarat in 1854, but none figured in the subsequent legal proceedings (although Italians and Germans did) and the assumption is that the American Consul at Melbourne hushed up the whole business, with British collaboration. It was an American named Freeman Cobb who established at this time the most famous of all Australian stage-coach services, Cobb & Company, celebrated in Australian song and story. Mention of Cobb & Company illustrates that the most important American influence in Australia has always been the technological. Americans were active in the pioneering of telegraphs and railways in Victoria in the gold-rush decade. Some who had tarried in Australia took a conspicuous role in the gold rushes in the South Island of New Zealand of 1862 and after.

American attention was directed toward the Southwest Pacific about this time in pursuit of another commodity of high value, though of less value than gold. This was guano, the gathering of which is an episode in history comparable in kind to the gathering earlier of sandalwood, bêche-de-mer, and so on. By an Act of Congress in 1856, during the administration of Franklin Pierce, discretionary power was conferred on the President to take sovereignty over islands on which guano was found and exploited by American citizens. About fifty islands were so claimed in the Pacific. However, three were claimed in duplicate under alternative names, eighteen under names still used today, twelve under names then correct but not now used, while fifteen which appeared on an authoritative list cannot today be identified and may never have existed in actuality. Of the islands claimed, the Americans worked, between the late fifties and the early seventies, only Howland, Baker, Jarvis, Canton, Enderby, Phoenix, and McKean. The British also took part in this guano trade — it led on for them to the mining of phosphate rock on Nauru — but worked islands other than those the Americans occupied, though they sometimes "cleaned up" an island after the Americans had left. The British operators worked out of Australia for the Australian market. The most famous figure in the trade was John T. Arundel. The American companies, mostly with headquarters on the Atlantic seaboard, based their Pacific operations at Honolulu. On the American side, the taking of sovereignty was done only to give security to the guano collectors while they actually were active. There was no policy of promoting permanent settlement on the islands, as the maintenance of sovereignty required. Most of them were promptly abandoned when the guano was exhausted. The islands involved were, in fact, largely unimportant, though some of them figured in history again later when islands for cable stations and airplane landing strips were in active demand, as some of them had figured earlier as discoveries of the whalers. The guano episode simply added an additional chapter to the complex history of sovereignty, or claims to sovereignty, now characteristic of many minor South Sea islands.

Quite fortuitously, the discovery of gold in 1851 coincided with a decided relaxation of the British navigation laws and with the granting of almost complete control over their tariffs to the Australian colonies. It was under these circumstances that the sharp upsurge in trade between Australia and the United States incident to the gold rushes took place. Up to that time, it was an extraordinarily good year in which American goods to the value of a quarter-million dollars were exported to Australia; suddenly the values shot upward toward three million dollars. While there was a decline to a lower average level in the latter years of the decade of the fifties, and the Civil War sharply reduced supplies, it was at this time that American goods really established themselves in the Australian market. While the Americans never for a moment menaced the British as the principal suppliers, they established themselves as most important secondary or tertiary suppliers. Yet the area of which Australia was a part — namely, Oceania — always has remained at the bottom of the list of outlets for American exports. The fundamental trouble became clearly evident at this time. It was that while Australians were receptive to American products, it was very difficult to find Australian products that could be sold in America. The trade was and remained completely unbalanced in favor of the United States, and the old complaint of the early days that the American rum sellers were drawing too much specie out of an indigent colony remained in essence true. The Australian commodity that might have filled the gap was wool. Australian wools were offered for sale on the Boston market early in the eighteen-thirties and have steadily been imported into the United States since that time. But it was not only that up to the eighteen-seventies the Americans got most of their Australian wools from London, rather than direct from Australia — this because all but a small fraction of Australia's wool was auctioned in London, but also because when the Americans supported the transfer of the auctions to Australia (they were chiefly interested in wool in the grease, easily obtainable at the place of production), they still did not take enough wool to redress the adverse Australian trade balance. The sudden reappearance of the Americans in the Australian market in force at the time of the gold rush led quickly to the discovery of the basic handicap on Australian-American trade: the fact that since most Australian exports were identical in character with goods in ample supply from domestic sources in the United States, a balanced trade on a strictly reciprocal basis was impossible. The trade therefore became restricted to the Australian capacity to find the dollars to pay for what was needed from American sources. It took a long time for need and capacity to raise it to any very remarkable heights. As we shall see, this situation made it difficult to maintain shipping services between Australia and the United States. The relative shortage of "back-cargo" made the services unprofitable.

Since the Australians and New Zealanders have for almost a century been anxiously concerned with the vagaries of the wool trade with the United States, a few observations on it are perhaps in order, prefaced by the observation that it appears never to have been intensively studied on an historical basis. Ordinarily the failure of the Americans to take as much wool as the Australians and New Zealanders would like is attributed to the American wool tariff. This is a simplistic thesis which often has overtones of the extraordinary Australian implication that the world has a moral obligation to buy Australian exports. It is hard to accept even in the light of the facts that are to be found on the surface of the record. From the record it appears that when Australian wools were wanted in the United States they were imported over the current tariff. Conversely, when there was no tariff, as was occasionally the case during the nineteenth century, this did not markedly increase imports from the Southwest Pacific. The key to the enigma seems to be (a) in the kinds of wool wanted by the American mills, (b) the influence of the fairly constant imports of fine woolen finished cloths from England on the foregoing, (c) the state of the domestic supply of wool, (d) the fact that the basic demand for imported wools was fairly consistently for carpet wools, not produced in Australia nor New Zealand, and finally (e) the ups and downs of the wool manufacturing trade. The last point is important because after the allegedly deliberately restrictive effect of the tariff, the chief Australian–New Zealand complaint had been irregularity from year to year of the quanity of wool the Americans have purchased, a complaint made not only back in the seventies and eighties, but down to the present day. The fluctuation of the sales to America has often been described as perverse, a perversity within the generalization that the Americans in any case have never purchased enough wool to satisfy the vendors, thinking, of course, of their adverse balance of trade. The trade has, over the many years of its existence, exhibited an irregularly upward trend in volume, but while the total quantity purchased has increased, taking a perspective of decades, the fluctuations have continued unabated.* The key to the problem is in the domestic American industry, and the role of the tariff is not central, but probably peripheral.

However, the influence of the United States in Australia was

* See, for example, *Statistical Handbook of the Sheep and Wool Industry* (Canberra, 1956), published by the Bureau of Agricultural Economics, tables 75 and 76, for the fluctuations in quantity and value in the period 1930–31 to 1954–55.

never wholly confined to personal contacts and commercial exchanges. There has been a steady influence at what may be called the "ideological" level. As far as the writer knows, nobody has ever worked out in coherent fashion the story of the role of "America" in the thinking of British colonials, but it does not take much knowledge of colonial history to make one realize that the idea of America, and American ideas, has played a very remarkable role, particularly in politics and cultural affairs. America has been held up as a model; it has been held up also as a warning. Time and time again colonial opposition to British measures allegedly oppressive or recklessly mistaken, has provoked invocations of the American Revolution. Time and again one discovers that colonial leaders have visited the United States one or several times and from their observations worked out ideas about how to build a society from scratch. Colonial legislators have often shown a surprisingly detailed knowledge of American legislation on specific matters of common interest, and they have used that knowledge to good effect, positively and negatively. American books and books about America consistently figured in the reading of the colonists.

All this was true of Australia and New Zealand, though of course in far lesser measure than of Canada. A dissident early Australian political leader like John Dunmore Lang had a fairly extensive knowledge of American history and political ideas and a firsthand acquaintance with American conditions as he saw them on a visit in 1840. Tocqueville on American democracy was widely read in Australia before 1850. Even a man like William Charles Wentworth, who violently attacked all "democratic" political proposals of an American flavor as vulgar Yankee notions, quoted copiously from Tocqueville in his speeches on the New South Wales constitution of 1850. Again and again in the days before the Civil War "America" was invoked in Australia to show how to do it, and how not to do it. The persistence of the American ideological influence is beyond dispute.

It may be suggested that this was because the colonial societies were not, like the society of the mother country, organic growths with deep historical roots, but were rather, like the American, devised in a wilderness by conscious acts of will, and, moreover, the American institutions were democratic, the direction in which both Australia and New Zealand were even then beginning to drift. American precedents were extremely useful, whether to guide or to warn, whether to support democratic proposals or to illustrate the dreadful consequences of succumbing to the democratic virus.

The Civil War sharply diminished traffic between the United States and the Southwest Pacific; the war nevertheless had a marked impact on the area. For example, the drying up of the flow of raw cotton from the South to England encouraged cotton-growing in Fiji, Samoa, and Queensland and even an exploration of the possibility of doing so in Western Australia. Similarly the Australians experimented with the production of tobacco to replace the supply no longer forthcoming from the United States. Americans resident in Australia offered counsel and advice. They also took a hand in the manufacture of certain goods hitherto imported from the United States, for example, buggies and wagons.

What the Australians thought of the war is unclear. (The New Zealanders were preoccupied with their war with the Maoris, which continued throughout the sixties in the North Island, while in the South Island the sixties were dominated by gold rushes.) There is some evidence that many Australians favored the North. At moments of tension between the United States and the United Kingdom during the war, there was talk in Australia about the need for improving local defenses against possible Union raiders, and there was even some drilling of volunteers. However at Sydney the militiamen sang, "We'll Hang Jeff Davis to a Sour Apple Tree" as they marched! But on the one occasion that it was possible to make a real demonstration of sentiment, favor was shown to the South. This was when the Confederate commerce-raider *Shenandoah* put in at Melbourne in 1865 to refit. The *Shenandoah*, second only to the *Alabama* in the dollar value of the destruction wrought on Union shipping, operated wholly in the Pacific, which it entered via the Cape of Good Hope, and left, on learning in August 1865 that the war was over, by way of Cape Horn for Liverpool. The upperclass people of Melbourne, including those in the government, taking their cue from their opposite numbers in England, not only acquiesced in the clear violation of British neutrality involved in the *Shenandoah's* presence at Melbourne for refitting, but showed their feelings by lavishly entertaining the Confederates as well. The Confederates were somewhat abashed by the warmth of the welcome. The visit became an item in the bill of particulars against England that was dealt with during the negotiations for the Treaty of Washington in 1871, and the so-called *Alabama* claims negotiations of 1872. The Melbourne misjudgment was paid for by the British in gold.

10. Economics, Technology, Ideology: 1865–1940

Between the end of the Civil War and World War II the Southwest Pacific continued to be of much less concern to the Americans than the North Pacific. The struggle over China and the repercussions of the rise of Japan, in initiating which the United States played such an important role in 1854, created a situation far more absorbing and fateful for the United States than anything that occurred in the Southwest Pacific. Insofar as the Americans can be said to have formulated an attitude toward the Southwest Pacific, it was viewed by them as an area ancillary to British interests and power in the Far East. The Americans had a trader's interest in the area, but it was not one of the major trading interests of the nation. As the two principal countries of the area were British colonies, it was not possible under the prevailing constitutional ideas for them to have formal political relations with foreign countries. Their foreign political relations were wholly in the hands of the United Kingdom Foreign Office, and insofar as the United States became involved in the high politics of the area, as it did during the struggle over the Samoan Islands, its dealings were with the United Kingdom, not Australia or New Zealand. It was during this time, moreover, that Australia and New Zealand attempted to achieve an isolation within their area, an isolation especially finding expression in an "islands policy" of which the gist was to see to it that the islands remain a British preserve and that all foreigners be excluded. This was partly to reserve the islands to British enterprisers for economic exploitation, partly to preserve as nearly unbroken as possible the defensive screen they allegedly provided against Britain's enemies. However, the United Kingdom did not share the colonial view of the islands, taking a far more tolerant and generous view of the rights of foreigners in them (including the right to take sovereignty over them), a difference of opinion that caused some intra-Imperial contention. Only once did the United States become entangled in the islands question. Her principal colonial opponent on that occasion was New Zealand, but of course the views of the United Kingdom ruled. It was only toward the end of this period that the colonies gained the right to some direct say about their foreign political relations, but Australia and New Zealand both lagged far behind the more adventurous British countries in taking advantage of this right. They did not appoint ministers to Washington until 1940–1942. And as to trade, Australia, as the principal country of the area, did not have any formal contractual relations with the United States until 1947. Both great changes were, therefore, consequences of World War II.

Whereas before the Civil War whaling brought Americans into the Southwest Pacific year after year in considerable numbers, of whom a few stayed on more or less permanently, the decline of the industry automatically eliminated these contacts and nothing comparable arose in its place. The residue of the great gold-rush influx into Australia naturally grew smaller and smaller as time passed, and was finally notable chiefly for supplying cherished American ancestors for a few Australians, some of whom achieved distinction. The Americans who now found their way into the islands, Australia, and New Zealand as more or less permanent residents were men of the type devoted to "knocking about" the world. They established themselves here and there in the available enterprises, but less as carriers of American influence than as Americans who were successful in local activities. They often remained identifiably American, were proud of being Americans, but they exerted an American influence only adventitiously or incidentally, and not always happily. Such individuals are to be identified in a wide range of occupations from mining to the theater, from agency business for American concerns to journalism. In the Australian theater there were Joseph Jefferson, Dion Boucicault, and J. C. Williamson, in journalism there was the cartoonist Livingston Hopkins. One runs across Americans here, there, and everywhere in the "literature" of the time: as captains in the disreputable kanaka trade (including that appalling rogue "Bully" Hayes of Cleveland, Ohio), as planters in Fiji, Tahiti, and Samoa, as mining engineers at Broken Hill, Kalgoorlie, and Mount Isa, as promoters of steamship services, as farmers who had followed the frontier clear across the Pacific, as irrigation experts like George Chaffey and Elwood Mead. By the 1920's the "American community" in the principal Australian cities, most visible when the Fourth of July was celebrated, consisted of a very mixed group of individuals indeed: headed by the consulate employees, it included oil company representatives, resident managers of American branch factories, a representative or two of American advertising enterprise, agents of American exporters of everything from automobiles to soap and corsets, the currently visiting theatrical performers and musicians, an academician or two either doing research or visiting Australia while on a sabbatical year world tour, and a variety of wanderers, from Mormon missionaries to persons of no readily identifiable occupation or profession. Outside the great cities it was easily possible to visit small towns and to find either that no American had been seen there "for years" or even that one was the first American ever to have appeared. Between the gold rushes and World War II resident Americans in Australia and New Zealand were relatively uncommon.

When the transcontinental railroads reached the Pacific Coast of the United States, beginning in 1869, there was an upsurge of optimism about the American economic future in the Pacific Basin, and naturally the Southwest Pacific figured in some of the calculations. During the seventies and eighties it was commonly assumed that San Francisco was destined to command the trade of the islands and to figure very prominently in that of Australia and New Zealand. There was an exceptional upsurge of optimism about the latter prospect at the time of the Spanish War. Hubert Howe Bancroft's *The New Pacific*, originally published in 1899 and revised in 1912 for a new career, a carelessly written, inaccurate book, gave flamboyant expression to the expectations. But while the quantity of trade with the Southwest Pacific did show an upward trend, it remained unbalanced in favor of the United States. Up to 1940, the Southwest Pacific ordinarily absorbed between 1 and 2 per cent of American exports,* while it supplied around 1 per cent of United States imports. Some figures are given in Table 2.

Table 2.   United States Trade with Oceania[a]

Year	Export value (thousands of dollars)	Import value (thousands of dollars)
1870	3,873	1,612
1880	7,437	4,619
1890	16,346	16,764
1900	40,751	28,640
1910	34,057	19,782
1920	171,605	80,014
1930	107,719	32,791
1940	94,483	34,673

[a] Source: *Historical Statistics of the United States, 1789–1945* (Washington, D.C.: G.P.O., 1949), pp. 250–251.

* Consisting of, for example, steel rails, railway cars and locomotives, steel bridges, electric lights, watches, irrigation pipes, tobacco, agricultural machinery, automobiles, office machinery, factory and mining machinery, and so on.

Naturally the composition of the trade changed somewhat over the long period, but probably more on the export than the import side. Speaking generally, one could say that the figures reflect the ever increasing economic activity in the United States and in the area and also the prevailing economic conditions from time to time. The figures which span World War I and the postwar prosperity reflect the fact that both parties were then in an exceptionally expansive mood. The 1940 figures show the effects of the Great Depression. But the single persistent characteristic was undoubtedly the failure of the area to achieve anything like a favorable balance of trade. Especially is this important when it is recalled that such "invisibles" as existed worked in favor of the United States also. It is this continuous unbalance that explains the Australian and New Zealand preoccupation with the American wool tariff.

As to long-term investments, by December 31, 1940, American direct investments in Oceania had reached a total of $120,-000,000 and portfolio investments $98,000,000 or 2 per cent of the American grand total of foreign investments. This was just a trifle more than American investments in Africa, which stood last on the list by regions of the world.

Nobody has ever worked out on an historical basis just where American private investment has been lodged in the economies of the Southwest Pacific. Most of it has probably always been in the Australian economy, but probably for the years up to circa 1950 in agency warehouses, assembly plants, and such. Branch factories appear to have been exceedingly uncommon until after World War II. American investment seems to have had but a minimal role in getting Australian industrialization going, though America had influence by way of technical advice. Probably the earliest American branch factory was that of the American Tobacco Company in the early eighteen-nineties; it did not long continue operations. Early in the 1900's International Harvester set a pattern of activities by establishing sales branches in both Australia and New Zealand. In the twenties the automobile manufacturers began to establish assembly plants: Ford Motor Company (of Canada, however) and General Motors in 1926. The Chrysler-Dodge group did likewise in 1939, but at the instance of an Australian collaborator. These enterprises soon began to use Australian-produced components, General Motors taking bodies from the Australian company of Holden, and this led on after World War II to the production of a wholly Australian car. This development was in fact pioneered by General Motors-Holden interests — the car was called Holden. In other fields, Wrigley's Gum and Heinz foods established branch factories in the twenties. But fundamental industrialization, like steel production, was carried out by Australian companies, many with large stockholdings by British investors, and the impulse to industrialize was unquestionably Australian. In its early phases the British were often accused of discouraging the effort. The Americans appear to have begun by taking advantage of what the Australians could supply by way of components in assembly operations and to have moved on, after World War II, to licensing of Australian producers and to direct entry into manufacturing themselves, with best results in terms of public relations, by joint investment with Australian capitalists, or in collaboration with Australian firms.

The idea that a regular steamship service between the American Pacific coast and New Zealand and Australia would be a major stimulant to the trade appealed to many men. It was concluded very early, however, that such a service could not be operated without subsidy, so the story of trans-Pacific shipping is also a story of struggles for and over subsidies, involving the Congress of the United States and the governments of New Zealand and New South Wales especially. In the colonies such men as Sir Julius Vogel of New Zealand and Sir Henry Parkes of New South Wales were heavily involved in the endless and intricate negotiations over subsidies, not always to their political profit. In the earlier phases of the business, Vogel and New Zealand were much more aggressively favorable to subsidizing a service than were Parkes and New South Wales. Vogel's favorite operator was the American W. H. Webb, Parkes' was another American, H. H. Hall. From the colonial point of view, the question at issue was not so much trade as the support of a fast mail service to London. By sending the mails across the United States by rail about two weeks' time could be gained over any route by sea. This was the beginning of the use of the United States as an avenue of travel between the Southwest Pacific and England.

H. H. Hall, who arrived in Sydney in 1867 as American commercial agent and acting Consul, was the pioneer promoter of the service. He started with sailing vessels and switched to steam. W. H. Webb, who had operated clippers from the east coast of America to Australia in the gold-rush period and after the Civil War had engaged in the West Indian trade, concentrated his attention on New Zealand and Vogel, but with Vogel's help he made great efforts to extend his service to Sydney. Actively assisted by Vogel, Webb started a service operating in 1871 and kept it going until 1874. He never received a subsidy from the United States government, and eventually failed, probably chiefly for this reason. It was Webb who directed attention to Pago Pago in Samoa as a desirable coaling station, with consequences to be examined shortly. Oddly, this also directed New Zealand's, or at least Vogel's, attention to Samoa also, and ever thereafter Samoa's status was a New Zealand concern.

Webb's line was succeeded by the Pacific Mail, with which H. H. Hall was closely identified. Pacific Mail carried on the service for ten years, 1875–1885, while Hall and Sir Henry Parkes remained keenly interested, but then they abandoned it. This line called at Kadavu, Fiji. The service was then taken up by the Union Steamship Company of New Zealand, operating one vessel, and the Oceanic Company of the United States, operating two. These companies carried on in collaboration from 1885 to 1901, when an American law excluded foreign ships from the coastal trade (including the Honolulu-San Francisco run), so the Union Company shifted its North American terminus to Vancouver, British Columbia. Oceanic then put three ships into the service to the Southwest Pacific and operated them independently of Union, continuing until 1907. Between 1907 and 1909 no service was operated between San Francisco and Australian and New Zealand ports, but Oceanic maintained a service between San Francisco and Tahiti. Union operated a shuttle service to Tahiti, connecting with the Oceanic line. Then in 1909 both Union and Oceanic returned to the North American-Southwest Pacific service. Oceanic, however, omitted New Zealand ports from its run, calling instead at Pago Pago, while Union operated via Tahiti, and had its American terminus at Vancouver. This in effect was sharing the run, but the two companies were independent. In 1926 the Oceanic interests were taken over by the Matson Line, which had operated between San Francisco and Honolulu from 1882. The Matson Line settled down to a run from San Francisco to Honolulu, Pago Pago, Suva in Fiji, Auckland, and Sydney; the Union Company started from Vancouver and omitted San Francisco but otherwise followed the same route. In the thirties, as a phase of the bad economic relations between Australia and the United States, a strong effort was made to exclude the Matson Line from the New Zealand-Australia run, but the laws passed for the purpose were never enforced. After a suspension during World War II, the Matson Line resumed its service and is today still the only American line in the service. Since World War II it has taken to calling at Tahiti on its homeward voyage. Competition is provided by the airlines, and a British line operating for the first time in the service. The gist of the story is, therefore, that while the steamship services have been indispensable to the support of the trading relations, they could not of themselves solve the deeper economic problems involved. Without subsidy, it is improbable that any service could have survived.

In terms of "influence" the trade and investment record is more meaningful than might at first appear, especially if one focuses on technological influence. The American technological influence was at work in the homes, as with Singer sewing machines, on the roads with American vehicles, on the railways with American equipment and managerial influences, in the fields with American farm machinery, on the dairy farms, as with the Babcock test and butter-factory organizations, in irrigation, notably through the work of the Chaffee family on the Murray River, on the sheep stations with imported Vermont sheep, in the mines as a result of the employment of American engineers (including Mr. Herbert Hoover) and machinery, in the steel mills (from 1915, when the modern industry was begun), in the shops and offices with business machines, and through technical publications, which have flowed freely from the United States to Australia for a long time. But this kind of Whitmanesque cataloguing — which, by the way, still awaits the historian's verification — gives a slightly false impression, for the American technological influence, persistent though it has been and still is, (1) has always been secondary to the British influence, and (2) has in any case been absorbed into a cultural matrix which has long been essentially Australian. It is safe to say, however, that the American technological influence on the Southwest Pacific has consistently been the most important single influence after the British and on occasion has achieved primacy as, for example, in road transport.

It is certainly this writer's impression that the American technological influence has been more constant, persistent, and considerable than the ideological influence. It is, also, even more difficult to isolate and describe the latter than the former. The American "ideological" influence on the Southwest Pacific, most readily identifiable in Australia, is at once elusive and pervasive. This is because while it enters the public and private mind in various ways at various levels of importance, it is at its best when it is assimilated creatively into an Australian context, and usually it is least desirable when it is uncritically imitative in nature. However, that said, it is exceedingly difficult to be sure that what one tentatively identifies as an American influence really is one, for it must not be forgotten that in Australia what we have is a new society largely built during the industrial era, since the French Revolution, highly urbanized, this assuring the appearance of pseudo-American phenomena which are local growths, not derived from across the Pacific. The society itself creates conditions, including intellectual conditions, which at once support pseudo-American expressions and provide the basis for the free acceptance of American ideas and things. This is why Americans have long been disposed to think that Australia is "American" — Henry Adams so reacted when he visited Sydney in 1891. This is a superficial view. But it is nevertheless true that history and the resultant social conditions dispose the Australians to be much like Americans in many ways. Even in New Zealand, where the rough sameness I am alleging is not nearly so visible or true, this is also the case, as can be illustrated by a quotation which, though literary in reference, can readily be given a wider connotation. The poet A. R. D. Fairburn once said, "I believe that from the point of view of the New Zealand writer, *Huckleberry Finn* is the most important novel ever written . . . we can understand Huck, the true colonial, where we can only pretend to understand Tom Brown, the English public-school boy."

Taking a hop-skip-and-jump approach to this fascinating but little studied matter, it may be pointed out that as the structure of the Australian Commonwealth government shows an American influence, so also there is readily discernible an American theme, with both positive and negative variations, running through the decisions of the Australian High Court. After all, the Commonwealth is a federal system, and the decisions of the American Supreme Court relate to such a system, quite apart from any other claims to attention they may have as part of the corpus of law. But the Australian constitution is normally interpreted by Australians as exerting a conservative influence, so it is natural that it should be interpretable with American help — for the United States to most Australians is a conservative country.

Yet it is up to those who subscribe to that interpretation of the United States to explain why so many American ideological influences in Australia, and New Zealand, too, have been radical in character. Equally as important as the constitution and the High Court is the labor movement. The historical backgrounds of the Labour Parties of both Australia and New Zealand cannot be thoroughly understood without reference to the writings of Edward Bellamy, Laurence Gronlund and Henry George. The most radical laboristic visitation Australia ever experienced before the coming of the communists after World War I — far more radical than Tom Mann's English socialism — was the American I.W.W. To say the least of it, this is a very odd way for a conservative country to exert its influence!

American painting has always been practically unknown in the Southwest Pacific and few American artists have ever worked there. Aside from Livingston Hopkins, the cartoonist, probably the most notable to work in Australia were those men associated with the production of the encyclopedic survey of the country, published in the eighties, called *Picturesque Atlas of Australia*. "The eight hundred illustrations," writes a historian of Australian art, "represented the finest examples of wood-engraving which had been done here." Three of the regular staff artists were Americans: F. B. Schell, the art editor, W. T. Smedley, and W. C. Fitler, the latter a graduate of the Pennsylvania Academy of Fine Arts. The staff of engravers was also headed by an American, Horace Baker. The two great volumes (18 × 14 inches) of this work are now a collectors' item.

American writers have usually done rather better, but not consistently so. Any nation's literature is apt to be exported in a haphazard, unpredictable, and often, from the critic's point of view, utterly senseless way. *The Australian Quarterly*, long one of the country's most distinguished periodicals, has consistently, since its founding in 1929, used a quotation from George Washington as its epigraph: "Promote, then, as an ob-

ject of primary importance, institutions for the general diffusion
of knowledge." The classic writers of the "flowering of New
England" had great prestige in Australia in the seventies and
eighties. Marcus Clarke sought the patronage of Oliver Wendell
Holmes for his classic novel of convict days, *For the Term of
His Natural Life*. Australian poets were flattered to be represented in Henry Wadsworth Longfellow's anthologies. Walt
Whitman had at least one Australian correspondent, the poet
Bernard O'Dowd, and another Australian wrote and printed a
small monograph on him that is today a rare item of Whit-
maniana. In the eighties the men who founded *The Bulletin*,
in its heyday a major power in the promotion of Australian
political and literary nationalism, closely observed American
journalistic methods. Mark Twain, whose reputation preceded
him, visited Australia and New Zealand when he was "following the equator"; he too saw Australia as quite American,
though he saw it rather more accurately than some, for he
described Sydney as "an English city with American trim-
mings." But slowly the Australian interest in American writing
seems to have fallen off. Henry Adams' visit of 1891 passed
practically unnoticed, and Jack London's of 1908 (when he reported the Burns-Johnson prizefight and did some pieces on the
labor situation) was not long remembered. Robert Louis
Stevenson appeared to be a far greater celebrity than any of the
stray Americans, so decidedly so that the day was to come
when an Australian critic could solemnly record the opinion
that Stevenson was a greater writer on the South Seas than
Herman Melville! By the nineteen-twenties and thirties it was
apparent that the Australians, speaking generally, had lost track
of American literature. They apparently began to lose track in
the nineties, never really taking an interest in such figures as
Norris and Crane. Dreiser, Anderson, Dos Passos, and so on
they simply passed by. When I went to Australia in 1927 H. L.
Mencken could think of but one Australian admirer, a newspaperman, and I discovered that he had been driven into such a
small corner as to be wholly without influence. Occasionally

Sinclair Lewis would be mentioned, for he could be read as highly critical of America, and Upton Sinclair was known on the left. Oddly the American writers of the twenties seem to have had more contemporary influence in New Zealand than Australia, which is hardly what one would expect. Frank Sargeson had obviously read Sherwood Anderson; John Mulgan, Ernest Hemingway. Only during and after World War II did an interest in American writing revive. Today one can find intelligent comments on American writers in the better journals. For several decades earlier this was hardly the case, first, because only such American books as were published in England reached Australia, and this was far from all of interest and significance; second, because it was a rather arid literary period in Australia anyhow, and third, because the reputation of the United States had been tarnished in World War I and was a long time recovering much luster.

What one nation thinks of another is rather a matter of speculation than of analytical description, but the testimony of competent observers who lived through the period is that America and Americans were "popular" in Australia and New Zealand in the years from the nineties to World War I, this popularity reaching a climax of a sort when Theodore Roosevelt's Great White Fleet visited Sydney in 1908. American neutrality in World War I made the United States very unpopular. It was regarded as showing a gross failure of moral insight and as somehow traitorous to the British cause. The Hughes-Wilson differences at Paris, to which we shall revert shortly, did not help matters, and the failure to join the League of Nations was resented. Between the two World Wars, "indifference," spiced by sniping, seems best to characterize the Australian attitude toward America, while the New Zealanders were rather more decidedly indifferent. Australians deplored what they believed to be the steady erosion of the "British" character of the United States by the rising influence of the non-British immigrants; they deplored the lawlessness of the prohibition era; they deplored American popular music and dancing; they deplored the movies; they deplored the sexy magazines; they deplored the Negro, particularly as entertainer, the role in which they saw him most often; they deplored . . . In 1926 an Australian named Maurice Groom published a gloomy book entitled *Within the Shadow*, in which he devoted several chapters to the United States. His verdict was that the Americans were "of the coarser kind, living in a civilization which showed marked signs of degeneration." The root cause of his gripe was American neutrality in the war. All else followed from that. Yet two years later another Australian published a small book wholly devoted to the United States and put forward a rather different view, though in a revealingly defensive fashion. This was the late Professor G. V. Portus; the book was *The American Background, Sketched for Australians* (1928). Professor Portus concluded:

> There is a fashionable pose of smiling in a superior way whenever the Americans are mentioned. I have no patience with this pose. Whether it comes from a Russian Communist, or an Australian Labour Leader, or a British businessman, it is a foolish affectation to pretend to despise the United States and things American. For what the Americans are doing, and still more, what the Americans will do, matters, and matters enormously, not only for this country, and for the continent of Europe; it matters enormously for the future of the whole human race.

The coming of the New Deal rather perked up interest in the United States in Australia and New Zealand, but it is doubtful if it was a very understanding interest. The Australians and New Zealanders had so little knowledge of the United States to work with that they tended to see the whole business as an effort to "catch up" with them in social legislation, quite overlooking that they had fallen behind the leaders in this area. New Zealand only "caught up" in 1935 and after, Australia during the war. At any rate it was still necessary at the end of the period for Australian writers like Professor Fred Alexander and Mr. R. J. Boyer to try their hands at explicating the American riddle anew. And it is the sorry truth that at the level of

government-to-government relations, Australian–American relations reached their very lowest point in the late thirties. It was
an odd prelude to the period of collaboration that soon
followed.

On the other hand, the Americans seem during these same
decades to have quite consistently entertained a favorable view
of the countries of the Southwest Pacific. They were hardly
overburdened with knowledge of them, but the general *impression* was good. The view was oddly compounded. The
American "Progressives" of the turn of the century took a keen
interest in New Zealand and Australian experimental social
legislation, *circa* 1895–1910. The interest found expression in a
spate of magazine articles — and in such books as Henry Dem-
arest Lloyd's *Newest England* (1903), Frank Parson's *The
Story of New Zealand* (1904), Victor Clark's *The Labour
Movement in Australasia* (1906), and P. S. Collier's *Minimum
Wage Legislation in Australasia* (1915). (Perhaps the most distinguished forerunner of this literature was John H. Wigmore's
The Australian Ballot (1889); it, however, referred to Australia's earliest experiments in political democracy, whereas the
later books concentrated on her later experiments in *social*
democracy.) This information, spiced with travelers' tales, fixed
at least three ideas in the minds of those Americans open to
impressions on the subject: that Australia and New Zealand
were politically radical, that they were daringly experimental
in general attitude, and that they were good countries in which
to live. For the rest it was thought that New Zealand was a
peculiarly beautiful country — true, of course — and that Australia was interesting for its kangaroos and aboriginals (thought
of as "the most primitive people in the world today"). And of
course it was a part of American folklore that the South Sea
islands were par excellence lands for those who adored lotus-
eating and contemporary romance, an impression assiduously
cultivated by certain writers and the entertainment industry.

11. The United States Acquires Territory in the Southwest Pacific

The story of how the United States came into possession of the island of Tutuila with its fabulous harbor of Pago Pago, and thus acquired a territorial foothold in the Southwest Pacific, is of incredible complexity and, by and large, utterly mystifying in its motivation, unless dreams are to be equated to reality. It was an adventure initiated for what appeared to be practical reasons, but history perversely destroyed the reasons almost before the story was completed, and the United States was left with a possession, the utility of which has not to the present day ever been proved.

The first Americans to take any interest in Samoa were the whalers, to whom it was one of several island groups near to a whaling grounds to which it was convenient to resort for "refreshment." For this reason Wilkes paid considerable attention to Samoa when he visited the islands on his exploring expedition, and he drew attention to the fact that the harbor called Pago Pago was probably the very best in all the islands of the South Pacific. This reputation it has ever since sustained: it *is* very lovely, as anyone who has seen it will testify, and its usefulness as a harbor is demonstrable. Unfortunately the assessment of it qua harbor was in the beginning and still is that of

mariners more interested in its character as such and its geographical position vis à vis its area and the routes from San
Francisco to Auckland and Sydney, and Panama to the same
destinations, than as a harbor with an economically significant
hinterland. It was this failure to take hinterland into account
that rendered the struggle for the harbor such a dubious enterprise. Insofar as the Samoan group has ever been assigned a
substantive economic potential, the island of Tutuila, the small-
est of the principal islands of the group (54 square miles), has
never figured in the calculation. Attention has always been
directed to the second largest island, Upolu (340 square miles),
and its harbor at Apia. Pago Pago has, in relation to the economy of the Samoan group, always been an outport. In con-
tending for Pago Pago the United States was therefore always
concerned with obtaining a port allegedly of great strategic
value, not one serving a hinterland subject to profitable development. If it had desired a port of the latter kind, it would have
done better to choose one in the nearby Fiji group, where at
one time it had a significant economic interest, but when as late
as 1869 it had a chance to take Fiji (in lieu of a claim on the
native king for $45,000 damages to the property of American
citizens), it passed the opportunity by. Oddly it was the same
President U. S. Grant who passed by Fiji who took a hand in
initiating the struggle for Pago Pago.

While the alleged usefulness of Pago Pago was asserted by
Wilkes about 1840, it was not until steam was replacing sail
and the need for coaling stations arose in the Pacific that any
American action with regard to it was taken. Two factors then
came into play: (1) the expansionist aspirations of President
Grant and (2) the commercial aspirations of the unlucky
shipping magnate, W. H. Webb, previously referred to. The
latter sought a coaling station for his ships running from the
West Coast to New Zealand and Australia, the former had a
passion for picking up stray bits of real estate, not shared, however, by the contemporary Senate. The notion that Pago Pago
was an ideal coaling station was confirmed to Webb by his

agent, Captain Wakeman, who had had experience as a mariner in the area earlier. Wakeman examined the harbor at first hand in 1871. The United States Navy then entered the picture.

Between 1859 and 1864 the American interest in Samoa was so feeble that no consul was posted in the group, though the first one had been appointed as far back as 1839, and between 1856 and 1869 no United States warship visited the group. In the late sixties, however, the practice of sending warships on tours of the islands, usually on a track that led from San Francisco to Honolulu, to Sydney and Auckland, to a South American port, and back to San Francisco, was re-established. When in 1871 Commander Richard W. Meade in the *Narragansett* was sent on such a tour, he fell under the influence of Henry Pierce, United States Minister at Hawaii, an ardent expansionist. Pierce persuaded Meade to be the agent for getting Pago Pago for the United States. At Pago Pago on February 14, 1872, Meade arranged a treaty with the local chief, granting the United States "the exclusive privilege of establishing in the said harbor of Pago Pago, island of Tutuila, a naval station." However, Meade's talking point with the chief had not been a *naval* station at all, but Webb's steamship line, a private commercial enterprise. It is to be assumed that he thought a naval station would be more appealing in Washington. Anyhow, the treaty was sent to the Secretary of the Navy, who passed it to the Secretary of State, who handed it to President Grant. Grant, consistent with his outlook in such matters, sent it to the Senate with a favorable recommendation. The Senate, consistent with its attitude, let it die. Nevertheless Samoa remained a live issue on the American agenda for a quarter-century thereafter.

Meade's tactic of talking up the private commercial aspect of the Pago Pago proposal and then writing a treaty for a naval station introduced a small ambiguity into the Samoan affair which has never really been resolved. Meade, however, made it clear that there were two sets of reasons for taking Pago Pago. That neither set was actually very compelling, then or later, only became evident in time. Meanwhile the theoreticians of commerce and war, collectively the expansionists, could play around with Samoa. Their first move was to try to find reasons for taking the harbor that might move the Senate to favorable action.

Before we become entangled in the convolutions of the Samoan story, its general context must be indicated. By going into Samoa the Americans came into collision with the British and the Germans, who had interests in the group, and they also tangled with the British colonials, specifically the New Zealanders. The two British views of Samoa were different in very important ways. Whereas to the United Kingdom Samoa and all the other as yet independent groups were remote and contingent interests of the Empire about which it was reluctant to do much, even in the seventies, beyond appointing consuls and backing them up occasionally with visits of warships. Taking sovereignty they regarded as an undesirable ultimate action or "solution" of a particular problem, not as a prime objective of policy. The British colonials, for their part, favored action to exclude all foreign powers from the islands and advocated the taking of sovereignty, or at minimum the declaring of a protectorate, as the primary policy. The colonials entertained the idea that the foreigners were intruders in what was rightfully a British preserve. Their doctrine was sometimes called "Monroeism," otherwise "Oceania for the Anglo-Saxons." On this basis the French in Tahiti, New Caledonia, and the New Hebrides were intruders, and so also were the Germans and the Americans in Samoa, or wherever else they might show signs of "taking over." The colonial attitude had its roots in the commission of the founding governor of Australia, in which the geographical boundaries of his domain were precisely defined north, south, and west, but not east in the Pacific, and the doctrine has been given expression since the middle of the nineteenth century by a galaxy of Australian and New Zealand leaders, including Sir George Grey, Sir Julius Vogel, Richard Seddon, Sir Henry Parkes, Alfred Deakin, William Morris Hughes, Herbert V. Evatt, and Peter Fraser. However, during the period when the islands were being parceled out among the powers — roughly from 1840 to 1900 — the colonials were not able to carry their policy into execution. They lacked the constitutional capacity to do so. They therefore were in the position of pressure-groups, exerting or trying to exert pressure on the Colonial and Foreign Offices of Great Britain to act in the fashion they favored. Nor did they until after 1900 really desire any other position, for they resisted all British suggestions that they might add responsibility to advocacy by assuming some or full financial responsibility for the islands they asked to have taken over. What they rather sought was the privilege of dictating island policy without responsibility, financial or administrative. They wanted to make Imperial policy without risking Imperial headaches, on the ground that their policy best served their own *and Imperial* interests. Mostly in the period here under discussion they failed to realize their aims in full — or even in very satisfactory part, and each frustration as it occurred was an occasion for execrating the blind leaders of Britain. Sometimes, however, they got what they wanted, as when Britain under Disraeli took over Fiji in 1874. But to them the Fiji victory was only satisfactory if identical action was also taken in Tonga and Samoa.

As remarked, the Imperial view was different. Whereas the colonials viewed the problem in terms of their area taken by itself, the British saw the area in a world context in at least three senses: (1) the Southwest Pacific was but one locale of a British Imperial domain which was already so vast that the authorities were reluctant to add to it; (2) it was clearly understood in London, if not in the colonies, that it was politically impossible, as the relations of nations stood, for the British to "grab" what was in sight regardless of the reactions of the competitive powers; and (3) the British tended to judge the islands of the Southwest Pacific, however the colonials might assess them, as often of insignificant value to Britain, and indeed properly to be traded off in realizing British aims elsewhere. In the Imperial perspective, the economic value of the islands was often trivial, actual or prospective, and the argument for the islands as a defensive screen was usually rejected. The British placed the emphasis on developing the defense potential of Australia and New Zealand themselves, if indeed the Imperial power needed any local strengthening. Hence the Imperial authorities did not share the Australian-New Zealand horror of foreign neighbors. The situation was complicated, however, by the fact that Imperial servants in the area often developed marked sympathy for the colonial point of view. Fiji was annexed partly because of the representations of "converted" Imperial agents.

The Germans first came into the Pacific as whalers, continued as traders and planters, and eventually, after Bismarck changed his mind about colonies, actively sought colonial possessions. They ended by holding, in the Southwest Pacific, not only a portion of the Samoan group, but also a piece of New Guinea and a number of important associated islands, including some geographically in the Solomon chain. During the period when the Germans were acquiring their colonies, the Americans were concerned only about their activities in Samoa, but the British were, of course, also concerned with German activities in New Guinea.

The German interest in Samoa can be dated from the establishment there of the pioneer trading and plantation firm of Goddefroy & Sons of Hamburg in 1857. The chosen island was Upolu and the headquarters town was Apia. In fairly short order the Germans clearly had the predominant material interest in Samoa. The British, who had been longest in the islands (for their missionaries had been active since the eighteen-thirties), were a rather weak second. The Americans were a poor third, and crude adventures like the Polynesian Land Company did not improve their position.

Although the Americans were chiefly concerned to protect their interest in Pago Pago, they had to do so by taking a hand in the politics of the group as a whole. This meant that the principal locale of the struggle was the island of Upolu and the town of Apia. It so happened that about the time the Meade treaty was dying in the Senate a petition from the natives of Samoa was received in Washington asking that the United States annex the islands. This was standard procedure in the islands at moments when the natives were for one reason or another discouraged about the possibility of maintaining their independence. This particular petition was forwarded to Washington by the Polynesian Land Company of California through W. H. Webb, the shipping magnate. The Polynesian Land Company was a speculative venture headed by J. B. M. Stewart, an Australian resident in San Francisco. It was decided that to get the background information needed to evaluate this petition, an agent should be sent to Samoa to make a firsthand survey. The agent chosen was Colonel A. B. Steinberger, a friend of Webb and President Grant. Steinberger did a good job, but he was bitten by the bug of ambition. He perceived that the core of the Samoan problem was the establishment of stable government. He got the notion that he could establish such a government, to be ostensibly a native government, especially if he could employ the authority of the United States in his support. However, the State Department refused to go along with his scheme, for it savored of interference in native affairs. Steinberger, while outwardly retaining his apparently close relations with the Department, negotiated with the Germans and promised them economic favors from the proposed new government in return for general support. He then proceeded to Samoa and on July 4, 1875, set up a government, nominally headed by a Samoan king, of which he was Prime Minister. In the political climate of the islands it did not survive twelve months. Within a year Steinberger was deported from Samoa at the instigation of the American consul with the help of the captain of a visiting warship from the British naval station in Australia. Steinberger was carried away to Fiji in the British ship and went from there via New Zealand to London. As a result of Steinberger's representations, the American consul was removed from office and the British naval officer was dismissed from the service. Later the British consul was transferred elsewhere. However, Steinberger was effectively smashed. The whole affair was "tropic vaudeville" of the O. Henry variety.

About this time the Germans began a campaign to influence the native government in their favor. The natives thereupon appealed to the British and the Americans simultaneously. The eventual American reply to the Samoan advance was a treaty formally recognizing the native government and promising advice and help when it was requested. The use (but not *exclusive* use) of Pago Pago was provided for. This treaty was signed at Washington on January 17, 1878. It was the work of President Rutherford B. Hayes' Secretary of State, W. M. Evarts of Boston. Meanwhile, the British, as represented by Sir Arthur Gordon, Governor of Fiji, made motions that seemed to reflect a desire to *annex* Samoa. The *New York Times* interpreted the American treaty as circumventing Sir Arthur's designs. The idea was that the British having lately taken Fiji, also coveted Tonga and Samoa to protect their strategic position in the islands and on the trade routes. This, however, was less a British aspiration than a colonial idea, especially a New Zealand idea. Sir Arthur was not really acting in a New Zealand sense, though unquestionably the New Zealanders were keen to have him do so. In January of 1879 the Germans signed a treaty with the Samoans, establishing *their* position. In August Sir Arthur Gordon at last arranged a British-Samoan treaty. What then became apparent was that a system of tripartite control of Samoa by the interested parties had been outlined by implication.

Such external, divided control was made difficult by the fact that the Samoans were themselves divided into two factions as to who should be king, and without a king there could be no native government at all. The "system" could only work if a reasonably stable native government existed. At one stage the Americans tried to solve the difficulty by arranging that one claimant be king and the other vice-king. As time passed it was the practice of the powers to back one or another faction of the quarreling groups.

In 1883 the government of Hawaii took notice of what was going on in the islands and protested to the United States against the ambitions of the colonists of Australia and New Zealand to extend British dominion over the still-independent islands. The Hawaiians spoke in the name of the islanders, especially the Polynesians. They had a special regard for the Polynesian Samoans. The United States made a most interesting reply: it put Hawaii and Samoa, in which it was keenly interested, on one plane, and said that their independence must be protected, and the rest of the islands not yet annexed were put on quite another. The latter, it said, were obviously within the "Australasian political system" and of no interest to the United States.

The German ambitions in New Guinea came plainly to notice in 1884 and the New Zealanders tried to establish the point that if Germany took New Guinea, then the British should immediately take Tonga and Samoa. This, of course, was but a new argument for an old wish. However, it was not the New Zealanders but the Australians who were really concerned about New Guinea, and they did not see it as a mere pawn in any game involving Tonga and Samoa. They pressed for the annexation of New Guinea as valuable in itself. In the end the Germans established themselves in northern New Guinea east of the Dutch portion of the island, and the British took the portion to the south of them. A definition of spheres of influence in the whole Southwest Pacific was arranged between the British and the Germans in 1886. This deal was much criticized in Australia and New Zealand, for it recognized the rights of foreigners in the islands. Three years before in a colonial conference they had declared strongly against further annexations by foreigners in the area.

While these adjustments were being made, the Germans began what appeared to be a planned campaign finally to take over in Samoa. The result was that in 1886 the United States, Germany, and Great Britain all sent special investigators to Samoa to find out what was really going on and to recommend a forward course to their respective governments. The matter was then canvassed at a conference in Washington attended by the Secretary of State and the German and British Ministers. The conference was abortive. Although nothing so horrendous actually emerged during the conversations, Secretary Bayard suspected that the British and the Germans had agreed to deal the United States out of the islands. At any rate the British recognized that the German interest in Samoa was much greater than theirs, and in the light of that discovery they set the New Zealand and Australian ideas about the future of Samoa to one side. This was tantamount to turning the group over to the Germans, unless the United States, perceiving how the game was going, insisted on remaining in it.

The United States did so insist, basing its position on the proposition that it had a moral obligation to protect the independence of the Samoans. The situation in the islands rapidly deteriorated as the struggling Samoan factions engaged either German or American support. To deal with the resultant muddle, the interested powers sent warships to Apia — three American, three German, and one British — and while they were there all but the British vessel were destroyed in a hurricane. The British vessel managed to get out of the harbor and to the open sea, where survival was possible. While the British said this was because of the ship's superior engines, the New Zealanders said it was because she carried New Zealand coal. The legend is that the hurricane averted war over Samoa; without ships there was nothing with which to fight. The truth is that violence between the ships was unlikely, but had it occurred it would not have led to war, for a conference in Berlin on the Samoan questions had already been arranged.

At the Berlin conference (1889) a condominium was devised to insure the independence of Samoa on the one hand and the accumulated treaty rights of the United States, Britain, and

Germany on the other, with a provision for joint intervention when required.

Thus well short of two decades after W. H. Webb had decided that Pago Pago would be an excellent coaling station for his (unprofitable) shipping line, and the United States Navy had decided that the port might serve it also as a coaling station for ships traveling around Cape Horn, the United States government had been moved step by step into a reversal of its traditional policy of "no entangling alliances." At Berlin in 1889 it accepted the first "entangling alliance" since that with the French in 1800. And it had also made a fateful step along the road to territorial imperialism, a step along a road that led fairly directly to the taking of the Philippines and Guam in 1898. As John Bassett Moore subsequently pointed out, it was shown at Berlin that the United States was prepared "to go to any length in asserting a claim to take part in the determination of the fate of a group of islands, thousands of miles away, in which American commercial interests were so slight as to be scarcely appreciable."* Why?

Secretary of State James G. Blaine, in office at the time of the Berlin Conference, provided a rationale: (1) the American interest in the Pacific was rising, (2) American commerce with the East was increasing, and (3) the anticipated canal at Panama would create changes in the Pacific of the first importance to the United States. Blaine said nothing specifically about the Southwest Pacific, to which Samoa presumably most directly related, rather blanketing it in under the general heading "Pacific." But it was entirely clear that the American Pacific interests were in the North Pacific, as the Spanish War was soon dramatically to show. It was, also, the commerce of the North Pacific that was most markedly increasing, not that of the Southwest. And as to the Panama canal, still a quarter-century away in any case, Samoa stood 5,656 miles to the west of it, so the practical relation of the two points was highly contin-

* Moore, as quoted in G. H. Ryden, "The Foreign Policy of the United States in Relation to Samoa" (New Haven: 1933), p. 520.

gent. Shipping from Sydney and Auckland for Panama coaled by preference at Rapa and Tahiti to the southeast, not at Samoa, as long as such coaling was necessary.

Nevertheless the Americans saw the matter through to the end. The condominium did not work. It was a modus vivendi, not a final solution. At the time of the Spanish War the Germans took the initiative in bringing it to an end. After ascertaining that the British could not be induced to take over Samoa, they worked out a maneuver by which the United States got possession of Tutuila and the harbor of Pago Pago, together with some minor outlying islands, while they took the rest of the group, including Upolu and its port of Apia. Britain was compensated by the resignation in its favor of the German treaty rights in Tonga and by a rearrangement of the earlier division of the Solomon Islands. The convention dividing Samoa was signed on December 2, 1899, and ratified by the Senate on February 16, 1900, but cession was not accepted, ratified, and confirmed by the Congress until 1929, a delay which is a commentary on the value attributed to the acquisition. The step might not have been taken even then had not Senator Hiram Bingham of Connecticut, whose family had a traditional interest in South Sea islands dating from early missionary days in Hawaii and Micronesia, taken the lead in pushing the matter through. From 1899 to 1951 American Samoa was administered by the United States Navy; since 1951 it has been ruled by civilians under the Department of Interior. American Samoa quickly became a small but exasperating problem in colonial administration, of which only a handful of Americans have been so much as aware. Far more have known that Pago Pago is the setting of Somerset Maugham's short story "Rain" than have known that Pago Pago is American territory. If it is asked how it came about that the Americans were so tenacious in their pursuit of Pago Pago, one can only reply that it is the dross of a dream dreamed ninety years ago which, because of startling changes in the technology of transport, it proved impossible to translate into any very tangible reality.

12. White Australia, The Islands, Versailles, the Washington Conference

The development of the resources of Australia and New Zealand was bound sooner or later to attract immigrants from not only Europe but also Asia and the islands. In actual fact, this has applied most forcibly in the case of Australia. Historically most of the immigrants have been of British nationality, and the Australians and New Zealanders have taken a good deal of pride in this background, even to the point of a certain intolerance of non-British immigrants at various stages of the story. Their firmest objection, however, has been to immigrants from Asia and the islands. The Australian objective has steadily been to maintain Australia "white" against all challenges. As is always true in such cases, the rationale of exclusion has been an inextricable mixture of racial prejudice, fear of economic competition, fear that certain immigrants would menace the prevailing standard of living, dogmatic assertions of unassimilability both physically and socio-economically — any and all arguments pointed to justify the means to the same end: a white Australia. A tangled complex of such ideas built up behind the policy in the colonial period until it was accepted by persons of all political outlooks, Labour or liberal or conservative. The policy had become the favored policy of the whole nation before it was comprehensively applied, and ever since it has been almost beyond argument as a national dogma. Only the exigencies of international politics since World War II have caused any marked moderation of its expression in law and administration.

During the gold rushes Chinese were attracted to Australia in considerable numbers. Their presence on the gold fields was resented by the white miners to the point of inspiring several very unpleasant riots. The colonial governments responded by levying a high poll tax on the Chinese in the country and trying to cut down the numbers entering by limiting the permissible immigrants to one to every ten tons of a ship's burden. As gold became exhausted, the flow from China fell off, Chinese in Australia went home, and during the sixties the anti-Chinese laws lapsed. The Chinese in Australia became a tiny, though fairly conspicuous, minority. Meanwhile during the sixties the importation of "kanakas," or Pacific island natives, to work in tropical agriculture in Queensland was begun. In the eighties the agitation against the Chinese immigration into California led in the United States to the Chinese Exclusion Act of 1882. It suggested to the Australians that the flow of Chinese abroad, deflected from California, might descend upon Australia, so the laws of the fifties were re-enacted. These laws were, in the late nineties, extended to apply to the Indians and the Japanese. All the colonies save Queensland fell in line. The legislation thereupon became an embarrassment to the Imperial authorities, whose relations with the Chinese, the Indians, and the Japanese were on a rather different footing from those of the Australian colonies. Joseph Chamberlain, then Colonial Secretary, tackled the problems in 1897 and advised the colonies how to have their cake and eat it too. He called attention to the dictation test devised by the Colony of Natal in southern Africa and suggested they adopt it as a way of excluding unwanted people without directly affronting nations with which Britain had to maintain the friendliest possible relations. Under the Natal law, "any person who, when asked to do so, failed to write out and sign in a European language an application for admission on a prescribed form set out in a schedule to the Act was to be deemed to be a prohibited immigrant." With modifications of a minor character, this device became the principal technical support of the White Australia policy. It was incorporated into Commonwealth immigration law in 1901. It was also adopted in New Zealand. The Australians were in complete earnest about remaining white and at federation cleared the remaining kanakas from tropical Queensland and embarked upon the experiment of developing the area exclusively with white labor, even though it proved to require constant subsidy of the principal crop, sugar, to achieve the end.

The point here is that the parallel treatment of the problem of Asiatic immigration in Australia and the United States (or at least California) led toward the end of the nineteenth century to the detection by the partisans of the Yellow Peril interpretation of the Pacific Basin situation of an identity of interest between Australia and America vis-à-vis Asia. It remained a foggy issue, but Admiral Mahan touched upon it as an important consideration in one of his magazine articles. It seemed to many Australians that the famous visit of Theodore Roosevelt's Great White Fleet to Sydney in 1908, while on its tour of the world, was directly related to it, especially since the fleet's tour was so obviously to be connected with the then existing tension between Japan and the United States over, precisely, immigration policy. But there was no way to translate the fellow feeling into anything more than that because of Australia's limited status in international law.

Whatever may have been the case in 1908, there was no great solidarity between Prime Minister William Morris Hughes and President Wilson at the Peace Conference of Paris ten years later. By that time the international status of Australia had been considerably enhanced, at least in British eyes, by her part in World War I. Prime Minister Hughes, as an ardent nationalist — and also an ardent Imperialist, a vigorous exponent indeed of the peculiarly British double-barreled patriotism — was of a disposition to take full advantage of his opportunities as he saw them. However this impulse to accept a higher international status was not strong enough in Australia to carry her to the lengths to which South Africa and Canada were shortly willing to go. But Mr. Hughes was entirely prepared to take full advantage of the special position given the dominions at Paris, which, in the end, allowed them separately to sign the Treaty of Versailles. He exercised his privileges in many ways, but the two ways that led to direct contention with Wilson involved the Australian islands policy and White Australia.

Early in the war Australia had taken over the German colonial possessions in New Guinea and associated islands, while New Zealand had taken over German Samoa. Germany's possessions north of the equator fell to Japan. It was Australia's expectation (and also New Zealand's) that the captured territories would be annexed in due course as spoils of war. Great Britain shared that view. In 1917 she promised Japan to support her claim to German Micronesia. The British share of New Guinea had been passed to the Australian Commonwealth in 1906 so the new addition would give the Australians control of the great island east of the Dutch portion — roughly half of it. Australia's traditional islands policy of course strongly favored annexation as against any alternative. New Guinea was peculiarly coveted both for economic and defensive reasons. Hughes always strongly emphasized that whoever controlled New Guinea controlled Australia. Prime Minister Massey of New Zealand supported Hughes, as Hughes supported him on Samoa. If Australia had coveted New Guinea from *circa* 1883, New Zealand had coveted Samoa from Sir Julius Vogel's time in the 1870's. Both drew support from Prime Minister Smuts of South Africa, who wanted to annex German Southwest Africa. Wilson's policy of no annexations put all these intentions in jeopardy, and Hughes' anxiety was increased by the strong suspicion that

Wilson did not even want to assign German New Guinea to Australia as a mandate.

The Hughes-Wilson clash was a clash of ideas and policy, but it was also a clash of personalities. All his political career — and it was a long one — Hughes was involved in bitter personality clashes. The Wilson episode was but one among many. It was, however, remarkably enduring: Hughes never forgave; he actively disliked Wilson, and the memory of Wilson, to the end of his days in 1952. It all seems to have begun in 1916 — though Hughes must have been prejudiced earlier by Wilson's neutrality policy — when Hughes, in Washington en route to London, called on Wilson, and rather foolishly (but understandably in view of its importance to him) poured out a discourse on his New Guinea policy. Wilson listened in absolute silence. Utterly disconcerted and repelled, Hughes sought the company of Theodore Roosevelt and fortified his now active dislike of Wilson with some of T.R.'s "evidence" against him. Hughes at Paris was a Clemenceau man, though he had some fondness for his fellow-Welshman, Lloyd George.

In the end New Guinea and Samoa were turned over to Australia and New Zealand as C-class mandates, described expressively by Hughes as "differing from full sovereign control as a ninety-nine years' lease differs from a fee simple."

The other clash between Hughes and Wilson involved White Australia. Hughes was a fanatical adherent to this doctrine. When the Japanese tried to get a racial-equality clause embodied in the Covenant of the League of Nations, Hughes took alarm. He interpreted it as an assault on the White Australia policy; he concluded that if it went into the Covenant, the Australian policy would collapse and thousands of Japanese would pour into the country. He therefore vehemently opposed it, even resorting to the shameless tactic of stirring up American West Coast newspapermen to cable home stories putting forth his interpretation of the clause as an indisputable fact, forecasting a Japanese flood into California as well as Australia, thus "building a fire" under Wilson. While in the end the declaration was carried on the votes, Wilson ruled that it had failed because the vote was not unanimous, as custom required when the Fourteen Points were involved. On this technicality, Hughes won his victory for White Australia.

After World War I two problems became intertwined in which the United States and Australia had the keenest interest as Pacific Basin countries: the limitation of armaments, especially armaments in the Pacific, and the position of Japan. Great Britain was equally concerned with both questions, in the case of Japan because the Anglo-Japanese Alliance, which dated from 1902, came up for renewal. Should it be renewed, with changes to make it conform to the League Covenant, or should it be abandoned? The Alliance was entangled with the limitation of armaments because it was so directly related to the power position in the Pacific. The United States was opposed to the renewal of the Alliance, and a satisfactory agreement about the distribution of political and naval power in the Pacific could be regarded as a substitute for it.

The Anglo-Japanese Alliance was originally entered into by the British as a contribution to the stabilization and strengthening of their position on the continent of Asia and in the Far East. In its original form it was directed against Russia; in the course of time it was turned against Germany; and as time wore on the Americans were not completely sure that it was not directed against them. Nothing the British did about revising the terms ever finally convinced the Americans it was harmless from their point of view.

For about half a century before the Anglo-Japanese Alliance was arranged the Australians had viewed the countries of Asia almost exclusively as possible sources of unwanted immigrants. They tended to take an apocalyptic view of the matter — the Yellow Peril — and Japan had become the principal horseman of the apocalypse. However one aspect of the situation, though it was little discussed by the more excited writers, was that British authority and power in the East was a guarantee that in the final analysis the apocalypse would never quite come off. However, not being much given to the close study of international relations, the more febrile Australians were not too sure that the Anglo-Japanese Alliance was, when it was first made, altogether to Australia's advantage, though in the long run that is the view they took of it. It was feared that the British in their struggles with the Eastern problem might conclude that Japanese friendship was of more importance than Australia's welfare and support the Japanese in an assault on White Australia. Dark references were made to the price Australia might have to pay for the protection of Britain's "nigger empire" in the East. On the other hand, when the Alliance was renewed in 1911 the Australians were worried lest it might bring the Americans down on their heads in case of an American–Japanese conflict, with Britain backing Japan. During World War I the Australians were not too pleased, on the one hand, that the Japanese assistance in liquidating the German Pacific empire brought them uncomfortably close to Australia — a position confirmed when German Micronesia was mandated to them — but on the other they were reassured by Japan's assistance in convoying Australian troopships and in naval patrol duties. When the question of renewing the Alliance came up after the war the Australians — their spokesman was still W. M. Hughes — were strongly in favor of doing so. The New Zealanders took the same line. By that time they had worked themselves around to the view that the Alliance put Britain in a very strong position to exert a moderating influence on Japan's policies. The Alliance was, in this fashion, regarded as an integral part of the Australian security system.

When the Alliance was discussed at the Imperial Conference of 1921 Hughes was the most forceful advocate of renewal. The context of the discussion made this a difficult position to sustain. The context was the problem of establishing the friendliest possible relations, regarded as indispensable to British welfare, between Britain and the United States, and the hard fact was that the United States took a critical view of the Alliance and wanted it terminated. The American view was strongly put at the conference by the Canadians. Hughes did not deny the importance of American good will; he simply took the line that terminating the Alliance might be too high a price to pay for it. (As a matter of fact, Hughes' ideas on the United States were very ambiguous and littered with curious misconceptions and questionable interpretations, especially as to that longstanding source of confusion for citizens of the dominions, the evaluation of Anglophilia and Anglophobia in the American outlook. Characteristically Hughes overvalued the former and radically misunderstood the latter, for to him, as to so many dominions inhabitants, Anglophile views were alone to be regarded as "sound" and worthy of the United States.) Hughes professed to understand the Canadian anxiety to meet American wishes. Canada very obviously had the tremendous direct stake in British-American relations. But Australia's position was rather different. There were things it did not seem wise to do to retain American good will, valuable though it was, and abandoning the Alliance was one of them. In his view it was more important to restrain Japan than to conciliate the United States. The result was that the Imperial Conference arrived at no decision on the Alliance. For the time, it remained in force. Its fate was finally determined at the Washington Conference on the Limitation of Armaments, 1921–22.

The preliminaries of the Washington Conference were marked by a curious comedy of errors revolving around the question of dominion representation. In traditional British practice, the United Kingdom was the diplomatic spokesman for the British Empire. The Americans clearly recognized this well-established fact. But British practice was changing, as had been shown by the position of the dominions at the Paris Peace Conference and at the League of Nations. Among the many objections to the Covenant of the League of Nations raised during the debate on it in the Senate was the point that separate representation of the British dominions in the League gave the British several votes as contrasted with the one allotted to the United States, a point given considerable weight if, as was apparently assumed, the dominions governed their voting by the rule of "the diplomatic unity of the Empire." However, it was not then clear how generally that rule would be accepted as a rigid dogma by the dominions. At any rate, Charles Evans Hughes, President Harding's Secretary of State, was prepared to accommodate to the new British practice and welcome dominions representatives to the Conference, though as members of the British delegation. On the other hand, as much for domestic reasons — to be able to exclude certain difficult Senators like Borah — as for any other, Secretary Hughes wanted all delegations kept small. The British Secretary of State for Foreign Affairs, Lord Curzon, welcomed the idea of small delegations, for this would make possible a "round-table" conference. But to keep the British delegation small the dominions would have to be excluded. This did not bother Curzon, a traditionalist in any case, but it did bother some of his fellow Cabinet members. So after accepting the principle of a small delegation, the British had to ask for room for dominion delegates. This was granted. Prime Minister Hughes, however, thought and said that Charles Evans Hughes "slammed the door" on the dominions. This was not true. Since the debate over the Versailles Treaty there is no evidence that the United States has ever been hostile to the assertion by the dominions of their rights as autonomous nations. In the Australian case, indeed, the United States quite consistently encouraged it forward, as will appear when the matter of the exchange of diplomatic representation is discussed below. If anybody slammed a door in 1921 it was George Nathaniel Curzon. And even his slamming was not final. Australia's principal representative at the Conference was Sir George Pearce, New Zealand's Sir John Salmond.

As curious as the contretemps over representation was the State Department information about Australia's foreign political views. Although Prime Minister Hughes' ideas about the Anglo-

Japanese Alliance were undoubtedly known, when a confidential information paper on Australia and New Zealand was prepared for the Conference, nothing but the policy with regard to the islands was set out. It was evaluated as exhibiting "expansionist sentiment." As far as was then known in the State Department, only in the islands had the Southwest Pacific dominions exhibited anything in the nature of a foreign policy.*

From the Washington Conference came a network of treaties intended to stabilize the situation in the Far East, protect the Open-Door policy and the integrity of China, determine naval ratios as among the United States, Britain, and Japan — the famous 5–5–3 formula — and provide in a Four Power (United States, Britain, France, and Japan) Treaty a substitute for the Anglo-Japanese Alliance. (The Alliance was formally renounced in Article 4 of the Treaty.) Australia and New Zealand "contracted in" on these arrangements more as associates of the United Kingdom than as autonomous nations. In effect the Conference arrangements left Japan the preponderant naval and military power in the Western Pacific, restrained by various self-denying agreements, and the United States the preponderant power in the Eastern Pacific, on a line running from Alaska to American Samoa (both ends in effect unanchored), pivoted on Pearl Harbor. In the face of this division of the Pacific, the Southwest Pacific dominions came to found their defensive positions on the British base at Singapore. Japan began throwing off the self-restraining agreements in 1931, thus

* The paper was one of many gathered into a bulky volume entitled *Papers in Relation to Pacific and Far Eastern Affairs Prepared for the Use of the American Delegation to the Conference on the Limitation of Armament, Washington 1921–22.* Confidential Information. Series D. No. 79. General No. 1. This volume was not reclassified as "unrestricted" until March 30, 1950. The paper referred to was prepared by Professor G. H. Blakeslee of Clark University. Immediately on his return to Clark from the Conference, Professor Blakeslee gave a semester discussion course on the Conference in the undergraduate college. The writer took that course, his introduction to international politics. In 1927 Professor Blakeslee gave a lecture on Far Eastern affairs at the University of Melbourne which the writer attended. Nothing was said about Australian policy.

initiating the chaos in the Western Pacific that led on step by fatal step to World War II.

In Australia, Hughes and his associates of the political right regarded the Four Power Treaty and the related agreements as a poor substitute for the old Anglo-Japanese Alliance. Hughes came to regard the Washington arrangements as initiating a British retreat in the Far East of fateful consequence to Australia. On the other hand the Labour Party and the political left felt a certain pleasure in being freed of an entanglement with Japan which might have led to difficulties with the United States. But while the division of opinion was discernible, it was difficult to say that it related to *public* opinion. Foreign affairs in Australia, as is true in most democracies, was then, and has largely remained, a minority, even an elite, concern. William Morris Hughes was rather rare among Australian politicians, not only at that time but for some years after, in having reasoned opinions of any kind on foreign affairs and the will to give them effect at the highest level. His original stimulus, of course, had been the war. The year after the Washington Conference he fell from power, never to be Prime Minister again, though he remained for many years after one of the very few politicians to hold strong views on foreign relations and willing to give them expression by tongue and pen.

From the Washington Conference to World War II Australia was largely quiescent about foreign affairs at the government level. It was felt that the great issues were best left to the British Foreign Office and that it was both wise and proper for Australia to follow the British lead, the right to be consulted, especially when Australia's interests were involved, understood. Certainly nothing was done during the twenties and thirties to follow up Hughes' precedent and give consistent expression to Australian views at the highest diplomatic levels *outside the Imperial circle*. Even Hughes himself saw no reason for giving formal constitutional support to the position he had assumed. The New Zealand position was similar, but by the chance that the New Zealand delegate to the Washington Conference,

Sir John Salmond, was a distinguished lawyer and wrote into his report a resounding rejection of the whole theory that the dominions had any independence in international law, the New Zealand retreat seemed more considered and studied. The cold reaction of the Australians and New Zealanders to the thinking eventually embodied in the Statute of Westminster (1931) further illustrates their semiphilosophical acceptance of what their more adventurous fellow dominions could only regard as an arrested nationalism. It took World War II to rouse the Australians and New Zealanders from their constitutional slumbers. Only then did they legislate acceptance of the Statute of Westminster and even then only on the ground of technical legal convenience.

From the middle nineteen-twenties, however, the intelligentsia, academic and lay, in both countries began to take a more and more lively interest in international affairs as they affected Australia and New Zealand and to raise the question of what national foreign policies might involve and mean. In 1925 there was formed in Australia an overseas branch of Chatham House, London, which in 1929 grew into the Australian Institute of International Affairs. New Zealand established its Institute in 1934. The Australian group in 1937 founded the first journal devoted to the discussion of foreign affairs the country had ever known, rather nostalgically entitled *The Austral-Asiatic Bulletin* (retitled more firmly in 1947, *The Australian Outlook*). The discussion thus encouraged, while somewhat academic, traversed the fundamentals of the subject and hammered out a coherent point of view. The coming of a Labour Government to power in New Zealand in 1935 — the first in the country's history — led that country to take the lead as between Australia and New Zealand in giving expression to a national policy, chiefly at the League of Nations. But when an Australian policy began to emerge in 1940 it showed that the academic discussion had had perceptible influence on the thinking of strategically important political figures.

With the end of the Washington Conference, relations between the United States and the Southwest Pacific reverted to the character traditional between them as trading partners. As long as prosperity lasted, the trade moved strongly upward in quantity and value as far as exports from the United States to the area were concerned, but the perennial problem of the failure of imports from the area to increase toward anything resembling parity with exports continued. In the early twenties, the state of Queensland taking the lead, Australian governments were optimistic enough about the future to obtain loans on the New York money market. (The move was, however, strongly disapproved of by those who doubted the wisdom of going outside the Imperial financial system for money.) The general position was tolerable as long as the idea of "triangular trade," under which the Southwest Pacific countries acquired their needed dollars otherwise than by direct sales in the American market, was the ruling idea in international trading. But when during the Great Depression the idea of bilateralism gained force at a time when the nation sought to insure markets by governmental negotiations, the Australians came to look critically on the situation. In 1934 and 1935 the Australian government asked the United States government to discuss the matter, but this the United States declined to do, chiefly because it was politically impossible, and economically hardly feasible, to take any action designed to increase the quantity of Australian exports to the American market. Australia's characteristic exports — and the same was true of New Zealand's — were largely competitive with American production. The American need was to increase its own markets for these things, not to augment supplies from abroad. The stalemate, the elements of which were widely known and understood, looked complete.

However, the Australians felt they could not afford to treat the situation as one of the uncomfortable "facts of life" about which nothing could be done. They were, of course, actively dealing with all aspects of their trade relations and to let the

American facet alone was probably impossible. Intra-Imperial relations — the most important being relations with the United Kingdom — had been dealt with in the Ottawa agreement of 1932. But two facets outside the Imperial trading system attracted close attention, the American and the Japanese. In 1936 an attempt was made to deal with them at the same time. The particular policy applied became known as the "trade diversion" policy and was designed to reduce the imports into Australia from Japan and the United States to protect the market of the United Kingdom there or to encourage production in Australia.

As to the Japanese, the Australians were concerned to cut down imports from Japan because these largely involved textiles. It was thought necessary to reduce textile imports to protect the market for United Kingdom textiles in Australia. On the other hand, in the American case the objective was to cut down the importation of automobile chassis with the ultimate purpose of encouraging the establishment of an automobile industry in Australia and the ad interim purpose of expanding the United Kingdom market for automobiles in Australia. The "cutting down" was to be accomplished under a licensing system. "Trade diversion" was, then, a confused and confusing policy. It was harshly criticized in Australia at the time, particularly in the case of Japan, by the wool exporters. It was questionable in both its economic and political aspects. The latter seem hardly to have been perceived by the government. It really made sense only in relation to two general ideas: the idea of a more or less "closed" Imperial trading system, and the idea of "autarky" for Australia. But neither idea fitted well with Australia's fundamental needs, which then required and today require her to maintain and diversify her trading outlets in an "open" trading system and to develop her economy without resort to anything more in the way of autarky than a tariff system.

"Trade diversion" had alienated both Japan and the United States. Here we are concerned only with the United States. The American response was to withdraw from Australia "most

favored nation" treatment of her exports to the United States
— to place Australia on a "blacklist" because, while an increase
in a tariff would have been accepted, discrimination by licensing
was quite another and intolerable proceeding. At about the
same time, to make matters worse, Australia and also New
Zealand — the latter, as a matter of fact, taking the lead — took
steps to exclude the Matson Line from the carrying trade in
passengers and goods between Australia and New Zealand, and
difficulties arose over the question of airlines from the United
States into the Southwest Pacific. Trade difficulties between
Australia and the United States only gradually returned to
"normal" after this. Late in 1937 the licensing discrimination
was replaced by a duty on motor chassis and in February 1938
the United States restored "most favored nation" treatment to
Australian goods. In 1943, as a wartime courtesy, Australia
extended "most favored nation" treatment to imports from the
United States.

The trouble over shipping never reached the point where
the proposed laws were applied, but in the case of the airlines
the question was unresolved at the outbreak of World War II.
The first flight between the United States and Australia was
made between May 31 and June 9, 1928, by a mixed Australian
and American team in the airplane *Southern Cross*. The flyers
were Captain (later Sir) Charles Kingsford-Smith and C. Ulm,
Australians, and H. W. Lyon and J. Warner, Americans. They
flew from Oakland, California, to Sydney via Hawaii, Fiji, and
Brisbane, 7,200 miles. Between October 20 and November 4,
1934, Sir Charles Kingsford-Smith and Captain (later Sir)
Patrick Taylor flew the reverse course from Brisbane to Oakland. The pioneering of a commercial service into the area
began in 1935 when Harold Gatty, representative of Pan American Airways, put a proposal before the New Zealand government. Like American shipping to the area, the air service was
to be heavily subsidized by the United States government.
This immediately raised the question of reciprocal landing
rights for any British line which might be established to follow

the same route to North America. The New Zealand government reserved the right to cancel its contract with Pan American if the rights were not granted by the United States. The point at issue was the British right to land at Hawaii and San Francisco. Pan American proposed to fly to San Francisco, Honolulu, Kingman Reef, Pago Pago, and Auckland. Although flights were made, the service was not firmly established by the outbreak of war.

As a phase of the effort to serve the Southwest Pacific by air, the United States took over by an executive order of March 6, 1938, the Canton and Enderby Islands in the Phoenix Group. The United Kingdom also claimed sovereignty over the islands. On April 6, 1939, the two governments arranged jointly to administer the islands under a condominium for fifty years, without prejudice to their conflicting claims to sovereignty.

Meanwhile Pan American had moved toward Australia as a logical terminus of a service into the area. In that direction it reached New Caledonia, but not its objective, Sydney. The Australians took a firm stand on the reciprocal-landing-rights question and, unlike the New Zealanders, were not prepared to make a contingent agreement with Pan American.

13. Australia Seeks a Foreign Policy

Until the middle thirties the interest of Australia and New Zealand in international politics was almost wholly expressed by consultation with the United Kingdom and by participation in the League of Nations in very close association with the United Kingdom. Since the governments were wedded to the "single voice" theory of Imperial relations with the outside world, the net effect of this was that they supported United Kingdom policy — which thus became their policy — both in regard to international affairs in general and in the League. In regard to the United States, the two Southwest Pacific dominions did not, like Canada, South Africa, and Southern Ireland, seek any special relation but rather went on the assumption that their interests were taken care of with complete adequacy while friendly relations existed between the United Kingdom and the United States. They in effect supported the policy of friendly relations which the United Kingdom was pursuing for its own reasons. In any deviation from it, real or apparent, as in the case of Manchuria in 1931, when Secretary Stimson fell out with Sir John Simon, they supported the British course.

Not until 1935 was the volume of business in foreign affairs sufficient for Australia to set up External Affairs (that is, foreign relations) as a separate Department of Cabinet rank. At about the same time New Zealand, in which, in 1935, a Labour government came to power for the first time, embarked upon a course in foreign policy which was one of the more remarkable demonstrations of dominion independence before World War II. This found expression almost wholly in the League of Nations, where New Zealand's spokesman, W. J. Jordan, became one of the most ardent exponents of the policy of "collective security," a line followed even when it was out of harmony with British policy on specific issues. The New Zealanders continued to follow their line as long as there was any chance that "collective security" might become effective. As the world situation continued to deteriorate, the New Zealanders slowly reverted to the policy of solidarity with the United Kingdom summed up by Acting Prime Minister Peter Fraser at the outbreak of war in 1939:

> Both with gratitude for the past, and with confidence in the future, we range ourselves without fear beside Britain. Where she goes, we go, where she stands, we stand. We are only a small and young nation, but we are one and all a band of brothers, and we march forward with a union of hearts and wills to a common destiny.*

Meanwhile, Australia, which had extended no support to New Zealand while she was a deviant, had followed the United Kingdom with limited enthusiasm for collective security. (Australian Labour, in parliamentary opposition at the time, was the only labor party in the British community which was not enthusiastic for collective security.) However, Australia and New Zealand arrived at the same destination in 1939. Both were at war because the United Kingdom was at war. Neither acted, as did Canada for example, to declare war on its own part. Neither, that is, accepted the implications of the Statute of Westminster in foreign relations.

The discussions of foreign policy in which the Australian intelligentsia engaged during the thirties were largely in the

---

* Quoted from F. L. W. Wood, *The New Zealand People at War: Political and External Affairs* (Wellington, 1958), p. 11.

nature of attempts to define the Australian national interest, or rather were efforts to discover whether or not there was any Australian national interest sufficiently unique and compelling to warrant special Australian action to advance and defend it. This was to attempt to distinguish an Australian interest from a British interest, not on the assumption of hostility between them but rather on the assumption that a peculiarly Australian interest might not be given the same weight and importance in London as in Canberra, because it was not so *vital* to London as to Canberra. Plainly such an Australian interest would be most likely to grow out of its geographical position. Hence very early in the discussion it was agreed that Australia's distinguishable special interests were in the Far East. To Australia the Far East was not a remote periphery of Empire. Rather it was the primary geographical context of her national being. It was not *far* but *near;* it was not Far East but Near North.

However, the recognition that Australia had a great stake in the shape of things in the Far East was not equivalent to establishing that Australia should have her own policy with regard to the Far East, especially if that policy was different either in emphasis or substance from British policy. In short, to discuss foreign policy realistically required the discussion of dominion status — of the position of Australia in the Commonwealth. This discussion was to take place in a mental and emotional context in which the traditional Australian position — here to be summed up as devotion to the theory of "diplomatic unity" of the Empire — was defended as "loyal" while proposals for autonomous action were stigmatized as anti-British. This is why Professor A. C. V. Melbourne, a pioneer in advocating autonomous Australian action, had to preface the printed version of a speech on "Australian Foreign Policy," made late in 1934, with the following remarks:

> As it has been suggested that the sentiments expressed in this paper are anti-British, it seems necessary to point out that this is not the case. The argument emphasises the value of the British connection to Australia, as well as the wisdom of insisting on

close co-operation between Australia and the other members of the British Commonwealth. The main purpose of the paper is to draw the attention to the peculiar circumstances of Australia, and to indicate a policy for adoption by the Australian Government additional to but not inconsistent with the policy which would be accepted by the United Kingdom and the other Dominions. This explains the emphasis laid on Australia's relations with the countries of Southern and Eastern Asia; the continuance of co-operation between Australia and the other members of the British Commonwealth as well as between Australia and non-British states, is taken for granted.

In every country there are emotional factors which are part of the context in which foreign policy is made, but in Australia in the thirties the primary emotional factor was actually an obstacle to the development of any autonomous policy which in expression would rise above the level of an attempt to influence the United Kingdom administrators and policy makers. Under the conditions obtaining in the Commonwealth this was not constitutionally obligatory on Australia, but it was the traditional position and definitively compulsive upon the top politicians of the country. Theoretically, Australia, like the other dominions, could do many things in foreign policy, up to and including declaring itself neutral in a war, but practically the situation was very different, both because of the fact that the Australians were completely unadventurous theorists about the rights and powers of the dominions with regard to foreign affairs and because the actualities of Australia's position as a nation required, or appeared to require, her to keep as close to the United Kingdom as possible.* Whether there nevertheless remained any small room for autonomous action was one of the questions at issue. Those who took their stand on "loyalty" — or tradition — argued there was not, while those who favored

---

* This difference between the constitutional capacity to act and the probability of a decision to act in the given situation of Australia is the theme of the writer's contribution entitled "Could Australia Remain Neutral in a World War?" to *Australia's Foreign Policy*, edited by W. G. K. Duncan (Sydney, 1938).

exploring the powers inherent in autonomy within the Commonwealth assumed there was, even at the risk of being stigmatized "anti-British." In the end the step toward establishment of separate Australian diplomatic representation abroad was made within a carefully guarded verbalization of the "diplomatic unity of the Empire" theory, but the door to autonomous action was nevertheless ineluctably opened.

The exploration of foreign policy possibilities went on in three areas: trade policy, political foreign policy, and defense policy. It might be argued that political foreign policy grew out of discussions of trade policy and that the arguments over defense arose from consideration of the ultimate risks of the situation in which Australia found herself. Professor Melbourne, for example, appears to have begun his campaign for an Australian foreign policy as a campaign for the appointment of trade commissioners in the East. The early books, pamphlets, and periodical articles are heavily weighted on the side of discussion of trade and trade problems. It was the recognition that the Far Eastern situation was not going to be resolved in terms of trade policy alone, but rather involved explosive political questions, that led the Australians on to the political questions. Since it was an integral part of Australia's traditional view of the East as a "menace" that an armed attack directly upon her was the ultimate expectation, defense policy naturally came up for debate.

In this continuing discussion the participants were many, among them a number who subsequently played conspicuous roles in Australian foreign relations: F. W. (later Sir Frederick) Eggleston, W. Macmahon Ball (subsequently Professor Ball), John G. (later Sir John) Crawford, and R. G. (later Lord) Casey, long Minister for External Affairs.

At the level of trade, the Australian fascination with prospects in the East was caused by the *fact* that the trade was increasing at the time and because the expectation was that it would continue to increase. The East was probably the one area of the world to which Australia could look for consistent expansion of trade by volume and value. The Australians never suffered as powerful a belief in an expanding "Eastern market" as the Americans did for several generations; they never developed such engaging theories as that about the great commercial benefits that would follow if the Chinese could be persuaded to add an inch to their shirt-tails; but they did have great hopes about rising sales of wool, wheat, and other Western-style foodstuffs. However, the perception was strongly conditioned by the recognition that the trade was supplementary, so to speak, to trade with British countries, particularly the United Kingdom, and might become competitive on the import side. This introduced an element of confusion into the apparent simplicity of exploiting to the full an expanding market, especially in an economic situation where it was suspected that there was an "iron law of trade" like the celebrated iron law of wages. This confusion was dramatized in 1936 when the "trade diversion" policy was instituted, for the gist of this in relation to the Eastern trade was to penalize the Japanese, the best customers in the area, for the benefit of United Kingdom exporters. The confusion thus caused had not been cleared up when World War II began.

At the political level the problem was, in essence, how to live with an expansionist Japan. Although certain Australians — notably the newspaperman Dr. G. E. ("Chinese") Morrison, author of the famous book *An Australian in China* (1895), and W. H. Donald, political adviser to Sun Yat-sen, Chang Hsueh-liang, and Chiang Kai-shek — had a personal identification with China, there was never any such feeling for the Chinese among Australians as was characteristic in the United States. Therefore there was no such automatic pro-Chinese reaction to Japanese adventures in China as there was in America. The Far East, in Australia, chiefly meant Japan. When after World War I Eastern studies were established at the University of Sydney, with Commonwealth government support, it was the Japanese language and Japanese history that were chiefly in question. The first occupant of the Chair of Oriental Studies was a specialist in Japanese history, James Murdoch, as was also his successor, A. L. Sadler. Only as the "China incident" developed did any considerable pro-Chinese sentiment appear in Australia and then chiefly on the political left as an offshoot of "antifascist" sentiment directed against Japan.

The most articulate Australian sentiment about the Manchurian affair of 1931 was in effect pro-Japanese. It found expression in a small book, *The Manchurian Area* by F. M. Cutlack, an influential journalist (Sydney, 1934). The argument was Japanese order versus Chinese anarchy and a plea for recognition of Japan's compulsive need to expand; and a subsidiary theme was that if the Japanese expanded onto the continent of Asia, they would be less tempted to expand south to menace Australia. When the Japanese began to bully the British in China, sentiment changed. It was less a matter of becoming pro-Chinese than a realistic assessment of the consequences to Australia of this clear demonstration of the further weakening of British power in the East. And as it became apparent that Japanese energies, while heavily engaged in China, were not going to be fully employed there but would also, in all probability, be used in southward expansion, the Australians became progressively more concerned. The climax of this situation came after the outbreak of war in Europe.

All through these developments Australia, at the diplomatic level, continued to operate within the confines of Imperial (that is, United Kingdom) foreign policy, presumably exerting influence on it through the machinery of consultation. (It is worth noting, incidentally, that even the partisans of consultation as an adequate form of foreign policy activity were rarely wholly satisfied with the machinery of consultation or the way it worked — but that is a point hardly worth exploration here.)

The evidence is that Australia followed the line of conciliatory temporizing with Japan and, after war broke out in 1939, favored appeasement, the clearest known illustration of this being its strong endorsement of, indeed pressure in favor of, Britain's action in closing the Burma Road in mid-1940. But it is hard to say what Australian policy really was for it was not conducted separately but within the confines of government-to-government discussions of United Kingdom policy proposals, discussions necessarily secret.* The essential difference between Australian and New Zealand policy in the later stages of the progress toward war appears to have been that New Zealand was less convinced of the uses of conciliation and appeasement than Australia. She recommended a stiffer line of resistence on principle.

The Australians — at least the articulate Australians — were convinced by around 1937 that their interests were irreconcilable with any Japanese ambitions that involved a southward course of expansion. Their response, however, was heavily conditioned by their convictions about their vulnerability to Japanese attack. But they misconceived the extent of their vulnerability by underestimating Japan's striking power — an error they made in common with the British and the Americans — and overestimated (even after discounting it from the pre-World War I level) British power of resistance in general and ability to give direct assistance to Australia in particular. The misconceptions or miscalculations were focused on Singapore. Some day a scholarly essay is going to be written around the "legend" of Singapore as a profound study in human illusions. Both the Australians and the New Zealanders were prime victims of the Singapore illusion.

This brings us to Australian defense policy, not to the details of expenditure as it rose in these years, but to the general conceptions on which it was founded. The orthodox conception

---

* A good illustration of the very low visibility of any Australian foreign policy at this time is the infrequency of references to Australia in the relevant chapters of such a standard British work as F. C. Jones' *Japan's New Order in East Asia: Its Rise and Fall 1937–45* (London, 1954). The New Zealand historian F. L. W. Wood has taken note of this in these words: "It is perhaps noteworthy that this scholarly book deals with British policy in the Pacific virtually without consideration of the importance of that policy to Australians and New Zealanders." Quoted in *The New Zealand People at War* (Wellington, 1958) p. 65 fn.

was succinctly stated by R. G. Casey in a speech at Chatham House, London, in 1938:

> Our policy generally, and in the simplest possible terms, is based on the belief that the British fleet, or some appreciable portion of it, will be able to move freely eastwards in case we in Australia get into trouble in our part of the world. And I think one can sum it up by saying that any world movement that appears to threaten the ability of the British fleet to move freely eastwards would be of great concern to us in Australia.*

From this ultimate expectation of assistance from the British fleet was deduced the conclusion that Australia's local defenses should be fundamentally naval. This was the origin of the Australian emphasis on naval power from the initiation of the Commonwealth navy in 1909. This emphasis thus predated Singapore by some years; and indeed Singapore was conceived as a base first for a British Eastern Fleet (as envisaged by Lord Jellicoe in 1919–20) and then as the base of a British fleet sent East in an emergency. In this conception the Australian standing army and the air force were supplementary to the navy in relation to the defense of Australia as such. (The Australian army and air force in World War I were wholly volunteer contributions to Imperial defense, a different matter from Australian local defense.) Singapore thus became at once a British stronghold in the East and the symbol of British naval cooperation in the defense of Australia.

Although both the ruling politicians and predominant public opinion were committed to the Singapore thesis in its ramifications right up to Singapore's fall, this is not to say that it was never questioned. As a matter of fact it was astutely questioned both by men of the Australian armed services and by interested civilian students of public affairs. One point made was that as it seemed likely that Japan would only move south toward Australia if Britain were deeply involved in a war in Europe, it was unlikely in such a case that Britain would be able to send

---

* Printed in *International Affairs* (London) March 1938.

any fleet to the East to oppose her. If this should turn out to be the case, then the whole problem of the local defense of Australia should be reconsidered. It was argued that emphasis should be shifted from the navy — since obviously Australia could not afford to build a navy capable of meeting that of the Japanese — to the army and air force. The Labour Party eventually took up the line that primary emphasis should fall on an air force and munitions-making. Another point was that Singapore was too far west to stop a Japanese approach to Australia, which would probably, it was thought, proceed through the mandated islands to New Guinea and the Solomons, around 4,400 miles from the great base. Hence defenses should be built in the islands. But however interesting these speculations are in relation to what eventually happened, they do not discount the fact that ultimate defense of Australia continued to be predicated on British power in the East, *in situ* at Singapore or sent to the East at the time of crisis. Only Labour opinion was much influenced by the critical arguments, and Labour in these years was mostly in opposition.

The x-factor in the whole situation was not reckoned at this time to be Singapore, or Britain's ability to deliver assistance, but the probable role of the United States in a crisis in the Western Pacific. There were two aspects of this question: (1) United States policy toward Japan and East Asia and (2) United States policy with regard to Australia. What the Australians were really asking about United States policy toward Japan was whether, when, and where would the United States draw a line over which the Japanese could not step in their territorial expansion without meeting American armed resistance.

In the prewar years the Australians found the United States enigmatic. They could not "make it out," certainly not well enough to predict in terms that served their purposes the probable course of policy with regard to the Far East. Their solid information about the United States was limited and they were not in a good position to interpret the information that reached them. It was clear enough that the Americans were opponents of the Japanese, but how would the Americans react if the Japanese were astute enough to move south without troubling American possessions? The result was that the Australians were unable to disentangle from American policy any clear conception of what the Americans would regard as a cause for war, and to them that was the real nub of the matter.

As they saw it, there was always the risk that as Japanese action and the diplomacy that it provoked unfolded, a point of no return would be reached and war would follow. They *hoped* it would not; they were prepared to conciliate to the maximum degree, but they really believed it would. And since they believed it would, the problem was how to stave off the war as long as possible and, if it came, to insure that the position of Australia was as strong as possible. Obviously the United States could be a source of strength. Rather more reluctantly, and with less worry about the risks of direct attack, the New Zealanders by 1940 had moved to the same position. The whole business was part of the process of recognizing that the United States was, after all, the *predominant power* in the Pacific and the ultimate guarantor of Australian and New Zealand security. Good relations with the United States became an indispensable reinsurance policy.

However, it was not at that time a situation in which the Australians, and certainly not the New Zealanders, saw any need to *sue* for American favor. It was rather a matter of speculating on America's course of action in certain imaginable contingencies (none of which remotely resembled that which arose in 1941–42). As a matter of fact, the solidest Australian opinion in late 1939 was to the effect that Australia's position was reasonably strong. An anonymous article entitled "America & Australia's Defence" in *The Austral-Asiatic Bulletin* for December–January 1939–40 (probably written by Mr. F. W. [later Sir Frederick] Eggleston) contained these revealing remarks, inspired by two American publications, a report of the Foreign Policy Association and an article in *Foreign Affairs* by Tyler Dennett:

The Association's report is important as a summary of influential American opinion on a matter of growing importance to Australia, though few will agree with the strategic views it expresses. The capacity of resistance of the Allies in the Pacific is seriously under-estimated . . . whilst the ability of America to wage war overseas in the present state of her defences is imperfectly appreciated.

It is a profound fallacy to reckon the Allied naval forces in terms of the peace-time distribution of their small Pacific squadrons. Whilst Italy remains neutral, the Allies have large naval forces free to move to the Pacific . . . Whilst these forces can operate from a first class naval base in Singapore . . . an attack upon Allied or Dutch possessions in the Pacific would be foolhardy . . .

The position of the United States in relation to naval action in the Western and Southern Pacific is anything but favourable. The United States do not possess secure bases in the Western Pacific and have scarcely the margin of naval superiority over Japan to engage in hostilities in this area unless allied bases and ports are available. Without the use of Singapore, close action to defend the Philippines would be a hazardous operation for the present American fleet.

It is a fact that the United States are in no position to embark in a major overseas expedition and that American experts are aware of it. . .

[Mr. Dennett] says: — "Uncertain of the degree of support which they may expect from the Admiralty, Australians and New Zealander almost without exception have expected confidently that American naval forces will come to their defence in their possible day of need . . . In both countries one heard the sort of petulant expressions that are associated with children who have been over-indulged."

He complains that Australians demanded effortless security at British and American expense, and that they wanted to have it not merely both ways but all ways. It is sufficient to observe that events since the outbreak of war have falsified Mr. Dennett's estimate of the Australian attitude to defence . . . he is mistaken in his belief that any considerable body of Australian opinion counts upon American support . . . The problem of Australian defence . . . is not dissimilar from that of the Philippine Islands . . . Australian conditions are much more favorable to defence against invasion, and defences have been greatly strengthened as the result of the war.

It is obvious to Australians that if their own defences are strong and the attitude of America towards Japan is hostile, the risks, such as they may be, of a Japanese invasion are greatly reduced. Now, the American attitude upon foreign affairs is unpredictable, and whilst few Australians have observed any noticeable American bias towards their country, their polite inquiries on the matter have been misconstrued . . . So far from Australian counting upon American support in the immediate future, the boot is on the other foot. In the present state of American rearmament, Allied and Australian bases and defended ports would become vital to America in an early conflict in the Western Pacific. Cooperation between two countries of similar world outlook and background is not aided by the preverted strategic ideas of the Foreign Policy Association, nor by the hasty and unjust generalizations of Mr. Dennett.

Thus the Australians hoped that American policy would be in close harmony with British policy and that any armed action would be collaborative, involving Singapore. *They believed that Singapore was vital to the United States,* an opinion the Americans were never persuaded to share. In large measure it was assumed and believed that as the resistance would be to Japan's southward drive, the net effect would be to keep the Japanese well away from Australia. Thus while it was not exactly a policy directly with regard to Australia, it was a policy from which Australia stood to benefit enormously.

Assuming, however, that the Japanese got into a position directly to attack Australia, what then would be American policy? Would an attack on Australia be regarded as a *casus belli* by the United States?

Granting that the mystification and insecurity of the Australians with regard to American policy had reason, and admitting that it was exceedingly difficult to estimate the balance of forces in the Western Pacific in the thirties, it was nevertheless inescapably the case that Australia (and New Zealand) had a stake in American policy, and power, however their direction, size, and significance might be reckoned. It was this perception, no matter how vague and contingent its formulation, that lay at the bottom of the fairly widespread feeling that Australian–American relations should be friendly.* And as time passed and tension grew in the Western Pacific, it became obviously necessary that relations be made formal. Thus out of the relations of Australia to its Near North grew the conviction that the time had come to take the steps necessary to establish formal diplomatic relations with the United States by an exchange of Ministers, in spite of emotional and constitutional inhibitions against such an exercise of autonomy. But in a game in which all moves had more or less portentous significance, the step with regard to the United States was balanced with an exchange of Ministers with Japan at the same time.

The case was stated by Prime Minister Robert Gordon Menzies on April 28, 1939, in his first policy speech after assuming office on the death of Joseph A. Lyons. He spoke as a traditionalist, hence the careful phrasing of the contextual remarks of his announcement, especially the references to the role of Great Britain and to "consultation," designed to protect "the diplomatic unity" of The Empire. (See also the note to the United States on November 30, 1939, quoted below.) The speech in a way was a triumph of the intellectuals who had so earnestly hammered out the fundamental thesis.

In the Pacific we have primary responsibilities and primary risks. Close as our consultation with Great Britain is, and must be, in relation to European affairs, it is still true to say that we must, to a large extent, be guided by her knowledge and affected by her decisions. The problems of the Pacific are different. What Great Britain calls the Far East is to us the near north. Little given as I am to encouraging the exaggerated ideas of Dominion independence and separatism which exist in some minds, I have

* This may be illustrated by a quotation from H. L. Harris' book *Australia's National Interests and National Policy* (Sydney, 1938), page 103, "America is not sufficiently known in Australia for Australian policy to be wisely directed . . . it is undoubtedly in the best interests of Australia to have a powerful and sympathetic friend in the great democracy on the other side of the Pacific." It is significant, perhaps, that these sentences occur in a discussion of trade!

become convinced that in the Pacific Australia must regard herself as a principal providing herself with her own information and maintaining her own diplomatic contacts with foreign powers. I do not mean by this that we are to act in the Pacific as if we were a completely separate power; we must, of course, act as an integral part of the British Empire. We must have full consultation and co-operation with Great Britain, South Africa, New Zealand, and Canada. But all these consultations must be on the basis that the primary risk in the Pacific is borne by New Zealand and ourselves. With this in mind I look forward to the day when we will have a concert of Pacific powers, pacific in both senses of the word. This means increased diplomatic contact between ourselves and the United States, China, and Japan, to say nothing of the Netherlands East Indies and the other countries which fringe the Pacific.

It is true that we are not a numerous people, but we have vigor, intelligence and resource, and I see no reason why we should not play not only an adult, but an effective part in the affairs of the Pacific.[*]

Although the United States was represented in New Zealand and Australia by consuls from the late 1830's, it was for a long time not constitutionally possible for the latter countries to reciprocate, and even after it became feasible in the nineteen-twenties, they were very reluctant to act. In the matter, the Australian attitude was decisive. The Commonwealth did not appoint even a Trade Commissioner until 1918. Almost immediately there was talk that Australia should be more impressively represented. It was proposed that a High Commissioner be sent to Washington. It is alleged that Prime Minister Hughes discussed this possibility with Wilson in Paris, but documentary evidence is lacking. At any rate in a political speech at Bendigo, Victoria, in 1920, Hughes said that he intended to establish a High Commissionership (higher in rank than a Trade Commission, lower than a Minister). This proposal was promptly attacked in the Australian press on two grounds: that a representative of diplomatic status would break up the diplomatic

---

[*] Quoted here from C. H. Grattan, *Introducing Australia* (Rev. ed., New York, 1947), p. 248, and there from a press release.

unity of the Empire and weaken Imperial ties, and that maintaining such an officer would involve the Commonwealth in unjustifiable expense. Nevertheless Sir George Pearce discussed the proposal in Washington during the Conference of 1922 and in the same year the government recommended that the post of Australian Commissioner-General to the United States be established. The following year an appointment was made. The post did not have diplomatic status. After five years, the then occupant of the post, Sir Hugh Denison, a Sydney newspaper proprietor, acting on his own initiative, sounded out Secretary of State Frank Kellogg as to American views on the appointment of a Minister, and he also discussed the matter with the United States Ambassador in London. Whatever the American reaction, Prime Minister S. M. Bruce vetoed the idea and the succeeding Scullin Labour Government also rejected it, on the old ground of unjustifiable expense.

By this time the Canadians, the Irish, and the South Africans were all represented in Washington by Ministers. On July 9, 1935, Prime Minister Joseph Lyons, in Washington on a visit, discussed the idea of an Australian Minister with President Roosevelt. Roosevelt was favorably disposed, but Lyons decided the proposal was "impractical." However the next year Sir George Pearce suggested that Australia appoint a Commissioner to work with the British Ambassador in Washington and on May 3, 1937, this led to the appointment of Mr. Keith Officer as "Counsellor in charge of Australian affairs" in the British Embassy. The State Department found this arrangement unsatisfactory because Mr. Officer was a very slow worker and because it proved impossible to discern anything particularly Australian in the views he expressed. The United States, through its Consul-General in Sydney, therefore indicated that it would welcome the appointment of a Minister.

On December 13, 1938, Mr. S. M. Bruce, Australian High Commissioner in London, stopped off in Washington en route to Canberra. Visiting the State Department to ascertain the American attitude on the question of Australian representation, he professed surprise when told that President Roosevelt favored the appointment of a Mnisiter, but said that he, too, had come to that view and would so recommend when he got to Australia. In May of 1939 Bruce was again in Washington on his way back to London. He confirmed that it was now the intention of the Australian government to appoint a Minister, as Prime Minister Menzies had said in a speech in Australia on April 28. Bruce said the decision had actually been made on January 9 by a Cabinet subcommittee consisting of Lyons, Hughes, Menzies, and R. G. Casey, before the death of Lyons and the succession of Menzies to the Prime Ministership. The American Consul-General had been instructed on April 29 to do all he could to encourage prompt action. On September 14, however, Mr. Officer told the State Department that there would be considerable delay in making the appointment because of preoccupation with defense problems. (A more likely reason was the precarious political position in which the Menzies government found itself.) In October the American Consul-General reported that Richard Gardiner Casey was the likely appointee. On November 27, 1939, the British Ambassador asked the State Department if the appointment of an Australian Minister would be agreeable. The Department stated that it would. On November 30, 1939, a note was handed to the State Department reading in part as follows (my italics):

His Majesty's Government in the Commonwealth of Australia have come to the conclusion that it is desirable that the handling of matters at Washington relating to Australia should be confided to an Envoy Extraordinary and Minister Plenipotentiary accredited to the United States Government.

This arrangement was not to denote any departure from the diplomatic unity of the Empire. In matters concerning more than one of His Majesty's Governments the principle of consultative cooperation among all His Majesty's representatives would be employed.*

On December 16 the British Ambassador requested the *agré-*

* Quoted from unpublished source.

ment for Mr. Casey, and five days later Secretary Hull told Lord Lothian that President Roosevelt would be glad to receive Casey as Minister. On March 1, 1940, Mr. Casey was received at the State Department and on the fifth he presented his credentials at the White House. The first United States Minister to Australia, Clarence E. Gauss, was confirmed in his appointment by the Senate on January 11, 1940, and presented his credentials in Canberra on July 17. Although the idea of appointing a Minister from New Zealand to Washington was broached as early as July 1940 it was not until February 16, 1942, that Mr. Walter Nash presented his credentials at the State Department. In the same month Patrick J. Hurley became first United States Minister to New Zealand.

PART III WORLD WAR II AND AFTER

14. Toward United States - Australian Collaboration

The exchange of Ministers between the United States and Australia was a significant development, but it did not in itself redefine their relations. It was, however, a useful preliminary to any redefinition that might come about. Although the Australians apparently entertained some hope that a vital redefinition relating directly to their security in the Western Pacific, chiefly visualized in terms of bases, might come about, the actual redefinition was, in the end, largely the product of events. It was, that is to say, less a product of diplomacy, or even of a rethinking or replanning of strategy and tactics, than of the misfortunes of actual war. The United States revised its thinking about the Southwest Pacific only when the Japanese in their southward drive had eliminated with unanticipated rapidity possible bases for resistance and counteroffensive right down to Australia. When the United States assumed primary responsibility for the war in the Pacific, it then had necessarily to use Australia as a base for any counteroffensive it might mount, and similar use had to be made of New Zealand and certain of the islands. In the context of actual war the primary substance of relations between the United States and Australia and New Zealand involved matters of strategy, tactics, and logistics rather than politics as such. There was discussion of goods, services, facilities, manpower, and so on, rather than political questions at the international level. The possible shape of a continuing politico-diplomatic-defensive relationship extending into the future did not begin to emerge until early 1944, by which time the war had moved north from Australia.

The road to war in the Western Pacific was long and devious, and there were astonishing miscalculations by all concerned, providing a rich field for critical historians operating *ex post facto*. It is impossible even to outline the story here, let alone to criticize the conduct of the principal actors, but some general points must be made to insure the intelligibility of the account which will shortly be given of American–Australian relations from early 1940 to Pearl Harbor.

(1) As to the diplomacy of the period, chiefly American-Japanese diplomacy, the Australians were primarily concerned to restrain Japan in her southward activities, while also averting or postponing armed conflict. So heavily did the Australians emphasize the necessity for avoiding actual war that they appear not to have shared to any great extent the American preoccupation with China, or to have been as disturbed as the Americans intermittently were by the association of the Japanese with Hitler. The Australians strove, right up to the end, to keep the diplomacy going, to keep the antagonists talking. However, they did not seek to bring their influence to bear directly, but in concert with the British diplomats in Washington. The British, for their part, after Churchill came to power, left the diplomacy largely in the hands of the United States, so the Australians suffered the disadvantage of acting with a party taking a more or less passive role. After the outbreak of war in Europe in 1939, the Australian commitment was to that war, and they could not contemplate war in the Pacific also with anything resembling equanimity. Commitment to Europe — or specifically in this instance to the Middle East — was their historic commitment, stemming from their membership in the Commonwealth and their close association with the United Kingdom. As time passed and war in the Pacific became an imminent possibility, the Australians found themselves

so heavily committed in the Middle East that very little of their armed strength-in-being was available for use in the Pacific, or for defense of the home country.

(2) The cutting edge of the predicament in which the Australians found themselves with regard to war in the Pacific was somewhat dulled by their continued confidence in Singapore. Whenever they had doubts about Singapore, the British succeeded in placating them. In common with the other members of the party of resistance to Japan, the Australians failed correctly to assess Japan's power to realize her strategic aims in the south if and when she chose to loose her armed forces there. Nevertheless the Australians had a keen appreciation of the significance of Japanese moves, as in Indo-China, but they did not forecast what the Japanese could accomplish in the first burst of actual war. What the Japanese accomplished was therefore a surprise to the Australians and to the other countries equally and perhaps rather more of a shock to the Australians, considering their heavy investment in Singapore and the weak defensive position in which they found themselves at home.

(3) The Australians, in common with the others concerned in this affair, rather vaguely conceived of a war with Japan as likely to be fought to the north of Australia. Australia's involvement was imagined to be through its participation in the war to the north — that is, at Singapore and along the so-called Malay Barrier, though surface, air, and submarine raids on shipping routes in the Tasman Sea, and possibly coastal raids, including landings, might occur. It was a minority view that the war might not be kept to the north by Singapore or any other factor, but rather that a front line might be established either in the islands close to the continent or actually on the continent itself. Hence Australia's weak defensive position in 1941 and 1942 related not only to a war in the north but also to continental defense.

(4) The situation in the Western Pacific was vastly complicated by the fact that the United States was not in a position to make firm commitments about the prosecution of a

war until a *casus belli* acceptable to Congress had actually occurred. Therefore such discussions of the hypothesis of collaboration in resistance to the Japanese as did take place were
not pursued far enough to iron out the disagreements such as
that between the Americans and the British over Singapore. As
Admiral Morison has said, "Conferences consumed much time
and thought, but had no substantial results . . ."

(5) However, one basic decision about the strategy of the
war was made quite early that was of profound significance to
Australia, though it was only so understood by the Australians
late in the day. This was the decision known as "Hitler (or
Europe) First," or the judgment that the first and primary task
was the defeat of Hitler. This decision was made before war
broke out in the Western Pacific, but it was not modified by
that event. The effect of the decision was to reduce the Pacific
war to second place, not to be prosecuted in an all-out fashion
until victory was clearly in sight in Europe. The Pacific war
was not to be a "holding war," as some people thought, but
rather a low-pressure war as long as Hitler's power was unbroken, the low-pressure expressed in terms of assigned manpower, materiel, and so forth. When war came the Australians
found themselves of necessity in opposition to this strategy and
its consequences.

(6) The factors here cited worked to make Australia a country of low visibility in Washington until the full impact of
Japan's war-making capacity was felt, when it appeared above
the horizon as an indispensable but menaced base. The first
American task became to secure that base and the sea approaches to it across the Pacific. At the time the Australians, at
least those outside official circles, got the impression that the
Americans came to rescue them from imminent peril. This was
not really the case. The Americans went to Australia to meet
unescapable strategical necessities of their own.* Even after
Australia's strategic indispensability was clear and its right to

* This is now fully recognized in both the Australian and American
official histories of the war.

a voice in decisions about the war conceded, her visibility from a political point of view continued rather low and the Australians had to wage a campaign for recognition and acceptance by those making decisions of effect on her future. In this campaign she had the support of New Zealand. The campaign led on to her recognition as a leading small, or middle, power with a primary interest in Pacific affairs and a significant stake in global affairs.

When Mr. Casey went to Washington as the Australian Minister, the war was in the last phases of its "phony" stage. No man really knew the shape of things to come, but the British had already concluded that they could not win the war without American help. From the British point of view, an item high on the agenda of politics was winning that support, and one of Churchill's great accomplishments was to carry through the task successfully, not without a good deal of eager assistance from Americans in and out of government. Churchill became Prime Minister in May 1940, when the war in its European phases had abruptly ceased to be "phony" and had become catastrophic. It was in this rapidly evolving context that Australia developed its diplomatic relations with the United States.

The disasters in Europe automatically intensified the already well-founded tensions in the Far East. The Japanese expansionists began a campaign to choke off the war in China to free the country for a southward drive directed against the orphaned colonies of the defeated European metropolitan powers. They began with pressure on French Indo-China. This raised the question of whether the threatening war in the Far East was to be considered a separate war or a phase of a global war directed by Hitler, a question made far more difficult to answer when the Japanese joined the Axis in September 1940. The Americans backed and filled on this question throughout the months that followed, but the verdict now seems to be that the Pacific war was a separate war, conducted to an extent by the Japanese in the light of what advantages the existence of a war in Europe gave to them. The Australians quite consistently thought of it as a simultaneous but definitely separate war, as the utterances of their public men can be cited to show.

In June 1940 Mr. Casey went with Lord Lothian, the United Kingdom Ambassador, to talk to Secretary Hull about the situation in the Far East. The British were then under very heavy pressure from the Japanese in China. The two diplomats sought Hull's views on how far the British could go in making a settlement without embarrassing the United States. Among other points they made was one to the effect that if the United States would send warships to Singapore it would strengthen the British arm and clearly indicate the American position. After consultation with the President, Hull replied that the Americans would not send ships to Singapore, for that would weaken the Atlantic defenses. However, the United States would continue to exert economic pressure on Japan. The British should judge for themselves how far they should go in conciliating Japan — Australia, for example, could grant Japan access to Australian iron ore, as had been suggested — but they should trade away nothing belonging to China. The climax of British conciliation of Japan came in the next month when they shut down the Burma Road, a major supply line of the Chinese. It was closed for three months. And in August Australia appointed Sir John Latham the first Australian Minister to Japan, in what was definitely a conciliatory gesture.*

The second half of 1940 was marked by the worsening of the relations between Japan and the United States. As tensions rose, Churchill largely passed responsibility for diplomacy with Japan to the State Department. While there was steady consultation between the British diplomats, including Mr. Casey, and the State Department, one gets the impression that a primary British interest was not so much to influence the diplo-

* The writer interviewed Sir John in Melbourne a few days after his appointment had been announced. He refused to be drawn on politics, contenting himself with the observation that he was glad to say that the Japanese loved children and flowers.

macy as somehow to induce the Americans to make concrete arrangements for the collaborative disposition of armed forces in the Western Pacific, thus at once providing a "show of strength" against Japan and improving the position if war should come. This was seen by the British as chiefly a matter of bases, their immediate and prospective use. The Australians could offer bases, either in their nearby islands or on their continent, or both. A veritable campaign to get the Americans committed to the use of the United Kingdom and Australian bases in the Western Pacific was pursued. Australian optimism about success in the campaign rose and fell as the Americans took action elsewhere which could be argued to be analogous to the wished-for collaboration with Australia, as for example the defense arrangements with Canada and the destroyers-for-bases agreement with Britain.

The campaign was pursued not only by Churchill with Roosevelt and by the British and Australian diplomats with the State Department, but very actively at the conferences that took place between the representatives of the British and American armed forces. The Americans were never induced to accept the British thesis about bases. Singapore was rejected with almost rigid consistency. Only very late in 1941 was there any initiative from the Americans about the use of Australian bases.

During these eighteen months the Australians were really in a disadvantageous position as far as wielding influence was concerned. The problem of the Western Pacific was theirs to contemplate, but the decisions about it were being made by the United Kingdom and the United States — increasingly by the United States. Reading the detailed account of the course of Australian thinking of this time one is struck by the fact that while the Australians certainly continued to remain within the ambit of British thinking, differences of emphasis constantly appeared and while theoretically the Australians could advance their views in consultation with the British, practically it was difficult for them to get them across effectively — or with any visible effect. The fundamental trouble was that while the Far

East was ever more obviously becoming a first priority for Australia, for Britain it was third on the list. In terms of defense, the Australians were contributing to the defense of Britain, the first priority of the United Kingdom, and the concentration of their effort was on the second, the Middle East, but Britain's third priority (which was becoming Australia's first) was being neglected by both. This is dramatized in defense terms by the story of the handling of the Singapore base. Britain consistently to the end did too little for Singapore, for understandable reasons, and while Australia took her Singapore obligations seriously, she could not within her limited resources do enough. What little she had to send was what was available after her Middle Eastern obligation had been met. This left Australian continental defenses excessively weak. Only by taking a radically independent line could Australia have changed this situation, and of the wisdom of this stand the Menzies conservative government was hardly to be persuaded. Alternatively, it might have increased Australia's defensive resources-in-being by increasing the intensity of Australia's war effort, but this would have been difficult politically. Actually the Menzies government was left in the position of gambling that things would turn out "all right" in the long run.

If the Australians were unable to use the consultative techniques with maximum effect in London, they suffered in Washington from their low visibility. Australia was undoubtedly perceived by the Americans as a close associate of the United Kingdom, not as an autonomous Pacific power, an ancillary character emphasized by Australia's own insistence upon maintaining the "diplomatic unity of the British Empire." Moreover the American perspective of the Western Pacific — focused as it was to the north — hardly allowed the Americans to perceive that Australia had a significance separate and distinct from general British power in the area, at least not a perception sharp enough to lead the Americans to brush aside the character the Australians had of their own choice assumed. Moreover, it must not be forgotten that at this time the Americans had more on their minds than the Western Pacific. They had already formulated the strategy of Hitler First; their minds were preoccupied with Europe. President Roosevelt, as the effective director of foreign policy, was particularly preoccupied with Europe, and he was only intermittently active in Far Eastern affairs. The negotiations with Japan were largely in the hands of Secretary Hull. Moreover, the naval strategy was in the hands of men who had not even toyed with the idea of fighting a Pacific war from south of the equator. The accepted strategy involved fighting a way westward through the Caroline and Marshall Islands, north of the line. The strategists thought of Australia's contribution in a war, if they thought of it particularly at all, in terms of its contribution to United Kingdom strength *north of the equator*.

Australia entered the war in September 1939 with a conservative coalition government, Robert Gordon Menzies Prime Minister, in office, but it was fated to participate in the Pacific War under Labour leadership. Mr. Menzies had won the leadership of the senior party of the coalition, the United Australia Party, on the death of Joseph A. Lyons in April 1939. The coalition had then been in office under Lyons' leadership since 1932, when it had displaced a Labour government. In the seven years since losing office, however, Labour had, under the leadership of John Curtin, largely repaired the disastrous disunity that in considerable part accounted for the reverse of 1932. By 1939 it was the conservative coalition in office that was beginning to suffer from internal dissention. The political tide was running in Labour's favor.

From April 1939 to October 1941 politics in Australia were marked by the rising strength of Labour and the disintegration of the United Australia Party and the coalition. In August 1941 Mr. Menzies was forced out of the Prime Ministership by his fellow-coalitionist, Arthur Fadden, the leader of the Country Party, who then took over the position. He held it but briefly.

In October Fadden fell and Labour took office with John Curtin as Prime Minister.

Mr. Curtin's Minister for External Affairs was Dr. Herbert Vere Evatt, who had resigned from the High Court to re-enter politics in the general election of 1940. His first statement to Parliament as Minister was made on November 27, 1941. "At the outset," he began, "I take the opportunity of stating that the recent change of government in this country does not imply any vital change in Australia's foreign policy." His principal remarks on the situation in the Pacific were as follows:

A year ago Japan entered into formal association with the Axis powers, proclaiming her national policy as the establishment of a 'coprosperity sphere' in greater East Asia. Early in the present year she signed a non-aggression pact with Russia. In July she made a fateful military incursion into French Indo-China. Both the United States and the British nations regarded this incursion as an unequivocal act of aggression which directly menaced their vital interests. They at once took counter measures against Japan in the form of stringent economic and financial restrictions. Next came the intervention of President Roosevelt after his return from the Atlantic talks with Mr. Churchill. It was then proposed that both Indo-China and Thailand should be neutralized under the joint guarantee of the Pacific Powers, provided that Japan withdrew her forces from Indo-China. What was called a 'moratorium' period then commenced, and preliminary conversations between Japan and United States took place. They have continued at Washington, and are now known as the Hull-Kurusu talks.

It should be emphasized that the talks are confined to the United States and Japan, though, of course, they are of very great concern to the British, Australian, Netherlands and Chinese Governments. We are quite content to allow the leadership and initiative in this matter to be retained by the United States, which is very directly affected by any armed aggression in the southeast corner of the Asiatic continent.

At the same time, I must express the hope that the talks will result in an agreement . . .

This Government's objective is to preserve the peace of the Pacific if that can be done without sacrifice of principle, without prejudice to national security, without endangering the solidarity of the democratic powers . . .*

From these remarks, attention being given particularly to the date of their making, it is apparent that the Australian government was not closely enough advised of what was happening in Washington to know that the talks on which its hopes were pinned had already broken down and that war was now inevitable.

Elsewhere in his speech Dr. Evatt made it clear that Labour had come to power with its hopes with regard to defense focused on Singapore, this in spite of the fact that its thinking had earlier been much influenced by the skeptics of Singapore. To support Singapore — or the so-called Malay Barrier — it was willing to collaborate closely with the Netherlands East Indies (with which an exchange of Ministers was impending) and the Portuguese in Timor. (The previous month Frederick William Eggleston had been sent to Chungking as Minister, but Australia took the British view of China, and Dr. Evatt made no particular mention of it.) A reference was made late in the statement to "the friendship and cooperation of the President and the people of the United States of America" but there was no concrete specification of what this might mean to Australia, at the moment or prospectively, beyond the careful statement of America's diplomatic responsibilities already cited.

As a matter of fact, up to the time of Dr. Evatt's statement there were only two bits of evidence of what "the friendship and cooperation" of the United States might concretely mean. In April 1941 some American cruisers and destroyers had been sent from Pearl Harbor into the Southwest Pacific. At Pago Pago they were split into two groups, one of which then visited Sydney, Brisbane, and Suva in Fiji, while the other visited Auckland in New Zealand and Tahiti. The *meaning* of this gesture was not clarified either to the men who executed it or

* Printed in H. V. Evatt, *Foreign Policy of Australia: Speeches* (Sydney, 1945).

to the officials in the places visited, as comes out in the "Pearl Harbor Attack Hearings." It was ostensibly a "good-will" move, but it was also designed to intensify any insecurity the Japanese might be feeling about American intentions in the Southwest Pacific or as a veiled warning to the Japanese about those intentions. A similar gesture north from Pearl Harbor was talked of but rejected as too provocative. (As a matter of fact, it is the writer's conviction that the Japanese were clear in their own minds as early as 1940 that the United States would take a hand in the defense of Australia in any emergency, but that an assault on Australia was scheduled for the second or third phase of their plan of conquest, so the prospect was remote. If this is true, the Japanese had reached clarity on a point about which the Americans and the Australians were in doubt until well after Pearl Harbor.) The other bit of evidence of the likely drift of affairs was that in September 1941 the United States, thinking of providing a backstop for the Philippines and a secure route from Hawaii to the islands, asked if air bases could be made available to it at Rabaul and Port Moresby in the islands, and Rockhampton and Darwin on continental Australia. Rabaul was also to be developed as a fleet base. The development of these points was to be a joint undertaking. But the odd thing about this proposal was that it was in the first instance addressed to the United Kingdom, not Australia, although every place mentioned was in Australian territory. The proposal reached Australia via the United Kingdom, which was, of course, quite powerless to dispose of Australian possessions. The episode vividly illustrates Australia's peculiar position in Washington at the time. Nothing had been done about these bases when the attack on Pearl Harbor set the Western Pacific aflame.

When Pearl Harbor came the Australians saw it chiefly as a guarantee that the Americans would fight, to them a supremely valuable boon, but in the immediate sequel Pearl Harbor was to them something else again. By crippling American power-in-being, though by how much was not then known, the attack practically guaranteed that the war could not be kept north of the equator and away from Australia, especially when, as soon emerged, it was apparent that neither Singapore nor the Philippines was invulnerable nor capable of as prolonged resistance as had been calculated earlier. The Pearl Harbor disaster was serious enough to insure, when taken in conjunction with the weakness of Singapore and the Philippines, that the Japanese would be able to complete the first stage of their plans and proceed early in 1942 to attempt to realize, in what they themselves called a fit of "victory disease," a second stage, the neutralization of Australia by the occupation of selected islands off its Pacific coast. Neutralization was what the Japanese planned, not direct and immediate invasion. Invasion might come later when Australia was weakened by prolonged blockade. Correctly seen, Pearl Harbor was an Australian disaster as it was an American disaster.

In the immediate sequel, then, the position of Australia was determined at Singapore and in the Philippines. The Japanese successes in those places opened the way for the Japanese to move south of the equator and attempt the isolation of Australia. If control could be gained of certain islands off her coast in the Pacific, Australia — or the heartland of Australia — could be blockaded. Any invasion or conquest of Australia could then be carried out at leisure if and when it became necessary. It was because the Japanese destruction at Pearl Harbor was not of as crippling a kind as was supposed at the time that the Americans were able to frustrate this program, relieve the Australians, and open the way to the free use of Australia as a base. The key event was the Battle of the Coral Sea, May 4–8, 1942.

Just when the Australian people first got a clear glimpse of what the situation to the north portended is difficult to say, but I think it a reasonable speculation that it came on January 10 with the sinking of the British warships *Repulse* and *Renown* by Japanese planes off Malaya, though the government saw the possibilities at least three weeks earlier. This was a clear indication that trouble lay ahead, for it was a plain notice that the resisting forces in the north were undersupplied with absolutely necessary equipment. This news was regarded as so bad in Australia that when it first came over the air, an official effort was made to keep it off the Australian radio on the ground that it was Japanese propaganda. It was only allowed to go out when it was confirmed by B.B.C.

Late in December an effort was made to coordinate the resistance to the Japanese along the Malaya Barrier by establishing a command embracing the American, British, Dutch, and Australian forces the (A.B.D.A.). After a moment when the idea of giving the job to MacArthur* was toyed with, the choice fell on Sir Archibald Wavell. But while the Australians were well pleased by the move — belated as it was in their book — they were chagrined to discover that they were to be given no direct representation on the controlling body far away in Washington. It was to be staffed, under Churchill and Roosevelt, by British and American officers. Here originated the long and arduous campaign of Australia for status and representation at the highest level in the direction of the war in the Pacific — later extended to the international political level. New Zealand supported this campaign.

The episode was but one in a long series of pinpricks and worse to which Australia was subjected, or felt it was subjected. The key decisions at this time were made by the United States and Britain, very often by Roosevelt and Churchill themselves. Roosevelt tended to support Churchill when the Australians showed they were restless. The Australian problem was not how to get into the war — it was in it by prior plan and was daily getting in deeper — but how to get some voice at the highest level in the important decision-making. It seemed grossly unfair, not to say derogatory of their importance as a nation, that they should be asked to supply men and equipment

---

* This provoked the Australian Minister to Washington to devise a masterly bit of understatement in telegraphing Canberra: "I understand that, although not devoid of human frailties, he is a good man."

without such a voice. As it became more and more obvious that the security of Australia as a nation was going directly to be jeopardized, the case for participation in decision-making became stronger and more urgent. More and more discernibly the decisions being made were having effect upon her national future. It seemed to the Australians holding political power that they should have something to say in what appeared from their coign of vantage to be a struggle for national survival. That struggle was one which national self-respect and dignity demanded that they at least help direct themselves. To preserve their national dignity and self-respect, they could ask no less, but as they had to ask it at a time when the big powers were rampant, and, moreover, committed to a basic war policy that Australia did not accept, they often appeared to be bumptiously assertive.

Nor was it an easy time in which to give expression to a rapidly burgeoning nationalism. Old assumptions were being dissolved, new policies were being evolved to meet unprecedented conditions. Not only was the world of events chaotic, but to adjust to the emerging situation required the rapid formulation of new policies, some of which did violence to established assumptions of a fundamental kind. These were not merely convenient operative assumptions; they were enshrouded in the emotional wrappings of the highest patriotism. It appeared ineluctably necessary that Australia (a) recognize and accept and publicly publish that British power in the Pacific was inadequate to the task confronting it, that this inadequate power moreover, was being eroded away to nothing at a fantastic speed, that there was no visible chance that it could be built up to any useful level in the predictable future, that therefore British assistance in insuring Australia's survival was rapidly ceasing to be a ponderable reality — that an idea and a fact about Australia's defense with which the Australians had lived for generations had suddenly lost all vitality; (b) conclude that this required Australia to act as a nation to insure her own survival, regardless of the violence that might appear to be done to ancient loyalties, a line sure to be interpreted by emotionally disturbed traditionalists as precipitate abandonment of those loyalties; (c) place her national survival above the universally acknowledged duty to sustain the Imperial military position and recover for use in domestic defense the trained men currently in the Middle East; (d) openly seek the closest relations with the United States as the Pacific nation which possessed the power to aid, probably decisively, in insuring Australia's survival. And this had to be done at a time when men's emotions were running high, when irrational responses to provocative proposals were sure to ensue, and when the temptation was practically irresistible to overstate the case for the new policies.

At the end of December 1941 the Labour Prime Minister, John Curtin, declared in a message to the Australian people:

> . . . the war with Japan is not a phase of the struggle with the Axis Powers, but is a new war . . . we refuse to accept the dictum that the Pacific struggle must be treated as a subordinate segment of the general conflict . . . The Australian Government, therefore, regards the Pacific struggle as primarily one in which the United States and Australia must have the fullest say in the direction of the democracies' fighting plan. Without any inhibitions of any kind, I make it quite clear that Australia looks to America, free of any pangs as to our traditional links or kinship with the United Kingdom. We know the problems that the United Kingdom faces . . . But we know, too, that Australia can go and Britain still hold on. We are, therefore, determined that Australia shall not go, and shall exert all our energies toward the shaping of a plan, with the United States as its keystone, which will give to our country some confidence of being able to hold out until the tide of battle swings against the enemy.*

This statement, particularly the reference to the ties between Australia and the United Kingdom, was widely misinterpreted, both in Australia and abroad. Mr. Curtin's hyperbole was really not necessary, for what he was in effect announcing — close collaboration with the United States — had been an element of the policy of Australia since 1940. The campaign for the use

---

* Originally a New Year's "message" to the Australian people, widely reprinted and broadcasted.

of Australian bases by the United States was a preliminary to what Curtin was now announcing. No abandonment of Commonwealth ties was necessary for the full implementation of collaboration. Mr. Curtin should have recalled the case of United States–Canadian relations with regard to defense. He apparently was provoked into the rather extravagant language by being aware that to the general public and the less realistic politicians, the proposal would suggest a radical change of Australia's position, though not a change without precedent in the affairs of other Commonwealth members. It was simply that Australia was not habituated to this kind of thinking and action and, momentarily oversensitive to the resistance it might inspire in Australia, Mr. Curtin overstated his case to his own immediate embarrassment. What the statement did signalize, however, was the end of Australia's unswerving allegiance to the dying dogma of the "diplomatic unity of the British Empire." That dogma is now so dead that it requires the exercise of the historical imagination to recover a sense of the operative and emotional meaning it once had to fervent dominion Imperialists.

During December the shape of things to come in American-Australian relations began to be traced. The Americans began to think of using Australia as a base, but as a base for supporting the operations to the north where it was still assumed the war in the Pacific was going to be fought. On December 9 Colonel Dwight Eisenhower, then on General Marshall's staff, but earlier with MacArthur in the Philippines, proposed that Australia be used as a base from which to supply the Philippines.* This proposal was apparently made in ignorance of a similar proposal for the use of Australia made in the previous September. Eisenhower's proposal was accepted by Marshall on the fifteenth; and presented by Marshall to Roosevelt, who adopted it. It was talked about in relation to the A.B.D.A. scheme and related to A.B.D.A. operations to the north men-

* Eisenhower tells about this in personal terms in *Crusade in Europe* (New York, 1948), pp. 21–23, and prints a map to illustrate his points.

tioned above. Darwin was the specific port in mind for transport by sea; various places were envisioned as useful for airplanes, of which Darwin was one and Townsville another. It was also suggested that Brisbane might be used. The pioneering of base building in Australia was in the end done by the air force, and it was the air force which managed the eventual shift from the idea of Australia as a staging point on the way north to a base-in-itself. If Australia was to be an American base, sea communications with it had to be kept open. When at the end of December Admiral Ernest J. King became Chief of Naval Operations and Admiral Chester Nimitz Commander-in-Chief of the Pacific fleet the task of insuring that the sea communications were kept open was one of the first to which they addressed themselves. They focused on the route running via Samoa and Fiji (that is, the established commercial route). Eventually there were American installations and troops on Palmyra, Johnston, Christmas, and Canton islands, on Samoa, Tonga, Fiji, Bora Bora, New Caledonia, and the New Hebrides, not to mention the numerous islands against or on which operations took place. The first considerable body of American troops to arrive in Australia were those of the so-called *Pensacola* convoy, which had been intended as reinforcements for the Philippines. Unable to reach the Philippines, they were diverted to Australia — specifically to Brisbane — where they arrived on December 22, 1941, "orphans of the storm."

These items of history are designed to make it clear that (1) the Americans came to use Australia as a base because of their own needs in prosecuting war to the north of Australia, and (2) they got into the islands south of the equator in insuring communications with the new base in Australia. The initiative was American, not Australian. And as the authors of the United States Army history, the volume entitled *Global Logistics 1940–43* (Washington, 1955), remark, "Like the base in Australia, the American defense and communications line along the Pacific islands west of Hawaii was *an outgrowth of circumstances rather than plan.*" (The italics are mine.)

It was disaster in war in the north that forced the use of Australia as a primary base. After the collapses in Malaya, Java, and Burma, the allied forces were split, some driven westward into India, others southwestward into Australia. When that great dispersal of survivors took place, Australia became *by force of circumstances* the anchor of the American line of defense in the Pacific.* The Americans, therefore, did not (to employ the words an Australian military historian used in undermining an Australian myth) arrive in Australia "solely to help Australia and in response to Australian appeals." Even the dispatch of General MacArthur from the Philippines to Australia was an American move to supply leadership at the base so adventitiously acquired. As an American army historian has stated, to cover MacArthur's apparent abandonment of the Philippines it was let out that he had left "in accordance with the request of the Australian Government." But Prime Minister Curtin did not know of MacArthur's assignment to Australia until he arrived, nor did Curtin know when MacArthur arrived for *what* he was destined. It was *arranged* that Curtin ask that MacArthur be made supreme commander, ostensibly at Australia's request. The Australians (and the New Zealanders) were, of course, fully prepared to accept an American Supreme Commander as they had made clear after an emergency Australian–New Zealand defense conference held in February. MacArthur's appointment was announced on March 17, and he assumed command on April 18. His top associates were the

* The Australians were in advance of the Americans in appreciating the strategical importance of their country in the unfolding war. This is beautifully shown in General Sturdee's paper of February 15, 1942, printed in full as Appendix 5 of Lionel Wigmore's *The Japanese Thrust* (Canberra, 1957), from which I quote a few indicative sentences as follows: "4. Our object at the present time should be to ensure the holding of some continental area from which we can eventually launch an offensive in the Pacific when American aid can be fully developed . . . 10. Even assuming the successful defence of Java, this island does not provide us with a continental base from which we could build up Allied strength to take the offensive . . . 11. The most suitable location for such a strategical base is Australia . . ."

American Brett of the air force, the American Leary of the navy, and the Australian Blamey in charge of ground forces. MacArthur focused the planning on New Guinea. It was the navy's job to keep the Japanese from carrying out their plans in the islands, the fundamental aspect of the task of insuring that communications between the United States and Australia not be interrupted.

The American way of looking at the situation confronting them resulted in a division of the Southwest Pacific into "areas" which put Australia into one and New Zealand into another, although the Australians and New Zealanders regarded themselves as linked together strategically and the New Zealanders accepted separation with some reluctance. Thus it came about that while MacArthur became closely and imperishably associated with Australia, he had little to do with New Zealand. New Zealand fell, along with the Pacific islands east of New Guinea, into the charge of the navy. Whereas the Australians saw a good deal of the American army and air force, and something of the navy, the New Zealanders saw chiefly the navy and the marines. Also the Australians brought back experienced troops from the Middle East to fight in defense of their homeland, even at the expense of a memorable dispute with Churchill, who wanted, with a recklessness now demonstrable, to throw some of them into Burma, while the New Zealanders bowed to Churchill's appeal and left their men in the Middle East. The result was that while the Australian army, air force, and navy all fought in the Pacific war, the fighting in the Pacific fell chiefly on New Zealand's air force and naval units.

Thus it fell out from the exigencies of war that the United States developed close relations with Australia and New Zealand at the level of the armed forces before the international political relations had had time to get beyond the embryonic stage. As long as the necessities of war dominated the scene, the relations between the Americans and the Australians and New Zealanders were dominated by the idea that Australia and

New Zealand were bases. The same was true of American relations with the administrations in the various islands, New Zealand, British, and French, at which ships and airplanes were serviced and on which troops were stationed. This situation lasted about two years; it was in 1944 that some inkling of the shape of future political relations began to show itself. There is unimpeachable testimony that in Australia the idea of Australia as a base dominated General MacArthur's headquarters and more or less determined the tone of the negotiations with the Australian civilian authorities. But of course the war dominated the Australian scene, permeating every aspect of the national life, and the concentration on the war was close to absolute. When Dr. Evatt, as Minister for External Affairs, visited Washington in these years he was less concerned with international political questions than with the direction of the war and with supporting the Australian view of it summarized in the opening sentences of Prime Minister Curtin's statement quoted above. This can be illustrated by reference to the campaign Evatt very vigorously waged for a Pacific War Council (an *advisory* body) in Washington — one already existed in London — which he achieved, with Australia as a very forward member, in March 1942. This was done in opposition to Churchill's views, but it was, however, as high as Australia reached in its campaign for recognition and status. It was not admitted to the Munitions Assignments Board or the Combined Chiefs of Staff Committee, but stood, as Dr. Evatt duly and sorrowfully noted, in the relation of a "petitioner" to them. Australia's views cohered very well with MacArthur's own views (and with the views of Admirals King and Nimitz also), so there was a very useful harmony between MacArthur and the Australian government on these basic points, though one cannot help wondering what MacArthur thought of working with a *Labour* government. All hands wanted "more" for the Pacific war and so all appeared to Washington like so many Oliver Twists. In relation to the "Hitler First" policy, the Australians and MacArthur were alike vigorous offsiders, never

reluctant to express their views. However, it is perhaps necessary to note that while this fundamental harmony existed between MacArthur and the Australians, this is not to say that
MacArthur was hero-worshipped. There is plenty of evidence
that the Australians saw him painfully clearly and were fully
aware that he was not "devoid of human frailties," including
errors of judgment, as about the relative quality of the Australian and American troops employed in the early fighting in
New Guinea. During this period more Americans were brought
into close relations with more Australians than at any other
time in history. An Australian who was closely in contact with
the Americans at this time rendered what seems to me to be a
classic Australian judgment of the Americans: "They are not
as good as they think they are, but they are a lot better than I
thought they were."

One aspect of the relationship that perhaps requires comment
is the revelation of American ignorance of the Southwest Pacific. Not only did the Americans not *plan* to use Australia as
a base, but they managed to remain remarkably uninformed
about it and its vicinity. The official American histories of the
operations contain such remarks as, "The Occidental world in
general had little exact knowledge of most of the Pacific areas
beyond Hawaii; more than one of the operational plans rested
upon data gathered in the eighteenth and nineteenth century
and never since revised, nor was there time to explore thoroughly the knowledge that did exist." Admiral Morison writes
of the use of "charts of Wilkes Exploring Expedition vintage"
and charts "based on the imperfect surveys of Bougainville,
D'Entrecasteaux and other navigators of the eighteenth century." There was an enormous ignorance of what Australia
and New Zealand could be expected to supply — animal, veg-
etable, and mineral — let alone what existed in excess supply
because of the wartime shipping shortage that hampered exports, and of course no knowledge of Australia's manufacturing
capacity. Although egregious errors were made in the things
dispatched to Australia, I do not think that General MacArthur

ever had to protest, as General Pershing did from France in World War I, that he "did not want bookcases, cuspidors, floor wax or lawn mowers." It was undoubtedly a great surprise to the Americans that Australian "lend-lease" to America came very near to evening out with American "lend-lease" to Australia.

15. Labour Directs Australia's Foreign Policy

The crisis of war in the Pacific found Labour parties in office in both Australia and New Zealand. In Australia foreign relations were in the hands of Dr. Herbert Vere Evatt, but in New Zealand Prime Minister Peter Fraser was his own Minister for External Affairs. Labour continued in office into the postwar period, in both Australia and New Zealand until 1949. Evatt was unquestionably the dominant figure of the time in foreign relations, so decidedly so that it was often speculated that Australian policy was his personal policy rather than a party-determined policy. However, it is easy to show that the Evatt policies, in general character if not always in their detailed emphasis, had their roots in traditional Labour Party, or labor movement, attitudes. These attitudes may never previously have found clear articulation, least of all at the level of foreign policy, but they were there and in the forcing-house of the period 1941–1950 found their spokesman in Dr. Evatt. By virtue of the fact that he was a man of powerful and authoritarian personality and vigorous intellect, with a conviction of the rightness of his ideas that was difficult to erode, Dr. Evatt made them vivid at home and abroad as nobody since William Morris Hughes had ever made Australian policies. Their thoroughly laboristic character was ratified in a significant fashion by their ready acceptability to the Labour Government of New Zealand, as in the Australian–New Zealand Agreement of 1944.

As the Labour policy developed — and it developed in response to events; it did not spring fully articulated from the head of Dr. Evatt — it became obvious that it was composed of three basic ingredients: nationalism, internationalism, and socioeconomic concerns. It was a small-power nationalism in a big-power world, a rule-of-law internationalism as against a power-politics internationalism, and socio-economically it was laboristic or, in the vague Australian–New Zealand sense, socialist. As a strategy of international relations it was designed to bring security and unalloyed national independence to Australia and New Zealand. Tactically it was usually, because Dr. Evatt, a former justice of the High Court, was a skilled lawyer and distinguished constitutionalist, legalistic in expression. Negatively, it was against power politics and anticapitalist. What the Australians and New Zealanders sought was national security and equality for small countries in a big-power world strongly disposed to power politics, accompanied by an assurance that socio-economic reforms, which they fully intended to pursue as nationalists, would have international support.

It turned out that a foreign policy for Australia, and in only slightly less urgent measure for New Zealand, involved juggling five "balls": (a) Commonwealth relations, (b) relations with the United States as the predominant Pacific Basin power, (c) relations with the Asian nations, (d) regional collaboration, as between Australia and New Zealand, and both and Asian countries, (e) the United Nations. Dr. Evatt gave a demonstration of how the five balls could be juggled. As the balls were not precisely of even weight, their juggling was a very nice exercise indeed, involving intricate "weighting" and careful balancing.

Labour's — and Evatt's — opponents, of whom in the Australian parliament the most able spokesman was R. G. Menzies, made at least five distinguishable general points against the policy, ignoring special points against specific applications of it: (1) that Dr. Evatt had seriously overestimated the power

Australia had to sustain the pretentions he made on the international stage — that the gap between Australia's pretentions and her actual and potential power, as currently forecastable, was dangerously wide; (2) that as an overardent Australian nationalist Dr. Evatt was recklessly riding upon and whipping up the centrifugal forces at work in the Commonwealth which Australia should in self-interest resist, thereby weakening Australia's traditional and still invaluable ties with Britain, though he was not, apparently, abandoning them; that as an overzealous nationalist and small-power spokesman he was failing to act so as to strengthen Britain's position among the powers; (3) that his highly suspicious attitude toward the big powers and his critical views of their policies were making it difficult to define a satisfactory relation with the United States; (4) that his laboristic anti-imperialism disposed him to be entirely too favorable to the Asian nationalist revolutionists, thus alienating the imperialist powers traditionally well-disposed to Australia; and (5) that he was dangerously wrong in thinking that all the difficulties Australia faced and all the dilemmas he had created for himself could be resolved by fervent devotion to, emphasis upon, and action in the United Nations. There were also, naturally, differences of opinion about the socio-economic policies the Labourites were seeking to advance through international agencies, especially about the wisdom of emphasizing full employment as against international trade, and some doubt about the wisdom of seeking to advance any through the United Nations.

In sum, the Opposition, frankly accepting a power-politics world, would have closely associated Australia with the Commonwealth, especially with Britain, and acted diplomatically to support and strengthen Britain's arm whenever possible, even at the sacrifice of Australia's own views when that involved no sacrifice of a national interest. It would have defined Australia's nationalistic pretentions in direct relation to its power, actual and potential, and therefore for more modestly than Dr. Evatt, and set about fortifying that power by sound relations with the

Commonwealth (that is, Britain) and the United States. It would have sought Asian friendship and good will but it would have been far more tender of the feelings of, say, the Dutch in the Indonesian situation. It would have removed the United Nations from the central place given it by Dr. Evatt, though it would not in any sense have abandoned it, putting in its place Commonwealth and United States relations. It would still juggle the same five balls on the same stage, but it would have handled them differently. The Opposition's chance to handle them came at the end of 1949. Its handling of them was sufficiently different clearly to mark a new era in Australian foreign policy.

It is not relevant to our purpose of describing Australian-American relations to trace the story of Australian foreign policy in all its aspects after 1941. Rather an effort must be made to pick out those policy statements and events which influenced the character of those relations.

The first major declaration of a political character bearing upon American relations with the Southwest Pacific after the outbreak of war was the Australian–New Zealand Agreement, signed at Canberra on January 21, 1944. This was a mixture of assertions of aspirations, definitions of policy with regard to specific questions, and provision for machinery to make collaboration easier and continuous in the future. The agreement was thought of as a *regional* pact entirely compatible with any universal international charter of organization that might eventually be written. As a pact, and as a regional pact, it was not in itself objectionable to the United States, and it was not objectionable to the Commonwealth governments either.

In part it was but a joint formal presentation of aspirations and policies which Australia and New Zealand had already entertained separately. Some of them had historical roots, some stemmed fairly directly from the laboristic ideology of the men who devised the agreement, while some were given an "edge," especially in wording, by recent affronts, official and unofficial, to the national *amour-propre* of the two parties.

Paragraph 7 dealt with "Armistice and Subsequent Arrangements" and asserted the right to "representation at the highest level in all armistice planning and executive bodies." Paragraph 14 asserted the right to participation in the planning and establishment of any future "general international organization." These assertions were in continuation of a campaign begun by Australia at the time of its chagrin at being left out of the highest direction of A.B.D.A. in 1941 and continued with the vigorous advocacy of the establishment of a Pacific War Council in Washington in 1942. It was a point of view considered imperative to restate on this occasion because of the failure to invite Australia and New Zealand to the Cairo Conference of November 1943 at which Roosevelt, Churchill, and Chiang Kai-shek agreed upon future military operations against Japan and formulated terms to be imposed upon Japan with regard to the restoration of territories to their rightful owners. Dr. Evatt had strongly resented exclusion from this conference, of which he had first obtained information from a newspaper dispatch. The argument for Australian–New Zealand representation "at the highest level" was variously supported, by reference to the sovereign equality of nations, by use of the argument from contributions to the prosecution of the war (or the "blood and treasure" argument), and by reference, in the case of the Pacific, to the imperative right to protect vital national interests. The position was obviously related to Dr. Evatt's — and Mr. Fraser's — critical view of the Big Powers and their assumption of the right to dispose of questions in which the small powers had an important stake. Paragraphs 7 and 14, therefore, both continued an old campaign and projected it warningfully into the future. The United States was conspicuous among those warned.

Paragraph 13 announced that "within the framework of a general system of world security, a regional zone of defence comprising the Southwest and South Pacific areas [much as defined for wartime purposes by the American military] shall be established and that this zone should be based on Australia and New Zealand, stretching through the arc of islands north and northeast of Australia, to Western Samoa and the Cook Islands." Australia and New Zealand did not claim exclusive responsibility for defense in this zone, but primary responsibility; they conceded a "share" to others. What this meant was not clear, for what was in question — the internal security of the areas, or their security against aggression from outside? Plainly for the latter much help was needed, as current events illustrated. The ambiguity was not resolved while Evatt was in charge of foreign policy. The matter was made more ambiguous than ever when Paragraph 13 was read in conjunction with 16: "The two Governments accept as a recognized principle of international practice that the construction and use, in time of war, by any power, of naval, military or air installations, in any territory under the sovereignty or control of another power, does not, in itself, afford any basis for territorial claims or rights of sovereignty or control after the conclusion of hostilities." The immediate provocation of this declaration was public but unofficial talk in the United States about "retaining" bases built in the two areas during the course of the war (then, of course, not concluded). The paragraph clearly forecast "trouble" over American proposals for the use of bases in the South and Southwest Pacific after the war. It came. The point of view expressed was elaborated in Paragraphs 26 and 27:

26. The two Governments declare that the interim administration and ultimate disposal of enemy territories in the Pacific is of vital importance to Australia and New Zealand, and that any such disposal should be effected only with their agreement and as part of a general Pacific settlement.
27. The two Governments declare that no charge in the sovereignty or system of control of any of the islands of the Pacific should be effected except as a result of an agreement to which they are parties or in the terms of which they have both concurred.

These paragraphs were a "swipe" at the Cairo Declaration of the previous November as well as the suggestions about bases current in the United States at the time. Taken together, the paragraphs cited can be read as a restatement in the context of 1944 of the old "Islands policy" of Australia and New Zealand, the oldest of their conscious foreign policies. Paragraph 13 embodied in modern dress the old concept of the islands as a defensive shield, Paragraphs 13 and 16, 26 and 27, a reassertion of the ancient point that sovereignty over the islands was a primary interest of Australia and New Zealand. But without their roots showing or pointed out, these declarations were open to the interpretation that Australia and New Zealand were proposing to fence off the South and Southwest Pacific and were asserting an active interest in the future of islands, like the Japanese mandates,* north of the equator and outside the two specified areas of primary responsibility. The United States was warned not to expect to get inside the fence (except in Eastern Samoa, where it had been established since 1899) by virtue of her wartime base-building activities, nor to dispose of islands elsewhere in the Pacific unilaterally.

Following also from the old "Island policy" but giving it a new "reformist" twist, was the group of paragraphs falling under the subhead "Welfare and Advancement of Native Peoples of the Pacific" (Paragraphs 28 through 31):

> 28. The two Governments declare that, in applying the principles of the Atlantic Charter to the Pacific, the doctrine of "trustee-

---

* Interest in the islands north of the equator was not a new interest for Australia. The Australians resented being virtually frozen out of Micronesia economically by the Germans before World War I and being "dealt out" of them in favor of Japan by a secret United Kingdom-Japanese agreement of 1917, the *quid pro quo* for the British being the taking of the German islands south of the equator by Australia and New Zealand. The New Zealanders had asserted their interest in the future of Hawaii as lately as 1896. It is unlikely that the negotiators of the Agreement had any inkling that the Americans regarded the 1917 arrangement (modified at the Peace Conference by turning all the islands in question into mandates) as a "mistake," an example of a mistake and worse the Americans associated with the "Secret Treaties" of World War I. See illustratively *The Forrestal Diaries*, ed. by Walter Millis (New York, 1951), entry for January 21, 1946, p. 131.

ship" (already applicable in the case of the mandated territories of which the two Governments are mandatory powers) is applicable in broad principle to all colonial territories in the Pacific and elsewhere, and that the main purpose of the trust is the welfare of the native peoples and their social, economic and political development.

29. The two Governments agree that the future of the various territories of the Pacific and the welfare of their inhabitants cannot be successfully promoted without a greater measure of collaboration between the numerous authorities concerned in their control, and that such collaboration is particularly desirable in regard to health services and communications, matters of native education, anthropological investigation, assistance in native production and material development generally.

30. The two Governments agree to promote the establishment, at the earliest possible date, of a regional organization with advisory powers, which could be called the South Seas Regional Commission, and on which in addition to representatives of Australia and New Zealand, there might be accredited representatives of the Governments of the United Kingdom and the United States of America, and of the French Committee of National Liberation.

31. The two Governments agree that it shall be the function of such South Seas Regional Commission as may be established to secure a common policy on social, economic and political development directed towards the advancement and well-being of the native peoples themselves, and that in particular, the commission shall —

(a) recommend arrangements for the participation of natives in administration in increasing measure with a view to promoting the ultimate attainment of self-government in the form most suited to the circumstances of the native peoples concerned;

(b) recommend arrangements for material development, including production, finance, communications and marketing;

(c) recommend arrangements for coordination of health and medical services and education;

(d) recommend arrangements for maintenance and improvement of standards of native welfare in regard to labour conditions and social services;

(e) recommend arrangements for collaboration in economic, social, medical and anthropological research; and

(f) make and publish periodical reviews of progress towards

the development of self-governing institutions in the islands of the Pacific and in the improvement of standards of living, conditions of work, education, health and general welfare.

These paragraphs caused no perturbation in American circles. The general approach was in line with Secretary Hull's proposals with regard to dependent territories of March 1943, which had the indorsement of President Roosevelt. The United States became a foundation member of the proposed commission, finally named The South Pacific Commission, when it was established at a conference at Canberra, February 6, 1947.

A set of paragraphs (17 through 23) enunciated an aviation policy, in gist a case for an International Air Transport Authority to operate services on "international air trunk routes." This was a projection of the Labourite belief in the virtues of government enterprise onto the international scene. In the terms used, it came to nothing. The United States, obviously, was the country least likely to support such a policy.

Notice must be taken, too, of two paragraphs (32 and 33) which signalized the return to the international scene of a subject which provided William Morris Hughes with the excuse for displays of emotion and Machiavellianism at Paris in 1918–1919 — the White Australia policy, followed also by New Zealand, though more discreetly. The operative paragraph (32) read:

> 32. In the peace settlement or other negotiations the two Governments will accord one another full support in maintaining the accepted principle that every government has the right to control immigration and emigration in regard to all territories within its jurisdiction.

In this careful disguise few Americans, in all probability, recognized the subject that gave Woodrow Wilson such trouble and Mr. Hughes the excuse for his spectacular maneuvers.

Inexplicable, however, was the omission of any reference whatever to the policy proposal to which Australia was soon to give assiduous attention: "full employment." That Australia proposed to seek support for a policy of full employment through international organizations was made clear at the Philidelphia conference of the International Labour Office in April–May 1944, and subsequent conferences on economic affairs. The Australian Government's own White Paper on "Full Employment in Australia" appeared on May 30, 1945. Paragraph 8 of the Paper read: "The Government has proposed in current international discussions that an employment agreement should be concluded whereby each country would undertake to do all in its power to maintain employment within its territories. The Government is also taking part in discussions relating to other forms of international collaboration designed to expand world trade and to mitigate fluctuations in prices of raw materials and foodstuffs. A domestic policy of full employment in Australia will prove of benefit to other countries." And, so the Australians always maintained, vice versa.

Pursuant to the consultative provisions of the Australian–New Zealand Agreement, a conference was held at Wellington during November 1–6, 1944. Among other matters, the whole question of General International Organization was canvassed. The conclusions were embodied in twelve short resolutions, some of which were entirely innocuous, others of a character which at once reflected Dr. Evatt's personal views on the general subject and forecast clearly the line Australia was to take at the San Francisco Conference to write a United Nations charter, April 25–June 26, 1945. Since New Zealand concurred in the Wellington resolutions, it is to be assumed that she found this line highly acceptable. As the concern here is with relations with the United States, a statement of the line as it eventually impinged upon those relations must be attempted. This is not easy to do, for much that was sought at San Francisco by Australia and New Zealand was of a general character, inherent in a particular conception of international organization and no more, and no less, aimed at the United States than at any other Great Power. Four points may be made: (1) that Australia and

New Zealand sought an international organization dedicated to the attainment of international justice, with the means (and the will to use them) to enforce its decisions and judgments; (2) that they sought to create a situation in which the rule of law would apply in international relations; (3) they sought a situation in which big-power leadership was conceded, but in which the small powers could actively participate in the control and direction of affairs; and (4) they looked for a situation in which socio-economic matters would be of major concern. What Australia and New Zealand feared, it is obvious, was that the prospective international organization might, if the Charter were not carefully drawn, pay more heed in its decisions to expediency than to justice, fail as the League of Nations had failed on the side of enforcement, be more political (in the bad sense) than legal in its judgments and arrangements, fall under big-power dictation, and neglect to deal with the socio-economic matters in which, as "socialists," the Australians and New Zealanders believed the seeds of war found nourishment. At the Conference Dr. Evatt became the most conspicuous spokesman of the Australian–New Zealand point of view; and since much that the Australians and New Zealanders wanted was inherently advantageous to the small powers, Dr. Evatt also became the leading spokesman for the small powers. In electing to become small-power advocate, Dr. Evatt of necessity had to appear as a contender against big-power policies and pretentions. However, while this was inescapably the case in many situations, most notably in the attempt to eliminate or reduce the scope of the veto power in the Security Council, in others it was really a carry-over of a fundamental bias, for some things the Australians and New Zealanders sought, the United States had no objection to having incorporated into the Charter. Examples are the enlargement of the powers of the General Assembly and therefore the enhancement of its importance, the amplification of the Trusteeship principle with regard to dependent peoples, and the rationalization of regional pacts and agreements. The veto, more than any other single matter, was a bone of contention between Australia and the United States. The United States, also, for example, took no pleasure in seeing the words "full Employment" incorporated into Article 55, nor would it accept the compulsory jurisdiction of the International Court of Justice. But except that it was, willy-nilly, a Big Power, it was hardly an offensive obstacle to Australia's progress as Dr. Evatt directed it.

All told, "out of some 38 distinct amendments of substance originally filed by Australia, 26 were either adopted without material change, adopted in principle or made unnecessary by other alterations."* The net effect was to make Australia one of the two or three most effective nations in the writing of the version of the Charter finally accepted.

The details of what went on, though fascinating even as incompletely revealed so far in public documents and personal reminiscences, are less important than the fact that at San Francisco it became clear how Dr. Evatt proposed to handle Australia's foreign relations in the future. He proposed to center them in a United Nations drawn as nearly to his specifications as could be managed. In the United Nations he saw a way to escape from big-power power politics, especially the use by the Big Powers of naked force to support decisions more expedient than just. His whole program was a flight from power politics, a game which he regarded as unspeakably evil and which in any case Australia could not play as an equal. Her only hope of achieving anything resembling the position of an equal was in a rule-of-law international organization. On occasion he hinted that he aspired to turn the relations of nations into the kind of politics characteristic under the British parliamentary system, with the United Nations General Assembly as the analogue in significance to the House of Commons. The tragedy was not that it was a bad or even a questionable ideal; the tragedy was that Dr. Evatt attempted to initiate his drama, and for a time actually tried to act it out, in a world rapidly de-

* *United Nations Conference on International Organization:* Report of the Australian Delegates (Canberra, 1945), par. 52.

generating into hostile power blocs, polarized around the United
States and the U.S.S.R. The Cold War put Dr. Evatt's world
into stygian shadow. A British parliament might be adequate
to contain the class war; its analogue could not contain an
international power struggle of the magnitude of that which
appeared after 1945.

To be sure, the United Nations was not destroyed by the
Cold War; it merely ceased to be of itself adequate to govern-
ing the world. It had to be supplemented by other arrangements
between nations to sustain and advance their positions, made
with a gesture of deference to the United Nations, but nevertheless founded on very different assumptions. Much of the
strength the United Nations showed in the difficult world it
came to inhabit can be attributed to Australian contributions
to its structure, many of its weaknesses to evils Australia tried
to correct. But Dr. Evatt found it excessively difficult to adapt
himself to the world of Cold War and undisguised power
politics.

Since Dr. Evatt placed such heavy emphasis on the United
Nations, there necessarily developed a certain measure of
ambiguity in relations with the United States. That the United
States was the predominant power in the Pacific was clearly
recognized, but it was not clear what special relationship with
the United States, if any, was called for, or would be welcomed
by the United States. It is a fact that the United States was not
at this time disposed to make special arrangements of a politico-
defensive nature in the Pacific. The willingness to do so came
later under very different circumstances from those of 1945–
1949.

The wartime accord early began to lose some of its warmth.
It was further cooled by virtue of the fact that the United States
was a central figure of the Cold War power struggle, a struggle
of which Evatt disapproved and which he appeared to "blame
on" the Americans, explaining Russian actions as defensive.

When shortly after the war's end the United States was planning its defense perimeter in the Western Pacific, it proposed

that the southern anchor be the great base on Manus Island, 200 miles north of New Guinea, built regardless of cost during MacArthur's progress from Australia northward to Japan. The island was an Australian responsibility, part of the Trust Territory. At the same time the Americans made a gesture toward acquiring some continuing rights in New Zealand's Trust Territory of Samoa, and they asked the United Kingdom to transfer sovereignty over Christmas Island to the United States. Australia, however, made difficulties, stemming apparently from the policies laid down in the Australian–New Zealand agreement, about the American proposal with regard to Manus, and in the end the Americans abandoned Manus, finally evacuating it in 1948. It was also the Australians who prevented the United States from acquiring Christmas Island, which the United Kingdom was quite willing to transfer. The defense perimeter as ultimately defined had its southern terminus at Manila. How far the abandonment of Manus was the consequence of onerous terms for its use in peacetime, laid down by the Australians, and how far it was caused by a rethinking by the Americans of the defense problem is hard to say. In Australia those who felt strongly that attachment to American power was indispensable condemned the government for its failure to handle the matter in an accommodating spirit. Nor was this the only occasion on which the Labour Government exhibited a touchiness that could be interpreted as hostility to the United States. It must not be overlooked that to the leftist Australian Labourites the United States was inevitably under suspicion as the world's leading exponent of free-enterprise capitalism. As an astute newspaper correspondent wrote in January 1949, "The truth probably is that no Socialist Government can work closely in peace-time with any American Government, Republican or Democrat, unless it is prepared sooner or later to adjust some of its values."[*] At any rate the Labour Government was noticeably dilatory about accepting the American proposal to use the balance due the United States under Lend-Lease (a mat-

[*] In *Manchester Guardian Weekly*, January 27, 1949.

ter of $5,000,000 only) as a fund to finance the exchange of university students and teachers, standing out for a large share in the administration of the fund, and asking if it could tax Americans visiting Australia under its terms. It refused also to consider abolishing so-called double taxation of investment earnings, thus with apparent deliberation discouraging American investment in Australia. But these things illustrate wariness of the capitalist giant rather than political hostility. Political hostility rather found expression, or the Americans certainly thought it did, when Evatt was President of the U. N. General Assembly in the Third Session, 1948. The Americans took particular exception to Evatt's actions with regard to the Berlin crisis of that year and to a letter he addressed to the Security Council criticizing American policy with regard to Indonesia. The latter provoked Robert A. Lovett to convey American dissatisfaction to the Australian Ambassador with the implication that he should make it known in Canberra. As President of the Assembly, Evatt was regarded by Washington as "an active source of both irritation and uncertainty."* But far more important than any of these were the differences over policy toward Japan.

The central place of Japan in Australian thinking about the Pacific was pointed out in reviewing the course of events in the prewar period. The war confirmed ideas about Japan that had been current in Australia for half a century before 1941. The defeat of Japan did not dissipate those suspicions, but rather seemed to freeze them into a rigid pattern. Although the Australians made every effort to gain a place in the decision-making about Japan at the highest level (in accordance with its policy in such matters), it nevertheless early became convinced that it was American policy, especially in the version of General MacArthur, that was ruling. It dissented from that policy. The Australians wanted a far *harder* policy than the Americans showed any disposition to enforce, a severe, even a punitive policy, especially designed to prevent the Japanese from ever

* See *Forrestal Diaries* (New York, 1951), pp. 532, 541.

regaining armaments, the technological equipment to build them, and the capacity to prosecute aggressive war. They insisted that Japan unquestionably be democratized, not merely be induced to exhibit the external stigmata of democracy; that its monopolistic economic organization be permanently broken up, not temporarily dismantled, only to be reassembled at a later time, and that it be replaced by a directed economy designed to provide security and freedom for all the people. The Australian policy was in large part dictated by fear of a resurgent Japan, a Japan capable of once more menacing Australia, while in substance it was a projection of a British laboristic program for democracy and welfare.

The Australians were well satisfied with the Allied policy toward Japan as it was formulated in the latter stages of the war and the immediate postwar period, especially with its emphasis on total and permanent disarmament and democratization. They fell out with the Americans, as the principal executants of policy, at first over details of the application of policy, then over the philosophy underlying American policy and about judgments of the actual effectiveness of the results in political, economic, and social terms, and finally and most violently over the shifts in American policy involved in changing Japan's status from "enemy to ally."

Professor W. Macmahon Ball of Australia was, during 1946 and 1947, Member representing jointly the United Kingdom, Australia, New Zealand, and India on the Allied Council for Japan. He carried the heavy burden of the intensifying disagreements over Japan between the United States and Australia. In terms of socio-economic policy, this is how he saw the situation:

> [There is involved] the difficulty of reconciling the American faith in individualism with a sound programme for Japan's economic reconstruction. It is possible for the United States, because of its immense wealth, to resist the kind of controls in economic life which other countries have adopted, and still maintain an endurable or, by comparison with some other countries, a comfortable standard of living for its poorest classes. Other countries cannot afford the wastes, or tolerate the inequalities, which such

a full measure of individualism invariably involves. Outside the United States it is widely accepted that a considerable measure of political control in the economic field is necessary or desirable. The degree and kind of control can only be decided in terms of changing situations. It is not an ideological battle between 'individualists' and 'socialists,' in which the belligerents hurl nineteenth-century epithets at each other. It is a practical problem of administration whether, in a particular country at a particular time, there should be public control of, say, the coal industry, and, if so, what particular technique of control will produce the best balance of economic welfare and personal freedom. The Prime Minister of the United Kingdom (Mr. Attlee) has recently described current British policy, not as diluted individualism, or diluted socialism, but as a positive effort to synthesize security and freedom. Such an approach avoids the rigidity of both 'socialism' and 'individualism.' To those who hold this view, Russian policy smacks of the 'extreme Left' and American policy of the 'extreme Right.'

I believe . . . that in helping Japan rebuild her industrial strength and restore her foreign trade, the United States will enable Japan to establish an industrial and economic supremacy in East Asia which her leaders will once again exploit for political purposes.*

Without stopping to debate the accuracy of the portrait of the United States or the elements of the rationale for a directed economy, it is clear that what the Australians were after was a domestic policy for Japan that would forever prevent her resurgence as a power in the Pacific. They were ineradicably suspicious of what she might do if she regained power.

It was in an effort to insure that the requisite restraints were imposed, to hold as far into the future as it was possible to contrive, that the Commonwealth countries, at the initiative of Australia, held a conference to discuss a possible peace treaty with Japan at Canberra, August 26–September 2, 1947. In effect this conference was an effort on the part of the participants — Australia, Burma, Canada, India, New Zealand, Pakistan, South Africa, and the United Kingdom — to find out how far they agreed on the terms of the prospective treaty, but in accordance

* W. Macmahon Ball, *Japan: Enemy or Ally?* (Sydney, 1948), pp. 198–199.

with Commonwealth practice, their disagreements were not brought to public notice. "Security against future aggression by Japan was a major concern of the Conference throughout all its discussion on all subjects." This beyond a doubt was the major concern of Australia and New Zealand. "The views of the interested Powers have already to a large extent found expression in certain key documents, notably the Potsdam Declaration and the basic policy decisions of the Far Eastern Commission . . . The acceptance of these two documents by eleven Powers encourages the hope among the delegations that agreement on the peace treaty itself may be reached speedily."*

The reference to the "key documents" was, at least on the part of Dr. Evatt, an effort to freeze policy toward Japan in the shape given it in those documents. The effort was to invest the documents and the policy they expressed with the authority and durability of the laws of the Medes and Persians and thereafter to argue that any deviation from the line taken in them — and American policy came to deviate radically — was of the order of breaking a solemn covenant. This extraordinarily rigid and highly legalistic attitude was coupled with an equally adamant refusal to admit that the world situation had changed, warranting changes in policy toward Japan. Dr. Evatt and his supporters were unwilling to adjust their view of Japan in the light of the Cold War. The Labourites were reluctant to admit that the locale of menacing power in East Asia had shifted from island Japan to the continent; they feared Japan but were not so disturbed about possible extensions of communist power in the North Pacific and South and Southeast Asia. The contention over Japan came to a kind of climax when the peace treaty with it was submitted to the Australian parliament and Dr. Evatt, as Leader of the Opposition, led an onslaught on it preliminary to the registering of a unanimous Labour Party vote against ratification.

* Quotations in this paragraph are from *Japanese Peace Settlement*, Report on British Commonwealth Conference, Canberra, 26 August–2 September, 1947 (Department of External Affairs, Wellington, 1947).

16. The Conservatives Direct Australia's Foreign Policy

At the end of 1949 Labour was displaced from office by a conservative coalition, with Robert Gordon Menzies as Prime Minister. The return of Mr. Menzies to office was a triumphant political comeback, for not only had he been forced to step down in 1941 by his own followers, but the party he had then headed had subsequently disintegrated. Mr. Menzies returned to office, not again as leader of the United Australia Party, but of a new creation, styled the Liberal Party. The minority of the new coalition was once more the Country Party.

The presumption was that the return of the conservatives — Australian-style conservatives, that is — would signalize a sharp reorientation of foreign policy, and that a conspicuous element of the new formulation would be a heavy emphasis upon close ties with Britain. That was in essence what came about, but with a very highly significant difference from what might have been anticipated. Before examining the shape the conservatives gave to Australian foreign policy, a few observations on Labour's attitudes toward relations with the Commonwealth and Britain must be made, lest it be supposed that Mr. Curtin's celebrated remarks of December 1941 represented settled Labour policy.

Mr. Curtin himself took the lead in reversing the implication of his hyperbolic statement. He addressed himself to the question of Commonwealth relations in public statements during August and September 1943 and in a speech to the Federal Conference of the Australian Labour Party in December 1943 which was designed to commit the party to his position. What Mr. Curtin sought was a way to make Commonwealth relations closer, with particular attention to the formulation of common policies, and to achieve this he advocated the establishment of a continuously functioning secretariat and regular meetings of the Prime Ministers, not always in London, but perhaps alternatively in the capitals of the overseas dominions. Mr. Curtin aimed to solve the difficulties which had been experienced with the machinery of Commonwealth consultation by tightening up the machinery and formally organizing it at the top. His statements and speech turned out to be contributions to a debate on the future of the Commonwealth, to which Field-Marshal Jan C. Smuts contributed in London on November 25, 1943, Lord Halifax in Toronto, Canada, on January 24, 1944, and which was vigorously pursued in the parliaments and press of the Commonwealth in late 1943 and early 1944. In essence the debate was between those who favored and yearned for the closer integration of the Commonwealth and those who favored the situation as it stood after the forces of devolution had done their work, especially since the end of World War I, and who would be prepared to accept further consequences of the centrifugal developments. Mr. Curtin and Lord Halifax, while their speeches were very different in expression, were on the side of integration, while Field-Marshal Smuts tried to combine the two positions in a peculiar fashion, though in the end he came out on the side of devolution. Mr. Curtin's position was harmonious with the Australian and New Zealand tradition of cherishing the Imperial ties. Neither country had adopted by legislation certain provisions of the Statute of Westminster, 1931, which supported the devolution of power from the United Kingdom to the dominions, until 1942, and then only

on technical legal grounds for reasons of administrative efficiency and convenience. Even this had severely upset the traditionalists of both countries, William Morris Hughes in Australia
opposing the move with the extraordinary allegation that the
statute "was enacted to serve the purposes of men and com-
munities who have proved themselves disloyal."* On the other
hand, Mr. Menzies had tried to get such legislation in Australia
in 1937 and hence saw Labour's point in asking for it in 1941.
It was not Mr. Curtin's purpose to retreat from the position
attained in 1943 but to regain a consultative intimacy which he
felt had been lost because of the informal and unsystematic
nature of the consultative machinery. He was also seeking a way
to make Australia's voice more effective in Commonwealth
counsels. The whole debate of 1943–44 on the Commonwealth's
future has, when examined ex post facto, an air of unreality
about it, for nobody, on either side, quite foresaw the true
nature of the changes which were to come in the Commonwealth after the war. On the whole, however, the devolutionists
were nearer right than the integrationists. The Australians and
New Zealanders were once more in the minority.

In the debate Dr. Evatt took no conspicuous part. He was in
practice on the side of the devolutionists, but he was by no
means against the Commonwealth in its "devolved" form. As
a Labour Cabinet Member, moreover, he was duty-bound to
support Mr. Curtin's position and proposals. Yet his public
statements on Commonwealth relations after the great debate
was over show no sorrow about the defeat of the integrationists.
For example, in a paper on foreign affairs presented to Parliament in February 1947 he wrote:

> The members of the British Commonwealth of Nations are
> fully grown and are ready to take over in an increasing degree
> responsibilities formerly borne by the mother country alone . . .
> The functions of the British Commonwealth and its members are

* This remarkable contribution to the pathology of Commonwealth
politics is preserved for posterity in Nicholas Mansergh, editor, *Documents and Speeches on British Commonwealth Affairs 1931–1952*, (London, 1953). Vol. I, p. 29.

not finally and irrevocably prescribed. The genius of the British race lies in its capacity to adapt itself to the changing circumstances of each generation. That is the condition of progress and indeed the condition of survival. There is much exchange of information and consultation between the United Kingdom and the Dominions. At the same time I have come to the conclusion that there may be ways in which the machinery of consultation and common action can be improved. The objective is day-by-day cooperation in a brotherly partnership which not only can exist with the United Nations to which we all belong, but which can and will actively assist the United Nations in carrying out its supreme objectives of peace and economic advancement of all the peoples of the world . . .*

And again, in an article in *The Times* of London (March 12, 1949), he said:

. . . the widening of the British Commonwealth group and the participation of its members as fully sovereign nations in world affairs will make full consultation and discussion of some aspects of policy even more desirable than before. The existing machinery is working well enough . . . However, some very practical improvements in the method of consultation were provisionally agreed upon at the last Commonwealth Conference in London and I am sure there will be an expansion in the practical side of consultation with more frequent meetings taking place in different member countries as convenience and the nature of the chief subjects of discussion might suggest . . . Just as in 1926, when the Balfour declaration was made, 'free institutions are its life blood, free cooperation is its instrument.'

From these statements it is apparent that the Labour administration had finally achieved what was believed to be a satisfactory balance between two deeply felt needs: the need for constant consultation and cooperation with the Commonwealth, and especially the United Kingdom, and the need to develop a national foreign policy for Australia. On coming to office, the conservatives were to find that while they could more strongly emphasize the former, they could not evade the latter, nor did they want to do so.

* See *Ministerial Statement . . . Tabled . . . 26 February, 1947* (Canberra, 1947), p. 13.

The first comprehensive statement on conservative foreign policy was made in the House of Representatives in March 1950. The new government's Minister for External Affairs was P. C. (later Sir Percy) Spender, who six years earlier had published a thoughtful critique of Labour policy as it then had found expression, in which he made it clear that his quarrel was more with emphasis and method than with direction.* The core of Mr. Spender's parliamentary statement follows, the rest being commentary on and elaboration of the points made or implied in these paragraphs.

Situated as we are in the South-West corner of the Pacific, with the outlying islands of the Asian continent almost touching our own territories of New Guinea and Papua, our first and constant interest must be the security of our own homeland and the maintenance of peace in the area in which our country is geographically placed. We could many years ago reasonably regard ourselves as isolated from the main threats to our national security. Our security, however, has become an immediate and vital issue because changes since the war have resulted in a shifting of potential aggression from the European to the Asian area, and our traditional British Commonwealth and U.S.A. friends have not yet completed their adjustments to the new situation. A very great burden of responsibility rests especially on us, but also upon the other British Commonwealth countries of this area.

The birth of new members of the Commonwealth, Pakistan and Ceylon and the Republic of India, the creation of new international entities in the form of the Republic of Indonesia, and the States of Vietnam, Laos and Cambodia in what was previously known as French Indo-China, are developments which have helped to shift the centre of gravity of world affairs more and more to this area. Our policy must be to ensure, to the full extent we can, that these new States co-operate with each other and with us in meeting positively and actively the new problems created in this area by the emergence of a communist China, and by the ever-increasing thrust of communism, which endeavours to ally itself, in the pursuit of its ends, with the national aspirations of the millions of people of South-East Asia. In other words, we

* The Hon. P. C. Spender K.C., B.A., LL. B., M.P., *Australia's Foreign Policy: The Next Phase*. (Privately printed, Sydney, 1944.)

should work with the new States, economically, commercially, in the technical as well as the political fields, in order to maintain newly-won independence.

Our foreign policy accordingly must be principally and continually concerned with the protection of this country from aggression, the maintenance of our security and our way of life. It is indisputably true, as I have already in other words indicated, that peace is indivisible and that what takes place in any part of the world concerns us. But it should at all times be stressed that here in this part of the world we are faced with special problems, and it is to a solution of these problems that our attention should primarily be directed.

Since the head and corner stone of the British Commonwealth is the United Kingdom, and since our security is to a large extent dependent upon her strength and influence in world affairs, we must be vitally concerned in her interests and safety. Next, therefore, to the maintenance of peace in the Pacific, and almost co-incident with it comes our interest in the maintenance of peace and security in Western Europe.

We also have a special interest in and duty to the British Commonwealth and to each of its members. It must be a constant purpose of Australian foreign policy to strengthen the different ties which exist between us and to build up and not to weaken our composite power and influence for peace. To this end the Australian Government will diligently and at all times direct its energies. It is, however, proper that we should understand that the British Commonwealth has, under the impact of the two forces, on the one hand nationalism and on the other hand internationalism, undergone fundamental changes during the last ten years necessitating a new approach to all questions which may affect it.

Thirdly, as the greatest Pacific power is the United States, and as, moreover, we have a common tradition, heritage and way of life, it is absolutely essential that we should maintain the closest and best possible relations with her and initiate and carry out our Pacific policies as far as possible in co-operation with her.

Fourthly, we are members of, and as a peace loving nation owe obligations to the United Nations, and must be in a position to discharge them. There is a danger of exaggerating not the importance of the aims or purposes or principles of the United Nations, but the extent to which in present circumstances it can exert real influence for the maintenance of peace in the world. It must never be forgotten that, as its membership includes representatives of all the groups of the world, it may contain those who are working to disrupt the order we believe in, as well as those who support it, although of course all are pledged to support the principles of the United Nations.

Of the Commonwealth, Spender had this specifically to say:

The British Commonwealth can be not only an organization with which we feel proud to be associated but an instrument of our security and prosperity . . . Should . . . the members of the Commonwealth insist on working as separate units, the importance of each is diminished . . .

I do not suggest that we can, or should, have identical policies, or duties. Australia and New Zealand have their special interests in the Pacific and South-East Asia . . . But we should not, in any emphasis on independence, be complacent about divergence. Unanimity freely reached should always be our aim . . . We can disagree on incidental issues but we must seek to resolve fundamental disagreements between the members of the family of the Commonwealth as a whole.

As regards organization, the association need not be rigid, but should provide constant means for consultation and contact. In theory these may be said to exist. In practice, except between Australia and New Zealand where close liaison is maintained by special arrangement, they have proved only too often to be insufficient or insufficiently used. Better means must be found and better advantage taken of existing methods.

But the most striking passage — the one that was widely featured in the world's press, especially by American newspapers, was that which dealt with Australian–American relations:

I have emphasized how essential it is for Australia to maintain the closest links with the United States of America for vital security reasons. But, our relations with the United States go further than that. We have a common heritage and tradition and way of life. During the war we built up a firm comradeship with our American friends. This friendship must, however, never be taken for granted. We propose actively to maintain the official and personal contacts and interchanges which resulted from the urgent needs of a common military effort.

Indeed, so far as possible, it is our objective to build up with the United States somewhat the same relationship as exists within the British Commonwealth . . . That is to say, we desire a full exchange of information and experience on all important matters, conceive our interests to diverge from those of the United States and consultation on questions of mutual interest. Where we on any fundamental issue, we shall, of course, firmly maintain our own point of view. But where our general objectives coincide, we shall seek to have done with petty disagreements and follow broad avenues of cooperation.

Taken in the Australian context, Mr. Spender's statement could be read to mean that while the conservatives were going to "weight" the ball of Commonwealth relations rather more heavily than Labour had done, even in the latter years of its period in office, they were also going to increase the "weighting" of Australian–American relations, but without diminishing the urgency of relations with the Asian states, old and new, and without in the least slighting the United Nations. Mr. Spender cited as contributions to closer relations with the United States the funding of the Lend-Lease balance to support the interchange of scholars and students, the abolition of double taxation and the encouragement of trade and investment. But the chosen instrument for formalizing relations with the United States in a rather more intimate posture than hitherto was described by Mr. Spender as a regional pact:

> It is therefore thought desirable that all Governments who are directly interested in the preservation of peace throughout South and South-East Asia and in the advancement of human welfare under the democratic system should consider immediately whether some form of regional pact for common defence is a practical possibility.

As a matter of fact, Dr. Evatt had thrown out the idea for one in 1947, but chiefly as embracing the nations geographically present in South and Southeast Asia, though the United States was sounded as to its attitude and its possible participation. Mr. Spender, however, came down heavily on the United States as a participant: ". . . the United States of America, whose participation would give such a pact a substance that it would otherwise lack. Indeed it would be rather meaningless without her." Nor was Mr. Spender's pact to be defensive only; he also had in mind the "promotion of democratic political institutions, higher living standards, increased cultural and commercial ties."

The working out of this program has been the substantive task of Australian foreign ministers since 1950. Mr. Spender himself relinquished the post of Minister for External Affairs in 1951 to become Ambasador to the United States. He was succeeded by Richard Gardiner Casey, whose identification with the policy became exceedingly intimate.

The conservative policy of developing close relations with the United States, though coupled with an equally emphasized policy of close relations with the United Kingdom, inevitably caused uneasiness among the traditionalists. Not satisfied with the knowledge that Prime Minister Menzies was as fervent an Imperial patriot as Australia possessed, and could be trusted to keep the Imperial relation highly burnished,* they worried about what Mr. Spender's declarations might really mean. For example, *The Age,* a newspaper of Melbourne, wrote (March 13, 1950):

> In his own words he declared that it was the objective of the Government to build up with the United States something akin to the relationships which exist within the British Commonwealth.
> If such words mean what they intend to convey, then Mr. Spender is attempting one of the most hazardous tight-rope balancing acts ever displayed in Australian foreign relations. Though he was careful to state that Australia was not contemplating a drift away from Great Britain, it is difficult to see how in a practical sense Australia can lean in two directions at the same time. If the lean is to become pronounced toward the United States then, quite obviously, the lean must become less pronounced toward the United Kingdom . . .
> Any departure from the existing relationship with the United Kingdom — a relationship through which there runs a blood vein of the strongest family sentiment and sustained by an enormous volume of trade — would be serious for Australia. Economically, it is still the United Kingdom which absorbs the bulk of Aus-

---

* Mr. Menzies selected three of his many statements on Commonwealth relations for inclusion in his book, *Speech is of Time* (London, 1958). See also the Suez episode below.

tralia's primary products and not the United States, whose imports from this country are a mere bagatelle by comparison.

What *The Age* and like-minded papers and individuals were obscuring by such worried comments was the terrible reality of what the New Zealand historian F. L. W. Wood later on called "the Anzac dilemma." On the one hand the Australians and the New Zealanders — the New Zealanders perhaps a bit more fervently — wished to keep their close ties with Britain in the very best of order for reasons of history, blood-ties, culture, and economics, while on the other they had, as realists, to recognize that Britain's power throughout the globe, and especially in the Pacific, had sharply declined and was unlikely to recover, even with dominion support, to a level that would justify neglecting to develop a special relation with the United States, now one of the world's super-powers, especially potent in the Pacific, where the Australians and New Zealanders had their being. The Anzac dilemma was created by a shift in the constellation of world power. The apparent price of survival in a power-mad world was to devise a scheme of relationships which would reconcile continuing the Commonwealth association in full force, while developing a new relationship with the super-power outside the family circle. It is no wonder that the Australians and New Zealanders developed a "we should — we shouldn't" frame of mind about how to deal with the dilemma. They might have learned a lot about how to handle it by studying the Canadian experience with it, but there is no evidence that they did so. It was not so much a question of "leaning," as *The Age* thought, as of *balancing*. Mr. Spender's definition was one conception of a desirable balance. As actually worked out over the decade after Mr. Spender spoke, the American relation was indeed a mixture, largely of power considerations but also of economic and cultural factors.

The pattern of relations developed in the decade 1950–1960 was not quite what was envisioned as ideal by the Australian conservatives. It was, moreover, far more the product of unpredictable circumstances of which astute advantage was taken than of deliberate planning. The failure of planning was not attributable to any weakness of wish or will on the part of the Australians. It was rather that they came up on the one hand, against Asian neutralism, which made any comprehensive pact impossible, and on the other the reluctance of the United States to erect in response to an argument by analogy any structure in the Pacific comparable to NATO in the Atlantic. The United States not only chose to wait until certain dust had settled, but also waited until the compulsion of events forced its hand in a direction that complemented Australian purposes.

Even before Mr. Spender made his comprehensive presentation of conservative foreign policy he had launched one proposal which in time was to become an integral part of the complex whole of Australian–American relations. This was, indeed, the particular aspect of Australian policy with which his name became most closely associated, the so-called Colombo Plan. At a meeting of the foreign ministers of the Commonwealth countries, held at Colombo, Ceylon, January 9–14, 1950, Mr. Spender proposed that a scheme be devised whereby the countries of South and Southeast Asia be assisted with technical advice, by the provision of educational opportunities in donor countries like Australia, and by capital grants with the purpose of strengthening their economies, emphasis to fall upon early (but not, of course, immediate) results in the way of fortifying and improving standards of living. This was in harmony with the diagnosis that the problem of South and Southeast Asia was poverty as much as, perhaps even more than, it was politics. But while the emphasis of Mr. Spender's proposal was on the assault on poverty, there was nevertheless a strong political overtone, not, however, related to the politics of eliminating colonialism, but of resisting communism. By attacking poverty it was Mr. Spender's expectation that the possibility of the infiltration of the area by the communists would be reduced. Thus the conservative government gave notice that its policy in world affairs was anticommunist, a point Mr. Spender elaborated in his parliamentary statement, but that its opposition to communism was not to be expressed negatively. Rather it was to have as its positive expression systematic contributions to the strengthening of the economies of the Asian countries, a good in itself and a contribution to the frustration of communist progress. Australia was joined as sponsor of the scheme by New Zealand and Ceylon. It was quickly worked out institutionally and got to work.

As originally conceived, the Colombo Plan was a Commonwealth plan. However, it was never the intention that the benefiting nations should be only those Asian countries which were members of the Commonwealth. It was at an early stage extended to non-Commonwealth countries like Indonesia, Burma, and Thailand. It was also recognized from the beginning — even before the plan was actually presented at the Colombo conference — that the better-off Commonwealth countries could not hope to make a very powerful assault on Asian poverty from their own resources. To gain maximum effectiveness, the association of the United States with the plan was absolutely necessary. The United States joined the Colombo Plan organization late in 1951 and quickly became the principal financial supporter of it. At the Jogjakarta meeting of the Colombo Plan nations in 1959 it was stated that the United States had contributed 95 per cent of the total of six billion dollars expended. Originally launched in July 1951, the plan was intended to operate for five years. Its life was extended to 1961 in 1955 and to 1964 in 1959.

The year 1950 was by the accidents of history a year of decision for Australia and New Zealand in more ways than one. It was the year of the outbreak of the war between North and South Korea. By the accident that an Australian Air Force unit (the 77th Squadron) and a contingent of Australian ground troops were all that remained in Japan at that moment of the Commonwealth occupation troops, the Australians were the first to join the United States forces in resisting North Korean aggression. The 77th Squadron was asked by General MacArthur, while he was en route by air to Korea on June 28, 1950, if it could participate in the action. After reference to Australia for a decision, the request was honored and the Australians thus signalized that it was to be a United Nations action, not solely an American adventure. This year — 1950 — was also the year in which Australia and New Zealand deviated from British policy in Asia by following the United States in not recognizing Red China. Both withstood not only the force of the United Kingdom precedent of recognition but also Prime Minister Nehru's advocacy of recognition at the Colombo meeting of foreign ministers and the subsequent meeting of Commonwealth Prime Ministers in London in January 1951. It became obvious that Australia and New Zealand had a firm intention of adhering to the American line.

It was, however, the negotiation of a peace treaty with Japan that provided the opportunity for Australia to make a beginning toward the kind of Pacific Pact envisioned in 1950. The attitude of the Conservative Government toward Japan differed from that of Labour in fundamental respects: (a) it was prepared to see Japan resume a place as an industrial nation, self-supporting by production and trade, (b) it was prepared to accept the argument that in the existing posture of world affairs Japan could not remain a "power vacuum," (c) it was disposed to accept the argument that the "menacing" power in East Asia was now Communist China, not Japan, and (d) it was at least prepared to gamble that Japan, in response to influence from the United States, would opt for the "free world" and reject both neutralism and leaning toward communism. However, it was at one with Labour in its fear that a resurgent Japan would be an aggressive Japan and that therefore a treaty which placed no limitations on Japanese arms was undesirable, and it also felt that any failure to provide for reparations for damages and losses arising from Japan's aggression in World War II would be deplorable. At Colombo Australia agreed that Japan should be allowed to strive without any impediments created by the occupying powers to achieve economic viability, but stipulated that a treaty should "contain proper safeguards against any recurrence of Japanese aggression." The New Zealanders agreed. What Mr. Casey later called "the principal architects" of the eventual treaty — the United Kingdom and the United States — did not accept the Australian propositions. When the chief American negotiator, John Foster Dulles, visited Canberra in February 1951 — significantly, he was accompanied by Sir Esler Dening, subsequently United Kingdom Ambassador to Japan — for discussions of the text of the proposed treaty with the Australians (led by P. C. Spender) and the New Zealanders (led by by F. W. Doidge) who were highly critical of the kind of treaty suggested, the idea of a defense treaty between the United States, Australia, and New Zealand was suggested. The idea was evolved alongside the development of the Japanese peace treaty. In its final form it was signed at San Francisco on September 1, 1951, and ratified by the Australian Parliament in March 1952.

The ANZUS (Australian–New Zealand–United States) treaty was hotly criticized both by political leaders and newspapers in the United Kingdom because the United Kingdom was not a signatory of it and participant in it. While the allegation was freely made that the United States had deliberately and insistently excluded the United Kingdom, this was never authoritatively established. The Australians were excoriated for accepting the alleged American position, especially without any known protest. The British criticism was, however, but a nine-day wonder, and no move was made to include the United Kingdom. It would appear that the outburst was in part a kind of last stand of those Britishers who held to the idea that a dominion should not have treaty relations with a foreign power without United Kingdom participation, in part a protest against the implication that British power in the Pacific had indeed become sadly diminished. The oddest aspect of the whole affair was that it was Australian conservatives, led by an Imperialist Prime Minister, whose actions inspired the fuss and who were not shaken thereby in their determination to take independent action in the national Australian interest.

The questions arise as to whether the ANZUS treaty was in effect a *quid pro quo* for the signatures of Australia and New Zealand on a Japanese treaty they did not like, and if so, whether the United States got anything more tangible than the signatures from the ANZUS treaty. It must be recalled that the Australian conservatives came to office committed to a policy of increasing the intimacy of relations with the United States, with the outcome envisioned as involving a treaty. The ANZUS treaty was certainly in line with that policy, though it was neither as highly developed — that is, it did not include reference to economic and cultural considerations — nor as comprehensive in the coverage of associated nations, as the treaty originally suggested. But it was a significant beginning, and its administrative structure provided the means for Australian and New Zealand participation in discussion of defense strategy and tactics in the Pacific at the highest possible level. Moreover, since in its text it was made clear that it was not simply a guarantee against the possible consequences of a recurrence of Japanese aggression, but left the source of aggression vague, it was a treaty useful to Australia and New Zealand in any contingency directly involving them likely to arise out of the acknowledged unrest in South and East Asia. On the American side, the usefulness of the treaty was that it associated the United States with what World War II had proved to be, on the one hand, the principal sources of strength in the Southwest Pacific and, on the other, had also proved to be bases of infinite value in dealing with aggression originating in the Western Pacific. As inheritors of total responsibility in the Western Pacific, the Americans could hardly do less than to gain all the support, and take out all the insurance, in the general area they could gain or take out. ANZUS was both insurance and support for the United States.

True, the treaty was evolved in an unpredictable circumstance of which astute advantage was taken by the Australians and New Zealanders, but if it can be shown that the benefits were in the end mutual, then what to some may be a "birth-

stain" can properly be minimized. Some writers find it difficult
to see any mutual advantages arising from defense treaties made
between countries of obviously disparate power, as is so painfully the case between Australia, New Zealand, and the United
States. To such writers, the advantages of the ANZUS treaty
are all with the Australians and New Zealanders, hence their
disposition to emphasize the circumstances of its birth. But a
reasonably careful examination of the uses of Australia and
New Zealand as considerable and growing powers (especially
rapidly industrializing Australia), and as fairly well-secured
bases in a highly disturbed part of the world, considerably
diminishes the force of the disparagement. Especially is this
true if Australia and New Zealand conceive the obligations
under the treaty as reciprocal.

They do. As Prime Minister Menzies of Australia pointed out
in an article in *Foreign Affairs*, January 1952:

> . . . the obligations are not all one way. Article II says that, "in
> order more effectively to achieve the objective of this Treaty
> the parties separately and jointly by means of continuous and
> effective self-help and mutual aid will maintain and develop
> their individual and collective capacity to resist armed attack."
> After the treaty has come into effect, our Australian defense
> preparations are not merely our own business; we owe them
> also to our friends, without whose help we cannot hope to main-
> tain our freedom against a major challenge. In other words, our
> defense effort ceases to be of merely local significance, but be-
> comes part of the concerted efforts of the free world. Americans
> who fought alongside Australians in the southwest Pacific will
> know that we mean this, and we shall do our part.

ANZUS was never regarded as sufficient for their purposes
by the Australians, for in spite of the fact that it brought the
ties with the United States into acceptable formal order at the
level of defense, it did not deal directly with the problems of
Southeast Asia. The Australians were acutely aware that there
was a gap in defenses between Manila and Singapore, an area
of fatal weakness in World War II and equally important with
the shift of the designated aggressor to the continent of Asia.

This was precisely the area where the pressure of Communist China was most likely to be felt in the forseeable future. How to close the gap was a problem of great delicacy, for many of the nations which should in logic be equally concerned with the Australians to close it were skeptical of the Australian and American view that China was to be asumed to be imperialist in outlook. This was particularly true of India and countries of a similar international outlook, like Burma and Indonesia.

The Australians were keenly concerned to develop and maintain the best possible relations with all the countries of South and Southeast Asia; they did not want to do anything offensive to them. They carefully studied the currents of opinion in these countries, especially the sensitivities about outside interference in Asian affairs founded in their reaction to colonialism and all that that portmanteau word implies. Yet while the Australians sought good relations with the Asian states, they did not feel that this meant that they must conform their own policies to Asian policies, either in substance or resonance. They conceived themselves as a nation with a profound and highly sympathetic interest in and concern for the Asian states and their future, but not as a state destined from motives of self-preservation to be assimilated to the emerging Asian political system, either gradually or precipitately. Australia they thought of as a nation which was and would remain by force of geography a close neighbor of Asia, but nevertheless to be maintained as a state of Europo-American social and cultural character. Its policies should, by preference, be sympathetic to the Asian states in every respect in which this was possible, but if Australian interests dictated support of policies the Asians were little likely to regard with any enthusiasm as policies they themselves could adopt, the plunge had to be made. These considerations applied with particular force and relevance to the Australian desire for a comprehensive pact embracing themselves, the New Zealanders, all the Asian states, and the United States of America, which they saw as necessary to protect their own integrity and the integrity of the Asian nations.

No fruitful opportunity to discuss such a pact with the United States came until April 1954. The oportunity arose when the French position in Indo-China, challenged by the communists under Ho Chi Minh, began to deteriorate. Up to that point the United States had resisted all efforts to involve it in any treaty which included commitments on the continent of Asia. It believed its interests were wholly served by close relations with the friendly nations on the island periphery of Asia, with the single exception of South Korea. Even South Korea had at one stage been excluded from the American perimeter, but it had been restored by the assault upon it by the communists of North Korea.

It was the American acceptance of the necessity to "do something" about the situation in Indo-China that led on to the devising of a pact of the kind the Australians wanted. Its gestation was complicated by that situation. It was only after the Indo-China problem was taken to Geneva and "solved" there, in the end, by the personal diplomacy of Prime Minister Mendès-France of France, that the pact the Australians wanted became a real possibility. Here again the Australians were enabled to get a pact in which their own and American interests coalesced by virtue of taking astute advantage of an unpredictable circumstance. The result was the South-East Asia Collective Defense Treaty, signed at Manila in the Philippines on September 8, 1954. The signatories were Australia, New Zealand, the United States, the United Kingdom, France, the Philippines, Thailand, and Pakistan. Laos, Cambodia, and South Vietnam were named as "designated" states to bring them under the protection of the treaty although they were not signatories of it. This was done as a warning to the communists not to try to upset the Geneva settlement by force. The pact came into force on February 19, 1955. The "treaty area" was defined as "the general area of Southeast Asia, including also the entire territories of the Asian Parties and the general area of the Southwest Pacific," but not including "the Pacific areas north of 21 degrees 39 minutes north latitude." The last phrase excluded

Hong Kong, Formosa, and so on. The treaty was so drawn as to provide for a permanent secretariat and the development of an organization: hence the designation "South East Asia Treaty Organization," SEATO. Its headquarters were established at Bangkok.

To insure that a satisfactory treaty could be drawn the Australians had to make a policy revolution, described and justified by Prime Minister Menzies in a statement to the House of Representatives on August 5, 1954:

> Honorable Members will have observed that preparations are now in hand for political conferences, in association with necessary military planning, to establish a South-Eastern Asia Defense Organization. It does not yet exist, nor is its prospective membership defined. We hope sincerely that when it is seen that the creation of such an organization is designed to help preserve the national integrity of Asian countries as well as those which are not Asian, some, I would hope all, of those Asian countries will be willing to participate. I emphasize in plain terms that this is not a question of color or race. It is a question of the maintenance of democratic freedom. But, so far as we are concerned in Australia, we must determine our own attitude and put it beyond doubt. We will become contributing parties. We will in association with other nations acting similarly accept military obligations in support of our membership.
>
> In the past it has been one of the traditions of Australian Government that commitments are not accepted in advance; that such matters are for determination of the Government and Parliament if and when the event of war occurs. There are sound reasons to explain why this should have been the tradition. In the two great world wars, Australia had an opportunity to decide what she was going to do and enough time to assemble, train, equip and dispatch armed forces. We cannot gamble upon this being our position any longer. If there is one thing that seems clear, it is that there will be no pause, no long period of stalemate, should the Communists determine to attack. All of the most dreadful instruments of war designed by man will be employable and employed. The first few months — indeed, the first few weeks — might do much to determine the issue.
>
> It is for these reasons that we have decided that in any great defensive organization of the kind envisaged, we must accept

military commitments. Honorable Members will not need to be persuaded by me that for us, as a democratic nation vitally at risk in these seas, to expect our great friends to accept commitments while our own attitude remained tentative and conditional, would be utterly inconsistent with the intelligence, character and record of our country.*

It was the Australian hope that the SEATO treaty would "have some economic provisions." In a statement before the negotiations began, Mr. Casey said:

If there is to be a healthy political life in South-East Asia, there must be a healthy economic life. We must sustain and if possible increase the flow of economic aid into South-East Asia, and, when possible, play a part in easing the economic difficulties of the region. At the same time, however, Australia does not want the Colombo Plan superseded. We want to keep economic aid separate from defense machinery.†

This was in accordance with the policy toward Asia announced by Mr. Spender in 1950 and first implemented by the Colombo Plan. In the Manila treaty, Article III provided: "The Parties undertake to strengthen their free institutions and to cooperate with one another in the further development of economic measures, designed both to promote economic progress and social well-being and to further the individual and collective efforts of governments toward these ends." As time passed, interchanges of a cultural nature were encouraged under the Treaty. And a phrase in Article II noted the problems raised by subversive activities across international boundaries: "to prevent and counter subversive activities directed from without against their territorial integrity and political stability." In time, preoccupation with subversion became almost central to the SEATO associates.

The Manila treaty was regarded neither as superseding nor as a substitute for the ANZUS treaty. The only true connection

* Quoted in R. G. Casey, *Friends and Neighbors* (East Lansing, Michigan, 1955), pp. 106–107.
† Quoted in Casey, *Friends and Neighbors*, pp. 108–109.

between them was the fact that the parties to ANZUS were also parties to SEATO. Yet it cannot be overlooked that they complement one another in relation to both Australian-New Zealand and American interests. In an important sense, more-over, SEATO represents an extension of Australian purposes in a direction Australia has sought to move since 1950. But even with SEATO Australia is still far from its objective and is likely to be so as long as Asian states give allegiance to the principles of neutralism. When in 1955 the Australian Govern-ment sent air force and ground troops into Malaya, then still a British colony, to assist in dealing with Communist "bandits," it was extending its commitments in Asia, but not within the ambit of SEATO, even though it obtained the tacit assent of the United States before doing so. It was rather extending its commitments as a member of the British Commonwealth. And although Australian and New Zealand forces have remained in Malaya since it has achieved dominion status (1957), as late as November 10, 1959, reflecting the influence of India and Indo-nesia, Prime Minister Tengku Abdul Rahman of Malaya stated in Melbourne, while on an official visit to Australia, that Ma-laya was unlikely to join SEATO. The prospects of extending the treaty system to other Asian states than those who signed the Manila Treaty therefore continue to be poor. On the other hand, the Australians can take satisfaction in the fact that the Malayans have spoken of their feeling of having a "special rela-tion" with Australia and New Zealand as the easternmost mem-bers of the Commonwealth.

If the Australians had not succeeded in realizing their policy aspirations in detail, they had gone a considerable distance toward realizing them and appeared, in the middle fifties, to have established an equilibrium in their relations with the United Kingdom, the United States, the Asian countries, and the United Nations that must have given them satisfaction. In 1956 this equilibrium was violently upset by the Suez episode and subsequently a good deal of energy had to be put into re-storing the *status quo ante*.

There were so many factors involved in the Suez affair that it is difficult to deal with it summarily only in those aspects that impinged upon relations with the United States. The crisis in Australian affairs induced by Suez was, in one aspect, a consequence of embracing too fervently one horn of the Anzac dilemma — the United Kingdom horn. The act of embracement was, I think, supported by the strongest of Australian traditions, and emotions, in foreign policy — support of Britain — and deeply infused with the nostalgia, not only for the easier, simpler days before the complexity of "balancing" occasioned by the dilemma showed themselves, when support of Britain was not only by policy automatic, but hardly likely to be questioned, and repercussions on relations with the United States were not a consideration, but also for the conditions of the nineteenth century when the use of force in the support of national policies considered "right," if self-judged "right" by the country initiating them, was normal, and moreover an established way of asserting and fortifying prestige. This emphasis on the factor of nostalgia in the Australian adventure is given additional force when it is recalled that the architect of Australia's Suez policy was Prime Minister Menzies, not the experienced Minister of External Affairs, R. G. Casey, for Mr. Menzies is, in one of his guises, an old-fashioned Imperial patriot with a liking, often commented on by political writers, for playing the "crusted conservative." It is also borne out by the fact that the sentiment that at Suez the United Kingdom was acting, thank God, like the old Britain of sacred tradition, found expression in some Australian newspapers. *Pax Britannia* had been revived. New Zealand went along with Australia, similarly under the influence of nostalgia.*

This way of putting the matter is more than an escape from

---

* Two important Australian post-mortems on Suez are Professor W. Macmahon Ball's article in *The Australian Journal of Politics and History* for May 1957 and Professor Norman Harper's article in Greenwood and Harper, eds., *Australia in World Affairs 1950–1955* (Melbourne, 1957). A New Zealand discussion is E. A. Olssen's article in the quarterly *Landfall*, no. 41, March 1957.

the task of reviewing the Suez story step by step, bringing in such questions as whether or not American policy in the Middle East had been ignorant, inconsistent, pro-Nasser, et cetera, whether or not John Foster Dulles merited Anthony Eden's personal distaste for him, or even whether or not Suez was a life-or-death issue for Britain.

What Mr. Menzies forgot throughout the Suez episode was that by supporting the Eden policy and, in doing so, justifying the use of force by unilateral decision, disparaging the United Nations, alienating Asian states, and embarrassing intra-Commonwealth relations, and getting far off-side from the United States, he was isolating Australia and ignoring the realities of its world position. Instead of thinking about how to keep all the balls of Australian foreign policy in proper relationship in the air, he allowed all but two to clatter to the floor: the United Kingdom and New Zealand. He did not even have the satisfaction of supporting a united United Kingdom, either in Cabinet, Parliament, or press, though this probably figured little in his calculations at the time.

The real significance of Suez in Australia–New Zealand–United States relations was, then, that by following Britain Australia and New Zealand alienated themselves for the time being from the United States. The episode was a cathartic experience for those in the two countries who felt an uncomfortable dis-ease about their national alignment with the United States, who enjoyed a more or less euphoric escape into a past when Britain was all that really mattered. Such flights from reality are necessarily costly in the world all parties equally inhabit. They are not, of course, really necessary as other Commonwealth nations — for example, India and Canada — demonstrated at the time. But they are temporarily comforting to troubled spirits. However, as long as global affairs remain in their present menacing posture, the Anzac dilemma is not going to be exorcised by pretending it doesn't exist. It still demands of those who confront it that they learn to live with it, inescapably in a continuous state of tension, a condition many understandably find it hard, and some utterly impossible, to endure. Suez in a remarkable way confirmed both the reality and the inescapability of that tension. The Australian Minister for External Affairs, R. G. Casey, carried out the "repair job" on Australian–United States relations after Suez with full knowledge of that fact.*

* Since Mr. Menzies, with a romantic persistence characteristic of him, still supports Anthony Eden's Suez policy, though he agrees it was not a success, we do not really know how he interprets the episode today. He acquiesced, of course, in the repairing of Australian–American relations and indeed has on occasion spoken of the United States with rhetorical warmth. On Suez apropos Sir Anthony Eden's book *Full Circle*, see his article in *The Age* newspaper of Melbourne, February 29, 1960.

17. New Zealand's Position

Since the coming into force of the Australian–New Zealand Agreement of 1944 there has always been the risk for the New Zealanders that they may be regarded as having surrendered the initiative in foreign policy to the far more aggressive Australians. Correctly understood, however, the agreement provided for consultation, not surrender. Paragraphs 38 to 42 inclusive of the agreement define the machinery. As there defined it was to consist of a Secretariat with offices in both countries attached to the offices of the High Commissioners. Formal conferences with attendant publicity were envisaged as exceptional; the routine was to be carried on through the Secretariat. There have been no formal conferences in recent years and as the work of the Secretariat is secret, it is not known what has gone on. As much of the policy enunciated in the agreement is now passé and some of it dead and irrelevant, it is difficult to draw any conclusions about current policy commitments from it.

It would appear, however, that the Australians hold the initiative in policy making. Significant differences are few. One difference is over recognition of Red China, to which the Labour Prime Minister Walter Nash is favorably disposed and Prime Minister Menzies' government is not. But Nash does not seem resolute to act on his own on this matter. Another difference is over Antarctica. The New Zealanders have long been more actively advocates of the internationalization of Antarctica than ever the Australians have been. If the Australians seem to hold the initiative in policy making, that is largely because, vis-à-vis the New Zealanders, they are the more substantial power, but since the problems with which they must perforce deal, whether rooted in geography, economics, politics, or culture, are fairly identical with those confronting the New Zealanders, though in many cases either inherently more urgent to the Australians, or evaluated by them as more urgent, it is rather improbable that the Australians would evolve a line fundamentally objectionable to the New Zealanders. It is highly significant that the process of consultation has now gone on through changes in the political character of the governments of both countries — from Labour to Conservative in Australia, from Labour to Conservative and back to Labour in New Zealand — with no apparent diminution of the considerable area of ready agreement.

A careful reading of the following paragraphs from *Report of the Department of External Affairs for the year ended 31 March 1959* (Wellington, 1959) will convey to the sensitive reader something of the subtleties of the New Zealand attitude at the official level. The reference is not to defense but to the politics of defense.

New Zealand's defence policy has never been purely or even predominantly local in character, and the battles fought to defend this country have invariably taken place far from its shores. In the past, our defence policy was so closely related to that of the United Kingdom as to be in all but its purely local aspects, a part of a single overall plan to guard the British Empire . . . The spread of war to the Pacific in 1941 brought something like a revolution in New Zealand's military thinking . . . These events underlined the necessity for closer contact between New Zealand and the United States on political and defence matters, and led to the establishment for the first time of direct diplomatic relations between New Zealand and a foreign country.

It is not to be expected that any future war will be fought on the pattern of the past. The areas of most concern to New Zealand in the future will almost certainly be the Pacific and South-East Asia and it is towards these theatres that our defence planning and commitments are now principally directed. New Zealand's defence policy is therefore no longer exclusively oriented to that of the United Kingdom, although, through the military working arrangement known as ANZAM, Australian, New Zealand and United Kingdom military authorities continue to work in the closest cooperation. It is significant that Australia and the United States belong to both of the regional collective defence treaties to which New Zealand has become a party since the end of the Second World War, ANZUS and SEATO. It is inevitable that in the changed strategic situation New Zealand, while continuing to cooperate as closely as possible with the United Kingdom, should look more and more to Australia, with its growing defence industry, and to the United States, both accessible sources of supply in time of war, for military equipment and training in the use of that equipment, and should seek to widen the basis of its defence planning accordingly.

. . . It follows that New Zealand's defence policy now has a larger foreign policy content than in the past. Negotiations on defence matters with foreign and Commonwealth Governments form an increasing part of the Department's work, and are likely to continue to do so.

Here we have fairly obviously conveyed New Zealand's continuing preference for the historical collaboration with the United Kingdom and the United Kingdom alone and the implication that it is the Australians who took the initiative in linking up with the United States, the New Zealanders apparently going along because of their increasing dependence on Australia in the first instance. Naturally the continuing link with the United Kingdom is emphasized. Naturally, too, the link with the United States is displaced from a primary to a secondary, perhaps a tertiary, position, after those with the United Kingdom and Australia.

This supports this observer's opinion that the New Zealanders have been consistently more reluctant than the Australians to accept the logic of their position in the Pacific as it has been defined since World War II. The New Zealanders have been far more reluctant than the Australians to accept in their hearts (as against their heads) the fact that their security can no longer be guaranteed within the Commonwealth alone. Their

heads tell them that this is the dreadful case. Hence they must
have some arrangement with the United States. But in their
hearts they deplore the necessity. Nostalgia for the good old
days of Pax Britannica is a far larger component of their foreign-political outlook than it is for the Australians, though
goodness knows it is an active ingredient for the Australians,
too. It is traditional with the New Zealanders to look west and
northwest from their islands, first toward Australia and, hurry-
ing on, to the United Kingdom. It was no particular wrench
to them to develop their association with the Australians, although the intimacy of that association has fluctuated over the
years since the British took sovereignty in New Zealand in 1840,
but the New Zealanders are well aware that the Australians
themselves are not, out of their own resources, able to meet
the challenge of a major power and are therefore themselves
ultimately dependent upon outside help for survival. Australia
can provide no final solution for New Zealand's security problem and only help with any of its other problems. In a decisive
crisis, as a matter of fact, the help Australia might be able to
give New Zealand might at best be very little, dictated perhaps
by the significance of New Zealand to the defense of Australia.
Thus even if New Zealand can shore up her security by association with Australia, she cannot wholly insure it by doing so. She
must look elsewhere. The traditional reinsurer has been, of
course, the United Kingdom. It has also been the traditional
reinsurer of Australia. The fact that the United Kingdom has
suffered a sharp diminution of capacity to reinsure either has
therefore confronted both with a dilemma — Professor Wood's
Anzac dilemma. The dilemma is only controllable by association with a power outside the Commonwealth: the United
States. This is the terrible logic of the situation. But the New
Zealanders have found acceptance of the logic far more uncomfortable than have the Australians, for although the Australians, as has been amply illustrated, and will be adverted to
again, have struggled with the task of reconciling continued
"loyalty" to Britain with intimate relations with the United

States, they have at least faced up to it in a bravura fashion, while the New Zealanders have been much beset by highly obvious doubts and hesitations. When Prime Minister Harold Macmillan of the United Kingdom was in New Zealand in 1958 he found it necessary to say:

> There are some who feel that the pact which New Zealand and Australia made with the United States has somehow weakened your links with us. But to my mind this argument has no force at all; for when members of a family make new friends there is no loosening of family ties . . . Upon the close co-operation and alliance of the Commonwealth and the United States almost everything today depends.

It is unlikely that even these reassuring words wholly resolved the disquiet in the minds of many New Zealanders. Heart and head will probably go right on warring.

In the position the New Zealanders confront, it is largely an irrelevance whether they "like" — or love — the Americans and the United States.* The craving so many Americans have to be loved by all foreigners with whom they have political-defensive relations is exceedingly tiresome, jejune, unhistorical. Since when have top-dogs ever been loved? Were the British loved during their ascendancy in the nineteenth century — even within the Empire? They were at best respected, not loved. The point is, surely, that the New Zealanders recognize the

---

* In a recent book on the New Zealanders, *The Fern and the Tiki*, by Professor David Ausubel of the University of Illinois (Sydney, 1960), the question of what New Zealanders think of Americans is labored but the discussion is largely vitiated by the undeclared assumption that they should love the Americans and himself as personifying them. Why? Much of Professor Ausubel's evidence based on personal experiences I can counter by my own personal experiences. When in a foreign country Americans should guard against identifying a reaction to them specifically with a reaction to Americans generically. It may also be pointed out that many of Ausubel's criticisms of aspects of New Zealand life could have been documented by reference to identical or parallel criticisms by New Zealanders. He did not cite these writings. Why? After all he objects strenuously to New Zealanders dwelling critically on aspects of American life to which Americans themselves have rancorous objection.

realities of international affairs and establish a proper political-defensive relation with the United States. This they have done, if reluctantly. United States–New Zealand relations are in good order today.

18. What of the Islands?

It can hardly be said that the United States government has a policy toward the islands of the Southwest Pacific. It has, however, at least three direct involvements in the islands: through its possession of American Samoa, through its participation in the South Pacific Commission (originally because of its possession of American Samoa but since 1951 because it has also associated its Trust Territory in Micronesia with the Commission), and through trade, ocean shipping, and air services. It might also be argued that the continuing concern of American anthropologists, academically located from Hawaii to the Atlantic coast, is also an interest, and even that the far less pronounced concern of the similarly scattered American geographers, historians, and writers of fiction and nonfiction is an interest. Its concern in island defense questions is presumably chiefly satisfied by knowledge of what the New Zealanders are committed to in Fiji and Samoa and the Australians in their territories.

However it can hardly be said that any nation has a comprehensive, carefully articulated policy toward the islands as a collectivity, or area, at the present time. Rather it is the case that the distribution of the island groups among the several sovereignties and administrations results in definitions of policy only in relation to the islands for which the particular nation is responsible. Such coordination of policy across sovereignty lines as occurs is minimal, as through the South Pacific Commission, the arrangements between the Australians and the Dutch in New Guinea, or the relations between New Zealand and the Fijian administration with regard to defense, education, and medical services. A vaguer coordinating influence is the general, if imprecise, acceptance of the trusteeship principal by all the nations, regardless of whether or not the islands for which they are responsible are actually trusteeships under the United Nations.

The South Pacific Commission took its origin from the Australian–New Zealand Agreement of 1944, Paragraphs 28 to 31 inclusive. It came into formal existence in 1947, with headquarters at Noumea, New Caledonia. The position of the Commission vis-à-vis the governments who maintain membership in it (Australia, France, The Netherlands, New Zealand, the United Kingdom, and the United States, responsible all told for eighteen separate island administrations) is advisory and consultative. It is chiefly concerned with social, economic, and health matters, and much of its work takes the form of research carried on, when this is obviously required, across the political boundaries, which issues in technical advice to the various administrations. The Commission cooperates with national and international institutions of a considerable range: for example in a recent year, with the Australian Commonwealth Library, Canberra, the Bernice P. Bishop Museum, Honolulu, the Institut de Recherches sur les Huiles et Oléagineux, Paris, the United States Department of Agriculture, Washington, and United Nations organizations such as UNESCO, WHO, and FAO. The Commission is thus not only an international organization itself but also it is an organization which brings to focus in the islands the interests and services of other international, and national, organizations. It complements its routine activities with occasional conferences of island peoples. It is an organization that year after year approaches the islands as an area. It is not, however, designed to promote the idea that the islands should be thought of areally, least of all to lead on to a comprehensive areal authority, organized federally or in any other way. The participation of the United States in the Commission does not define an American policy toward the area. It merely signifies that the United States is favorably disposed to the Commission's approach to the technical problems with which it deals.

The area approach today can only be made by more or less playing down, or ignoring, the division of the islands among the six sovereignties and eighteen administrations, or precisely the principal obstacle to the area approach. This reduces the political utility of such an approach and certainly discourages the formulation of an islands policy. It should not, however, discourage the promotion of the area approach as such. In fact there is reason to suppose that it is going to be increasingly required if the problems of the islands are going to be brought under control. It is an indispensable intellectual tool; it provides an indispensable frame of reference. But today there is little apparent disposition on the part of the metropolitan powers, including Australia and New Zealand, to think beyond the groups for which they are politically responsible. Australia and New Zealand appear to be in a trough of the wave of their traditional general interest in the islands.

Obviously, then, there is little active foreign political interest in the islands on the part of the United States government. It is characteristic that with regard to the only active international dispute in the islands — that between the Dutch and the Indonesians over Irian in New Guinea, in which the Australians support the Dutch — the United States maintains a position of neutrality. It may be supposed that the United States government is officially informed about the political developments in Western Samoa, which is to become independent in 1961, for they have an impact upon the politics of American Samoa, but what cognizance is taken in Washington of the complicated crisis in Fiji, of developments of a political and economic character in Australian Papua–New Guinea, or of developments in the French islands is impossible to say.

As these remarks suggest, all is not quiet on the island front. The several administrations all face problems of an economic or political character, or both intertwined, of varying degrees of difficulty. In dealing with some of the problems of an economic character, the help of international agencies like the Colombo Plan, the International Bank, or a derivative lending institution of the Bank, may become indispensable. In that case, the United States may perforce define an attitude. It will presumably be sympathetic and helpful, but how knowledgeable and in what frame of reference is impossible to say.

19. Antarctica

From the time of the Wilkes expedition to the Antarctic in the early eighteen-forties until the late nineteen-twenties, the Americans took little active, though some theoretical, interest in Antarctica. Matthew Fontaine Maury, the great student of ocean winds and currents, contributed notably to keeping alive an interest in Antarctica, but efforts by anybody to investigate the area at first hand were uncommon until the end of the nineteenth century. To be sure, it was an American ship sailing according to Maury's ideas that discovered Heard Island in 1853 while carrying passengers to the Australian gold rush, and it was an American sealing party that, a few years later, was the first ever to winter on the island. An American expedition to observe a transit of Venus visited the Isles de Kerguelen in 1874–75. And an American subsequently involved in controversy damaging to his reputation, Dr. Frederick A. Cook, was with the famous Belgian expedition of 1897–1899 under Adrian de Gerlache. But before the Americans were able to return in force to Antarctica the classic expeditions, like those of Scott, Shackleton, Amundsen, Charcot, Drygalski, Nordenskjold, and Mawson, were already history.

By the time the Americans returned the Australians had established a brilliant tradition of activity in the far south, largely as individuals attached to British expeditions, but with official and unofficial financial, scientific and moral support

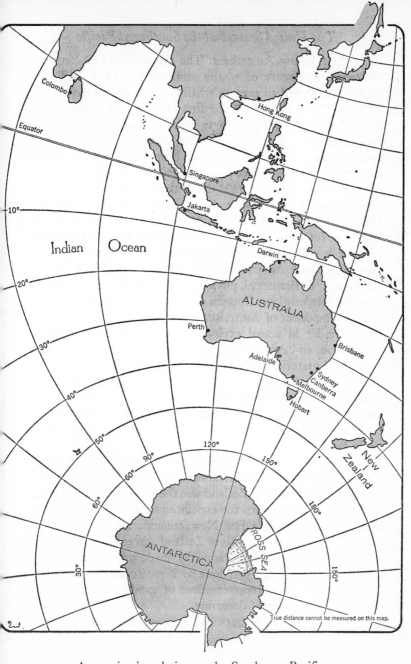

Antarctica in relation to the Southwest Pacific

from their fellow Australians. The Australians had long encouraged the pursuit of whales south of 60°. H. J. Bull's expedition, designed to explore whaling resources, to Antarctica in 1894–95, during which the first landing was made on the main Antarctic continent, was originally projected in Australia and took off from Melbourne, though it was in the end financed by Sven Foyn, the great Norwegian whaler, and is ordinarily classed as a Norwegian expedition. And C. E. Borchgrevink's expedition of 1898–1900, the first to winter on the continent — at Cape Adare — was, while officially classed as British, closely associated with Australia, where Borchgrevink had lived for some years as a schoolteacher. From these beginnings it is possible to trace a tradition of close association of Australians with Antarctic exploration and to list such famous names as L. C. Bernacchi, physicist to the Borchgrevink and the first Scott expeditions, Douglas Mawson (subsequently the outstanding exponent of Australia's scientific interest in Antarctica and a leader in actual exploration of the stature of Scott, Shackleton, and Amundsen), and Edgeworth David, who first went to Antarctica with Shackleton in 1908, Griffith Taylor and Frank Debenham, who went with the second Scott Expedition, on which Scott met his death, and so on right down to the present day. David and Mawson, Australians, with a Scottish collaborator, were the first to reach the South Magnetic Pole.

The New Zealand association, which began with Captain Cook, was until much later almost entirely geographical, based upon the fact that New Zealand was the ideal jumping-off place and point of first return for expeditions utilizing the Ross Sea entryway. However, a few New Zealanders were staff members of expeditions; the New Zealand government and individual New Zealanders occasionally made grants and gifts to expeditions, and much was done by New Zealanders in a managerial way as local representatives of expeditions using New Zealand as the point of departure.

The identification of both Australia and New Zealand with

Antarctica was given greater official formality when Great Britain transferred to these countries large segments of the continent hitherto assumed to be British, which it was now thought wise to associate more directly with a claimant. By an Order in Council dated July 30, 1923, that part of Antarctica "between the 160th degree of east longitude and the 150th degree of west longitude which are situated south of the 60th degree of south latitude," called the Ross Dependency of New Zealand (770,000 square miles), was placed under the jurisdiction of New Zealand, and on February 7, 1933, an even vaster area, described as "all the islands and territories other than Adelie Land which are situated south of the 60th degree of South Latitude and lying between the 160th degree of East Longitude and the 45th degree of East Longitude" (2,472,000 square miles), was transferred to Australia.

All this was of great interest to the Americans after they resumed, in the late nineteen-twenties, their activities in Antarctica, for they then began to use New Zealand as *their* principal point of final departure and first return and also did much of their actual work on the continent in New Zealand's Ross Dependency. After World War II, this association grew in intimacy. However, in accordance with its policy, the United States did not extend recognition to the territorial claims of either Australia or New Zealand. The exemplary figure in promoting and directing American activities in Antarctica from 1928 to 1947 was Richard E. Byrd.

As American activities in Antarctica have increased since Byrd initiated the American return there in 1928, so have the common interests of all parties. The activities of all have markedly increased since the close of World War II. This is particularly true of American Antarctic activities that involve New Zealand, for the Americans have come to use the Ross Sea area as their principal, but not exclusive, point of entry to Antarctica, and this is not only in the sector to which New Zealand lays claim, but is normally approached by using a New Zealand port or airfield as the final point of departure from civilization. American activities have also been extended into Australian-claimed territory to the west of the New Zealand sector, but this has involved little activity in the Australian homeland. Although the United States does not recognize any national claims to possession of portions of Antarctica, which diminishes in American eyes the significance of the point that they have carried on activities in claimed territory (even, in recent years, to the extent of building "permanent" facilities), it has long been the practice of the claimants to grant the Americans *pro forma*, unsolicited permission to do so. The difference of views on claims is all that divides the three countries, but it has consistently been kept in the background of relations, except when there has been compelling reason publicly to "reserve" a claim.

The American disposition latterly to make its activities in Antarctica continuous has made its relations with New Zealand vis-à-vis Antarctica more important. In 1958 they were regularized in an "exchange of notes constituting an agreement between the Government of New Zealand and the Government of the United States regarding the provision of facilities in New Zealand for United States Antarctic expeditions." The exchange involved a letter in which was enclosed a "Memorandum of Understandings" sent by Prime Minister Walter Nash to the American Ambassador in New Zealand on December 24, 1958, and the Ambassador's acknowledgement.

The substance of the "Memorandum" in part reflects the kind of problems which arise when the United States establishes a base in the territory of another sovereign nation. There are provisions covering the handling of "offences against New Zealand law" and the handling of "meritorious claims for loss or damage caused by acts or omissions (whether committed on or off duty) of United States personnel" and New Zealanders in American employ. Provision is also made for waiving passport, visa, and immigration laws and regulations, for exempting from taxes and customs duties goods imported into and exported from New Zealand for use in Antarctic operations by the Americans, exempting American personnel from New Zealand income taxes, and so on. But the most interesting passages are such as the following:

> The New Zealand Government will provide as far as possible facilities in New Zealand requested by the United States authorities in connection with United States operations in Antarctica. It agrees to the establishment of operational headquarters in New Zealand [at Christchurch] and to the transit of United States personnel, ships and aircraft through New Zealand. United States personnel may be accommodated in New Zealand and United States aircraft may be based at agreed airports within New Zealand.
>
> The New Zealand Government agrees to the establishment and operation of a military and affiliate radio station in New Zealand by the United States authorities, under arrangements to be made with the Royal New Zealand Air Force.

And the reciprocation provided for thus:

> The Government of the United States of America for its part will provide as far as possible logistic support requested by the New Zealand authorities in connection with New Zealand operations in Antarctica.*

The reciprocation clause was, as a matter of fact, a way of stating in formal fashion a helpful relationship the Americans had already established upon the entry of the New Zealanders into active participation in the work in Antarctica for the first time during the Geophysical Year.

Because of the circumstance that no American expedition to the Far South since that of Charles Wilkes in 1840 has used an Australian port as a point of departure, nor until lately worked much in the Australian sector of Antarctica, the relations of the United States and Australia with regard to Antarctica

---

* The foregoing quotations are from "Exchange of Notes constituting an Agreement between the Government of New Zealand and the Government of the United States of America regarding the Provision of Facilities in New Zealand for United States Antarctic Expeditions," New Zealand Treaty Series 1958, no. 2 (N.Z. External Affairs Publication no. 188).

have been of a different character from those with New Zealand, though not less friendly. Australia has done far more than New Zealand to secure its territorial claim in Antarctica, including the extension of the law of the Australian Capital Territory to the sector and active scientific and exploratory work since 1947, though not in a fashion or with an effect disturbing to its relation with the United States. Starting as far back as Sir Douglas Mawson's expedition of 1911–1914, there has been steady cooperation on the scientific side and since World War II frequent exchange of personnel. Sir George Wilkins, who made the first airplane flight in Antarctica in 1928, backed by American money (as indeed were so many of his explorations and adventures), was an Australian. When in 1935 Lincoln Ellsworth made his celebrated flight, in stages, from Dundee Island to the Bay of Whales, where he was temporarily marooned, he was succored by the British research ship *Discovery II* at the instance of the Prime Minister of Australia and was taken to Australia for a twelve-day visit. Ellsworth subsequently — in 1939 — surveyed by air what he called "American Highland" back of the Ingrid Christensen Coast in the Australian sector and ended his expedition at Hobart, where his ship was sold. During the International Geophysical Year the Americans established a station called "Wilkes" in the Australian sector. In 1958 they turned over this station entirely to the Australians as a gesture of good will, and it is now operated as an integral part of the Australian group. (As to Charles Wilkes, the Australians have, by their exploratory and mapping activities along the continental coast Wilkes said he saw in 1840, gone far to vindicate Wilkes against his numerous and often scornful critics of the last twelve decades.)* The Americans are, it goes without saying, active and willing cooperators with the Australians in all scientific activities. By way of illustration, they cooperate with the weather analysis center and

* See p. 1 of the *New York Times* January 10, 1960. When I visited the office of the Director of National Mapping at Canberra in April 1960 I was shown other maps that further vindicate Wilkes.

the teleprinter and radio-telephone center for Antarctica, both of which have headquarters at Melbourne.

Australia and New Zealand were signatories late in 1959 of the American-sponsored treaty demilitarizing Antarctica and reserving it for exclusively scientific uses. But whereas New Zealand announced at the beginning of the formal negotiations that it "would be prepared to consider the relinquishment of national rights and claims in Antarctica if such a step towards the establishment of a wider regime were generally agreed," in accordance with their policy favoring internationalization, the Australians were among those powers that reserved their territorial claims before entering into negotiations. The treaty concluded did not affect claims but rather put them, very appropriately, into a kind of diplomatic cold-storage where, it is probable, they will remain until the resources of the continent are revealed and it is feasible to begin their active exploitation, or where they will perhaps wither away entirely. It is not, however, the presence of the Americans in Antarctica, even as the disposers of by far the most elaborate exploratory and scientific equipment, and the most numerous personnel, yet taken to the continent, that has disturbed the Australians, but rather the presence of the nearest competitor of the United States in scale of activities, the U.S.S.R. And the U.S.S.R. all the more so since its stations have all been set up in the Australian sector. The treaty will dissipate such fears.

20. Final Thoughts

Situated as they are, and culturally, politically, and economically related to the world scene as they are, the Australians and New Zealanders are keenly aware of their implication in world politics in their widest expression. Nevertheless, as has been made clear earlier, they tend to focus much of their attention upon the Near North and to calculate their national future in relation to their expectations, their hopes and fears, about that part of the world. Unfortunately much Australian thinking about the Near North is in terms of the "population explosion" and an anticipated swarming of peoples, a peculiarly alarming business to amateur commentators, introducing *fear* as a basic constituent of their thinking, always a disaster to rationality. Unfortunately too, many in both countries who are articulate on the subject are sentimental leftists quite incapable of an objective evaluation of communism as a political force in the world and not too sure that communism is not preferable to American capitalism. A current academic concern is with the development of expertise about the Near North — its geography, history, politics, economics, languages, its past and current condition generally. The New Zealanders are stirring in this respect also. Neither country has as yet gone any great distance in this direction and the stream of information flowing to the general public is shallow and murky indeed. (This is not to imply that the United States is vastly better off in this regard.) American foreign policy is often evaluated most urgently in terms of its impact upon the Near North, and irritation with American policy generally is often no more than a reflex of an expressed, or unexpressed, vote of "no confidence" in American policy in Asia. The "no confidence" vote is usually related to the political outlook of the person giving it, not to superior knowledge of Asia. However, skepticism of American insight into the problems of South and East Asia is fairly widespread. Expectations of disaster are associated with a fear of some monumental American blunder which will, so to speak, bring the Near North down on Australia's head. American action in, and with regard to, the Near North is, therefore, closely watched indeed.

A besetting fear of the Australians is that when it comes to the pinch, no assistance will be forthcoming from the United States, treaty or no treaty. Any statement by any American that can be interpreted to support this conclusion, whether accurately or not, is sure of wide publicity in Australia. The Australians cannot easily be persuaded that the basic purpose of the United States is to prevent the development of a situation in the Near North out of which a direct attack on Australia could possibly emerge. It is axiomatic, surely, that an attack on Australia could come only out of a radically deteriorated situation in the Near North. Nobody can confidently forecast that such a situation will *never* emerge, but surely it is the task of all hands — the Asians, the Americans, and the Australians — to try to prevent its emergence. This is fundamentally a task in political, economic, and cultural relations. The role of arms is as insurance against potentially disastrous contingent developments. But surely it is a distorted view to insist in advance that the effort at solving the problems of the Near North by peaceful means is certainly going to fail and to place all the emphasis on obtaining a guarantee that in the case of failure the Americans will defend Australia. Even an amateur analysis of the lineaments of the crisis from which an attack on Australia could emerge, leads inexorably to the conclusion that the world situation would then be completely out of American or anybody else's control. Australians must surely concede that the Americans are no more able to guarantee what they will be able to do in the face of such a devastating disaster in the Near North than the British were in the early nineteen-forties. They will, it must be assumed, do the best they can within the confines of a total situation of which the attack on Australia will be a part.

On the other hand, there is certainly on the American side great need of far closer attention to the uses of Australia as an ally which has, after all the chatter dies away, identical purposes in the Near North — that is, the promotion of economic progress and political stability — and of its uses as a base in the Western Pacific. All too often the so-called strategic foothold of the United States in Asia is assessed by Americans without any reference to Australia whatever. All too often Americans do not take Australia into account in their thinking about Asia — strategic, political, economic, cultural. They have not yet intensively explored the full meaning of Australia as an associate in the Western Pacific. Americans have, unfortunately, a powerful tendency to revert to the conception that relations with the Western Pacific and Asia are best thought of exclusively in terms of "across the North Pacific" only, thus placing the Southwest Pacific in a peripheral position in their thinking or outside it altogether.

It is true that from the American point of view, the Southwest Pacific has historically been a peripheral, not a central concern, in the context of the Pacific, let alone in a global perspective. Australian writers on relations with the United States warn their countrymen that they are still today only a peripheral interest and concern to the Americans. They point out that the impact of the United States around the world has increased since World War II and allege that the Southwest Pacific has simply received its roughly proportionate share of that increase. They point out that American interests are global and Australia and New Zealand are only two of over a hundred nations about which Americans must think in making policy and obviously not among the most conspicuous. They suggest that the Australians and New Zealanders not be misled into overestimating the position of their area in the American scale of interest by provincially assuming that since the United States bulks large in their eyes, they must bulk large in American eyes. This is a salutary exercise in correcting a distorted perspective, chastening an overly exuberant national pride, and contributing something to a proper understanding of the relations of the nations, but whether one can arrive at a wholly accurate definition by a process of systematic deflation is doubtful.

It is the writer's impression that as the Pacific has long been a major preoccupation of the American people and in some respects an alternative to the traditional concentration on Europe, the improvement in the status of the Southwest Pacific in Pacific Basin affairs as a result of World War II represented a very considerable and permanent upgrading of the area in American interest and concern. It is the writer's further impression that, while the force of the case for a peripheral position is fully admitted, nevertheless the periphery has been so greatly drawn in in the Western Pacific in recent decades that the Southwest Pacific is, after seventeen decades during which the Americans have been dodging in and out of it with their minds really concentrated elsewhere, now fairly firmly planted in the American consciousness as an area of great importance to them in a rapidly changing world. What they now need to do is to get it into perspective, to see it more accurately, to place it more intelligently in relation to the Pacific and Asia. The prospects are good that they will do so, in the process slowly eroding away the sense that the Australians and New Zealanders have that they are, in American eyes, on the outer edge of things.

BIBLIOGRAPHICAL NOTES

This bibliographical is not intended to supply an exhaustive list of books of direct or inferential relevance to the subject matter of this book. Rather it is intended to give the reader some hints as to books he can consult for an enlargement of information about points covered rather summarily here. The "literature" on all the several parts and aspects of the area is enormous, but one never knows what books published in the area or London are available in the libraries of the United States. The writer hopes he has sent no American reader on a wild-goose chase, but he cannot be certain he has not. He has solved his own problem in this regard by acquiring the books for his private collection insofar as possible.

There are very few books dealing with the Southwest Pacific as a whole and none which includes Antarctica. The most useful is, I think, a geographer's survey, K. B. Cumberland's *Southwest Pacific* (Christchurch, 1954).

On Australia's geography, climate, resources, and so on one can profitably consult *The Australian Environment* (Melbourne, 1950), prepared by the Commonwealth Scientific and Industrial Research Organization and also the numerous *Bulletins* published by CSIRO, Dr. John Andrews' authoritative series of pamphlets collectively entitled *Australia's Resources and Their Utilization* (Sydney, *ca.* 1956), and the series of maps with pamphlet commentaries (not yet complete) issued by the Commonwealth Department of National Development, Canberra, under the general title *Atlas of Australian Resources* (Canberra, 1953–   ). The Commonwealth issues a *Year Book* which compendiously covers the statistical data and includes short articles of great value. Up-to-date statistical data and also narratives of events in various fields can be found in *Australia in Facts and Figures,* issued at irregular intervals by the Australian News and Information Bureau, Department of Interior, Canberra. *Land Utilization in Australia* by Sir Samuel Wadham and G. L. Wood (various editions since 1939) is a standard work. On population the writings of W. D. Borrie are the very best available. See, for example, *Population Trends and Policies* (Sydney, 1948). The publications of the Australian Institute of Political Science, Sydney, are authoritative — see, for example, *Australia's Power Resources* (Sydney, 1955) and *Australia's Transport Crisis* (Sydney, 1956). There is to the writer's knowledge no satisfactory study of the rise of factory industry in Australia and no analysis of the present-day industrial structure is up-to-date even when it is published, because the situation is changing so rapidly. See, for example, *The Structure and Capacity of Australian Manufacturing Industries* (Canberra, 1952). A useful analysis, published as a pamphlet, is F. G. Davidson, *The Industrialization of Australia* (Melbourne, 1957). Details of United States investment in manufacturing are occasionally published in pamphlet form in the Department of Trade's "Investment Series." On politics, see *Australia's Government and Politics* by J. D. B. Miller (2nd ed., London, 1959), *The Parliamentary Government of the Commonwealth of Australia* by L. F. Crisp (Adelaide, 1949), and *The Australian Labour Party* (Melbourne, 1955), also by Professor Crisp. There is a study, *The Country Party,* by Ulrich Ellis (Melbourne, 1958), but none of the dominant conservative party in all coalitions, in spite of the interest its strange instability inspires in observers. Current political developments, federal and state, can be followed, even if belatedly, in the chronicles published in *The Australian Quarterly* (Sydney, AIPS) and *The Australian Journal of Politics and History* (Brisbane, University of Queensland Press). On the administrative aspects of Australian government, see R. N. Spann, editor, *Public Administration in Australia* (Sydney, 1959). On the government of the states, to which renewed attention has lately been given by the political scientists, see S. R. Davis, editor, *The Government of the Australian States* (Melbourne, 1960). On recent economic policy there is a rich collecton of documents, Sir Douglas Copland and Professor Ronald Barback, editors, *The Conflict of Expansion and Stability* (Melbourne, 1957). It covers the period 1945–1952 — that is, the period in which the switch-over from Labour to conservative direction was made — and another volume covering later years may be expected. The Commonwealth Government issues an annual White Paper, *National Income and Expenditure*, and usually a special analytical and descriptive report on the state of the economy and its prospects. Current economic developments are analyzed and criticized in *The Economic Record* (Melbourne), an academic periodical, and in *The Australian Financial Review* (Sydney), a general journal. An accurate idea of how the Australians currently see their history can be obtained from *Australia: A Social and Political History*, edited by Professor Gordon Greenwood (New York, 1955). In his Preface Professor Greenwood refers to "the admirable interpretative essays of Hancock, Grattan and Crawford." The reference is to *Australia* by Sir Keith Hancock (New York, 1931), *Introducing Australia* by C. Hartley Grattan (New York, 1942, 1947), and *Australia* by Professor R. M. Crawford (London, 1952). See also *Australia*, a symposium, edited by Grattan (Berkeley, 1947).

The New Zealand Government issues a compendious *Year Book* annually. The best detailed account of the two islands as geographers see them is K. B. Cumbeland and J. W. Fox, *New Zealand: A Regional View* (Christchurch, 1958). The excellent periodical, *The New Zealand Geographer* (Christchurch, 1945–   ) should be consulted. There is no strictly political history of New Zealand which meets with universal approval, but see Professor Lipson's *The Politics of Equality* (Chicago, 1948). Current political developments are usually analyzed in the periodical *Political Science* (Wellington, 1948–   ). The publications of the New Zealand Institute of Public Administration can be consulted with confidence: for example, *Welfare in New Zealand* (Wellington, 1955) and *Economic Stability in New Zealand* (Wellington, 1953). A first-class study of the administrative organization is R. J. Polaschek, *Government Administration in New Zealand* (Wellington and London, 1958). A comprehensive and provocative analysis of the New Zealand economy is C. Westrate, *Portrait of a Mixed Economy: New Zealand* (Wellington, 1959). The standard economic history to 1935 is J. B. Condliffe, *New Zealand in the Making* (2nd ed., London, 1959) but Condliffe's continuation of the narrative in *The Welfare State in New Zealand* (London, 1959) has not won a similar status among New Zealand experts. Professor C. G. F. Simkin's *The Instability of a Dependent Economy* (London, 1951) must unfailingly be consulted. The government publishes an annual *Economic Survey*. Good general histories of New Zealand are W. P. Morrell and D. O. W. Hall, *A History of New Zealand Life* (Christchurch, 1957) and Keith Sinclair's Penguin book,

History of New Zealand (London, 1959). A book of great use in understanding New Zealand is H. Belshaw, editor, *New Zealand* (Berkeley, 1947). The best comprehensive descriptive analysis of New Zealand life by a single hand is F. L. W. Wood's *This New Zealand* (latest ed., Hamilton, 1958).

In addition to K. B. Cumberland's geographer's survey of the islands in *Southwest Pacific*, see also F. M. Keesing's *The South Seas in the Modern World* (New York, 1941) and Douglas L. Oliver's *The Pacific Islands* (Cambridge, Mass., 1951). The histories available, chiefly political in emphasis, stop short of the present day and are usually not absolutely comprehensive within their limits: the principal histories are G. H. Scholefield, *The Pacific: Its Past and Future* (London, 1919), Jean I. Brookes, *International Rivalry in the Pacific Islands 1800–1875* (Berkeley, 1941), J. W. Ward, *British Policy in the South Pacific 1786–1893* (Sydney, 1948), and W. P. Morrell, *Britain in the Pacific Islands* (London, 1960). Anybody at all interested in understanding the islands should read the anthropologists: Bateson, Firth, Belshaw, Beaglehole, Stanner, Oliver, Hogbin, Mead, and so forth. For reviews of the anthropological literature, see A. P. Elkin, *Social Anthropology in Melanesia* (Melbourne, 1953) and F. M. Keesing, *Social Anthropology in Polynesia* (Melbourne, 1953).

The best way to get a clear conception of what Antarctica is like and to acquire ideas about its use to mankind is to read the narratives of the explorers and scientific workers. Only a few attempts have been made at comprehensive description and analysis, notable among them the survey edited by F. A. Simpson for the New Zealand Antarctic Society, *The Antarctic Today* (Wellington, 1952). The Introduction to Walter Sullivan's *Quest for a Continent* (New York, 1957) is useful in this respect. *The Polar Regions in their Relation to Human Affairs*, by Laurence M. Gould (New York, 1958) is valuable. President Gould's book prints the Bowman Memorial Lectures of the American Geographical Society. *Antarctica in the International Geophysical Year*, a symposium (Washington, D.C., 1956), includes discussions of geography, geology, atmosphere physics, flora, fauna, and so on, by American experts. Much can be learned from *Sailing Directions for Antarctica* (Washington, D.C., 1943, with mimeographed supplements), and also from *Geographic Names* of Antarctica (Washington, D.C., 1956), the one published by the United States Hydrographic office, the other by the United States Board of Geographic Names. The most comprehensive bibliography on Antarctica is *Antarctic Bibliography*, published by the Department of the Navy (Washington, 1951). A useful up-to-date history of polar exploration — that is, Arctic and Antarctic exploration — not devoid of errors of fact and judgment, is L. P. Kirwan, *The White Road* (London, 1959).

There is no comprehensive history of external relations from which the story of relations with the United States might be teased out for either Australia or New Zealand. However, for New Zealand there is Professor F. L. W. Wood's *New Zealand in the World* (Wellington, 1940), the emphasis of which is on the country's position within the Empire, not the world exactly, but perhaps seemingly so to New Zealanders up to 1940. Professor Gordon Greenwood's *Early American-Australian Relations . . . to the Close of 1830* (Melbourne, 1944) interprets the word "American" as referring, quite properly, to South as well as North America. He covers some of the ground on which the United States stands. Professor Werner Levi's *American-Australian Relations* (Minneapolis, 1947) is an attempt at a comprehensive coverage, but somehow it never really rises above its footnotes, fails to convey a sense that it is a story of fallible men acting, and is deficient on the Australian side of the story.

The story of the exploration of the Southwest Pacific is an integral part of Professor J. C. Beaglehole's wonderful tour de force, *The Exploration of the Pacific* (London, 1947). Beaglehole is also responsible for *The Discovery of New Zealand* (Wellington, 1939) and *Abel Janszoon Tasman and the Discovery of New Zealand* (Wellington, 1942), and he is editor of the Hakluyt Society's edition of *The Journals of Captain James Cook*, vol. I, (Cambridge, 1955), the volume that covers the rediscovery of New Zealand and the discovery of the vital Pacific coast of Australia. The standard work on the discovery of Australia is *The Discovery of Australia* by G. Arnold Wood (London, 1922), but the story has been amended in the last thirty-odd years, so one should consult the subsequent literature. On the exploration of Polynesia see *Explorers of the Pacific: European and American Discoveries in Polynesia* by Te Rangi Hiroa (P. H. Buck) (Honolulu, 1953). A volume on Melanesia identically planned and executed would be most useful.

The role of Cape Horn in the story of American enterprise in the Pacific is indicated in *Cape Horn to the Pacific* by R. A. Rydell (Berkeley, 1952). Useful information about Americans in the fur trade, the China trade, and so on, is to be found, expertly handled, in Professor S. E. Morison's *The Maritime History of Massachusetts 1783–1860* (Boston, 1941). The story of the incursion of the sealers into Antarctica is told in *America in the Antarctic to 1840* by P. I. Mitterling (Urbana, Illinois, 1959). *The Voyage of The Huron and The Huntress* by Edouard A. Stackpole (Mystic, Conn., 1955) helps set straight the story of the discovery of the Palmer-Graham Peninsula. Mr. Stackpole's *The Sea-Hunters: The New England Whalemen During Two Centuries 1635–1835* (Philadelphia, 1953) gets the story into the Pacific, but the bulk of that part of it will be in his second volume. The story of whaling as told by Americans tends to neglect its impact on the islands, New Zealand, and Australia. The Australian-New Zealand aspect is in the forefront in Dakin's *Whalemen Adventurers* (Sydney, 1934). On the whalers in the islands the best material is in the narratives of the missionaries, allowance being made for bias. There is no good critical comprehensive account of the impact, but one can enjoy Ernest Beaglehole's *Social Change in the South Pacific* (London, 1957), which deals only with the islands of Rarotonga and Aitutaki. *Puritans in the South Seas* by L. B. Wright and M. I. Fry (New York, 1936) deals with the missionaries, but more to scoff than to wonder what effect they and their contemporaries really had on the poor islanders. An example of an American "show the flag" narrative is *A Visit to the South Seas* by C. S. Stewart, 2 vols. (New York, 1833). The official account of the Wilkes Expedition is *Narrative of the United States Exploring Expedition* by Charles Wilkes, 5 vols. plus atlas (Philadelphia, 1845). A comprehensive bibliography of the expedition is *The United States Exploring Expedition . . . and its Publications* by D. C. Haskell (New York, 1942). The only (and very disappointing) life of Wilkes is *The Hidden Coasts* by Daniel Henderson (New York, 1953). Mitterling (see above) covers Wilkes in Antarctica.

As to the early contacts of the Americans with the settlement at Sydney, it is perhaps best to tease the story out of the *Historical Records of Australia*, series 1, the volumes of which began to appear in 1914. There are some useful articles on early Australian–American relations by L. G. Churchward in the professional periodical, *Historical Studies: Australia and New Zealand* (University of Melbourne). On the Americans in New Zealand in the early days, information can be gleaned from the books of Robert McNab. In Mr. McNab's *Historical Records of New Zealand*, vol. II, (Wellington, 1914) can be found letters to Washington from the first American Consul at Kororareka.

For a study of the Australian and New Zealand gold rushes in the context of the nineteenth-century rushes, see W. P. Morrell, *The Gold Rushes* (London, 1940). For an authoritative account of the Australian "ducks" in California in the days of the great rush see Mary Floyd Williams, *History of the San Francisco Committee of Vigilance of 1851* (Berkeley, 1921). The classic account of an American on the Australian gold fields is C. D. Ferguson, *The Experiences of a Forty-niner During Thirty-four Years Residence in California and Australia* (Cleveland, 1888). Another "American in Australia" narrative is *Knocking About* by A. B. Peirce (New Haven, 1924). George Francis Train told his story in various volumes, including *My Life* (New York, 1902). A perceptive Australian study of Train is *Bonanza: The Story of G. F. Train* by Clive Turnbull (Melbourne, 1946). The story of Cobb & Company is told under "Coaches and Coaching Days" in *Australian Encyclopedia*, vol. II (10 vols., Sydney and East Lansing, Michigan, 1958) in which also can be found biographies of other Americans than Cobb, including Livingston Hopkins, J. C. Williamson, "Bully" Hayes, and so on.

On the steamship lines, see W. Lawson, *Pacific Steamers* (Glasgow, 1927). A useful life of Vogel is *The Life and Times of Sir Julius Vogel* by R. M. Burdon (Christchurch, 1948). There is no really good life of Sir Henry Parkes.

The standard work on the struggle for Samoa from the American angle is *The Foreign Policy of The United States in Relation to Samoa* by George H. Ryden (New Haven, 1933). See also *The Origins of International Rivalry in Samoa 1845–1884* by Sylvia Mastermann (Stanford, 1934) and *The Rise and Fall of Germany's Colonial Empire 1884–1918* by Mary E. Townsend (New York, 1930) as well as the life of Sir Julius Vogel just cited.

The standard account of the development of the White Australia policy is Myra Willard, *History of the White Australia Policy* (Melbourne, 1923), but there have been several important journal articles on it in recent years, for example, in *The Australian Quarterly*. The story is wide open for re-examination.

On Australian trade policy since federation see *Australia's Trade Relations* by D. F. Nicholson (Melbourne, 1955).

The best account of the extraordinary career of William Morris Hughes thus far is W. Farmer Whyte, *William Morris Hughes: His Life and Times* (Sydney, 1957), but it is lacking in critical perception. For an account of Australia at the Peace Conference in 1918 see *Official History of Australia in the War of 1914–18*, vol. XI. This volume is also important on Hughes as political leader in wartime.

On the Australians and New Zealanders in Antarctica see Arthur Scholes *Seventh Continent: Saga of Australasian Exploration in Antarctica 1895–1950* (London, 1953). David's narrative is to be found in Shackleton's *Heart of the Antarctic*, vol. II (London, 1909). See also the books on their Antarctic experiences by Bernacchi, Taylor, Priestley, Debenham, and especially Mawson, *The Home of the Blizzard*, 2 vols. (London, 1915). Byrd records his reception in New Zealand in his narratives, *Little America* (New York, 1930) and *Discovery* (New York, 1935).

The story of the first flight from the United States to Australia is told in *The Flight of the Southern Cross* by Charles Kingsford-Smith and C. P. Ulm (New York, 1929). On the development of aviation in Australia, see *Air Transport in Australia* by D. M. Hocking and C. P. Haddon-Cave (Sydney, 1951).

The discussion of a foreign policy for Australia can be followed in the periodical mentioned in the text and in such pamphlets and books as the following, as well as the mimeographed data papers provided by the Australians for IPR and RIIA conferences. *Australian Foreign Policy 1934* (Melbourne, 1935), *Australian Foreign Policy 1935–36* (Melbourne, 1936), *Australia and the Far East*, edited by I. Clunies Ross (Sydney, 1936), *Australia's Foreign Policy*, edited by W. G. K. Duncan (Sydney, 1938), *Australia's National Interests and National Policy* by H. L. Harris (Melbourne, 1938), *The British Commonwealth and the Future*, edited by H. V. Hodson (London, 1939), *Australia's Interests and Policies in the Far East* by Jack Shepherd (New York, 1940), and *Australia and the United States* by Fred Alexander (Boston, 1941). See also *The British Commonwealth and International Security: The Role of the Dominions 1919–1939* by Gwendolen Carter (Toronto, 1947) and *Survey of British Commonwealth Affairs: Problems of External Policy 1931–1939* by Nicholas Mansergh (London, 1952).

As to New Zealand, it may be well to begin by calling Professor Wood's book to mind (see above). Reference has already been made to Sir Julius Vogel in connection with Samoa and steamship services. The New Zealand version of the Islands policy has its roots in the thinking of Sir George Grey, especially his reaction to the French proclamation of sovereignty in New Caledonia in 1853. There is no good, modern life of Grey in existence, but one is being written by Professor Rutherford, probably to be published in 1960. The Islands policy came to full expression in the ideology of Prime Minister Richard Seddon ("King Dick"), in office at the turn of the century. Seddon was proud of New Zealand but he was also a very ardent Imperialist. See *King Dick: A Biography of*

Richard John Seddon by R. M. Burdon (Christchurch, 1955). Foreign-policy questions are treated in the following handbooks of New Zealand affairs: *New Zealand Affairs* (Christchurch, 1929) and *Contemporary New Zealand* (Christchurch, 1938). The volumes by Carter and Mansergh, cited above, deal with New Zealand in the Commonwealth context, as also does the Hodson book cited earlier. I. F. G. Milner's *New Zealand's Interests and Policies in the Far East* (New York, 1940) complements Jack Shepherd's volume on Australia's interests.

The volumes of the official history of Australia in World War II — *Australia in the War of 1939–45* — contain a great deal of information indispensable to understanding how Australia and the United States arrived at intimate collaboration. See, for example, Lionel Wigmore's *The Japanese Thrust* (Canberra, 1957), Dudley McCarthy's *South-West Pacific Area — First Year* (Canberra, 1959), and the volumes of "Series 4 Civil," *The Government and the People* by Paul Hasluck, vol. I (Canberra, 1952) and *War Economy*, vol. I, by J. S. Butlin (Canberra, 1955). In accordance with historical logic, these latter works go as far as the attack on Pearl Harbor, but the rest of the story is reserved for the second volumes, which are not yet available. Other volumes of this tremendous series should not be passed by because they deal with events outside the Pacific, for frequently an introductory chapter provides valuable general background of relevance. The plan of the series provides for no special study of American-Australian relations, but the writer suggests that one would be a highly appropriate added volume.

The relevant volumes of S. E. Morison's *History of United States Naval Operations in World War II* contain valuable information relevant to the theme of this book. One can also read with profit such volumes of the official publication, *United States Army in World War II*, as *Global Logistics and Strategy 1940–43* by R. M. Leighton and R. W. Coakley (Washington, 1955), *Victory in Papua* by Samuel Miller (Washington, 1956), and so on. The *Report* and *Hearings* of the *Investigation of Pearl Harbor Attack*, Senate Doc. 274, 79 Cong. 2 Sess., Hearings Parts 1, 5, 9, 15, 16, 26, 32, contain useful documents and statements. The various lives of General MacArthur that have appeared should be looked at, but none to date deals adequately with his role in American-Australian relations. See also the reminiscences of soldiers and sailors who served in the Southwest Pacific, for example, *From Down Under to Nippon* by Walter Krueger (Washington, 1952), *Our Jungle Road to Tokyo* by R. L. Eichelberger (New York, 1950), *Admiral*

Halsey's Story (New York, 1947), though not with the expectation of finding much data directly relevant to our theme. There is a good deal of illuminating detail in *Blamey: The Biography of Field-Marshal Sir Thomas Blamey* by John Hetherington (Melbourne, 1954).

An early Australian reaction to Australia's position after Pearl Harbor is *Australia and the Pacific*, a symposium (Princeton, 1944). The Preface begins optimistically, "The Pacific War has done much to dispel the prevailing North American ignorance of and indifference to Australia as a nation . . ." An American reaction is *The Southwest Pacific and the War*, a series of lectures (Berkeley, 1944).

Dr. Evatt's principal speeches have been collected: *Foreign Policy of Australia* (Sydney, 1945) and *Australia in World Affairs* (Sydney, 1946), covering his utterances from November 1941 to May 1946. The Introduction to the first by W. Macmahon Ball and the Foreword to the second by Sir Frederick Eggleston should be carefully read as sympathetic analyses of the Evatt point of view. Dr. Evatt's views of a later period are recorded in *The United Nations* by H. V. Evatt (Melbourne, 1948), the Oliver Wendell Holmes Lectures at Harvard for 1947, and in *The Task of Nations* by H. V. Evatt (New York, 1949).

On the Evatt case for adopting certain provisions of the Statute of Westminster, see *Statute of Westminster Adoption Bill: A Monograph* (Canberra, 1942).

Professor Julius Stone's book, *The Atlantic Charter* (Sydney, 1943) may profitably be read as the reaction of a learned professor of law to a famous international document.

On the Australians at the San Francisco Conference on International Organization, see the White Paper, *United Nations Conference on International Organization: Report of the Australian Delegates* (Canberra, 1945). For a formal government paper, this is a highly personal document, but all the more illuminating for that very reason. It is generally understood that it was composed by Dr. Evatt himself. For Australia's role in the United Nations, see the excellent volume, *Australia and the United Nations* by Norman Harper and David Sissons, one of the Carnegie Endowment's *Studies on International Organization* (New York, 1959).

A first-class book by one of the pioneers in the development of a distinctive Australian foreign policy is Sir Frederick Eggleston's *Reflections on Australian Foreign Policy* (Melbourne, 1957). Sir Frederick contributed the chapter on "Foreign Policy" to *Australia*, edited by C. Hartley Grattan (Berkeley, 1947). An essay which can profitably be read for an understanding of what Australians may mean by the expression, a socialist foreign policy, is "Foreign Policy" by H. Wolfsohn in *Policies for Progress: Essays in Australian Politics*, edited by Alan Davies and Geoffrey Serle (Melbourne, 1954). A fascinating exercise is to try to discover in what respects, by this definition, United States policy is not socialist! The best academic writing, or writing by academicians, on current foreign-policy developments is to be found in the chronicle "Problems of Australian Foreign Policy" in *The Australian Journal of Politics and History* (Brisbane: University of Queensland Press, vol. I, no. 1, November 1955). The most skilled of the academic writers — for example, Julius Stone, Fred Alexander, N. D. Harper, Geoffrey Sawer, John Andrews, Leicester Webb, W. Macmahon Ball — sooner or later take charge of this excellent feature. Important occasional articles on Australian policy appear in *International Affairs* (London) and *Foreign Affairs* (New York). Minister of External Affairs R. G. Casey has collected some of his papers in *Friends and Neighbors* (Melbourne and East Lansing, Michigan, 1954, 1955). A series of volumes on Australia in world affairs was initiated with *Australia in World Affairs 1950–55*, edited by Gordon Greenwood and Norman Harper (Melbourne, 1957). The book contains also an account of the Suez episode of 1956. A valuable service would be to extend the coverage back to *circa* 1940 in a special volume. The book contains an able essay on "Australia and the United States" by N. D. Harper; and it is relevant to call attention to Gordon Greenwood's essay, "The Commonwealth." An examination of Australia's place in the Commonwealth is to be found in *The Commonwealth in the World* (London, 1958), by J. D. B. Miller, an Australian resident in England. Indispensable on Australia in the Commonwealth context is Nicholas Mansergh's *Survey of British Commonwealth Affairs: Problems of Wartime Co-operation and Post-War Change 1939–1952* (London, 1958). Professor Mansergh is also responsible for a monumental collection of documents in two volumes covering the period of the volume just mentioned and also that of the book by him cited earlier — *Documents and Speeches on British Commonwealth Affairs 1931–1952*, 2 vols. (London, 1953).

Australia's relations with Asia are, of course, always included in any comprehensive study of foreign policy.

The first postwar book wholly devoted to this aspect of Australia's problem was *Near North: Australia and a Thousand Million Neighbors*, edited by R. J. Gilmore and Denis Warner (Sydney, 1948). Professor Werner Levi's *Australia's Outlook on Asia* (Sydney, 1958) is useful as an opinion survey. Professor Macmahon Ball's two books, *Japan: Enemy or Ally?* (Melbourne, 1948) and *Nationalism and Communism in East Asia* (Melbourne, 1952), are valuable intrinsically and for the light they throw on the point of view of a prolific writer on foreign affairs. Attention should be called to the White Paper, *Japanese Peace Settlement: Report on British Commonwealth Conference, Canberra, 1947*. My copy happens to be one issued by the New Zealand Government, but all the governments involved issued similar papers. The only book on Australia and Korea of which the writer has knowledge is George Odgers, *Across the Parallel* (Melbourne, 1952), an account of the Australian 77th Air Squadron in the fighting. A British study of SEATO is *Collective Defence in South East Asia* (London, 1956). On Suez, see Part III of Prime Minister Menzies' collection of speeches, *Speech is of Time* (London, 1958).

Presuming that readers are familiar with the books by Byrd, Ellsworth, Ronne, Dufek, Siple, and others on American activities in Antarctica, we may direct attention to *New Zealand Activities in the Antarctic* by A. S. Helm, a pamphlet reprint from the *New Zealand Official Year Book of 1958* and, for Australia, to *ANARE: Australia's Antarctic Outposts* by Phillip Law and John Bercher-vaise (Melbourne, 1957) which covers the period 1947–1957. Later Australian activities are regularly reported in *Australia in Facts and Figures*. The treaty between the United States and New Zealand is published as *New Zealand, Treaty Series 1958, No. 2*. The comprehensive treaty negotiated late in 1959 is to be found in the *New York Times* for December 2, 1959. Walter Sullivan's expert news stories on the negotiations and the treaty should be attentively read.

The most important book on the impact of the Pacific war on New Zealand is Professor F. L. Wood's *The New Zealand People at War: Political and External Affairs* (Wellington, 1958) in the series *New Zealand in the Second World War 1939–45*. Walter Nash's *New Zealand* (New York, 1943) throws some light on New Zealand's first response to the crisis in the Pacific. *New Zealand and the Statute of Westminster: Five Lectures*, edited by J. C. Beaglehole (Wellington, 1944), throws ample light on that question. Attention may also be directed to the files of *The New Zealand Geographer*, published in Christchurch, and *Political Science*, published in Wellington, for valuable articles on foreign affairs, to Professor Wood's admirable "The Anzac Dilemma" in *Interna-*

tional Affairs, April, 1953, and to Sir Leslie Munroe's "New Zealand and the New Pacific," in *Foreign Affairs*, July 1953, especially important in view of Sir Leslie's distinguished representation of New Zealand as Ambassador to the United States and the United Nations. See also Sir Leslie's book, *United Nations: Hope for a Divided World* (New York, 1960). Articles on foreign-policy questions appear occasionally in the quarterly *Landfall* (Christchurch, 1947–), and it may be expected that articles of relevance to foreign policy will appear in the new bi-annual *Pacific Viewpoint* (Wellington, Victoria University, vol. I., no. 1., March 1960), though it is to be primarily devoted to studies in the social and natural sciences.

Detailed information, intelligently analyzed, about current developments in the islands is hard to come by in the United States. It is impossible to point to satisfactory sources of news and documents for the islands, least of all collectively. *Pacific Islands Monthly* (Sydney) is the voice of the "intruders" and something of a news magazine. The same publishing house issues a useful handbook, *Pacific Islands Year Book*. *South Pacific Bulletin* (Sydney) is the journal of the South Pacific Commission. The Commission also publishes important monographs on subjects falling within its range of interests, for example, V. D. Stace, *The Pacific Islander and Modern Commerce* (Noumea, 1954), E. J. E. Lefort, *Economic Aspects of the Coconut Industry* (Noumea, 1956). The governments controlling the several groups usually publish annual reports that reveal the official viewpoint. The governments also occasionally publish valuable special documents, as the Fiji government in recent years has published at Suva *The Pattern of the Fiji Economy: The National Income 1950–53* by Carleen O'Loughlin (Council Paper No. 44 of 1956), *Report on the Census of the Population, 1956* (Council Paper 1 of 1958), *The Fijian People: Economic Problems and Prospects* by O. H. K. Spate (Council Paper 13 of 1959), and *Report of the Commission of Enquiry into the Natural Resources and Population Trends of the Colony of Fiji, 1959* (Council Paper 1 of 1960). Books that deal in some measure with "current affairs" include C. S. Belshaw, *Changing Melanesia* (Melbourne 1954), C. S. Belshaw, *The Great Village*, a study of urbanization of the Papuans of New Guinea (London, 1957), and the AIPS publication, *New Guinea and Australia* (Sydney, 1958). Two books that describe the postwar situation in several island groups and which have been practically standard references are W. E. H. Stanner, *The South Seas in Transition*

(Sydney 1953), dealing with Papua-New Guinea, Fiji, and Western
Samoa, and Linden A. Mander, *Some Dependent Peoples of the
South Pacific* (New York 1954), dealing with Papua-New Guinea,
Fiji, Western Samoa, the British Solomon Islands, Tonga, and the
New Hebrides.

INDEX

Index

No attempt has been made to index every mention of Australia, New Zealand, United States or Britain.